365 Meditations for Grandmothers
by Grandmothers

365 Meditations *for* Grandmothers *by* Grandmothers

Sally D. Sharpe, editor

Sylvia M. Corbin Berry,

Martha Chamberlain, Ellen Groseclose,

Georgia B. Hill, Nell W. Mohney,

Helen C. Scott-Carter

DIMENSIONS
FOR LIVING
NASHVILLE

365 MEDITATIONS FOR GRANDMOTHERS BY GRANDMOTHERS

Copyright © 2006 by Dimensions for Living

This book is printed on acid-free, elemental-chlorine-free paper.

Library of Congress Cataloging-in-Publication Data

365 meditations for grandmothers by grandmothers / Sally D. Sharpe, editor; Sylvia M. Corbin Berry . . . [et al.].
   p. cm.
ISBN-13: 978-0-687-33353-0 (pbk. : alk. paper)
   1. Grandmothers—Prayer-books and devotions—English.   2. Grandmothers—Religious life.
3. Devotional calendars.   I. Sharpe, Sally D., 1964-   II. Berry, Sylvia M. Corbin.   III. Title:
Three hundred and sixty-five meditations for grandmothers by grandmothers.
   BV4847.A14 2006
   242'.6431—dc22

                                                                                    2006018698

06 07 08 09 10 11 12 13 14 15—10 9 8 7 6 5 4 3 2 1

MANUFACTURED IN THE UNITED STATES OF AMERICA

Contents

Introduction

Grandmothering:
Awesome Opportunity, Priceless Gift

"Just about the time a woman thinks her job is done, she becomes a grandmother." —Edward H. Dreschnack

Grandmothering is not the same as it was a generation ago. More and more grandmothers today are helping to raise their grandchildren—whether this involves participating in daily childcare responsibilities or providing regular support. For some, grandmothering may, at times, seem more of a "job" than a gift.

Actually, grandmothering *is* a job—a holy assignment, if you will, given by God. It is something to be taken seriously and with great care and responsibility. Grandmothers have the awesome opportunity not only to care for and nurture young lives but also to leave a lasting legacy that will shape future generations. For Christian grandmothers, this legacy is grounded in an enduring faith in Jesus Christ. The apostle Paul tells us in his second letter to Timothy of the unmistakable legacy Timothy received from his grandmother Lois: "I am reminded of your sincere faith, a faith that lived first in your grandmother Lois and your mother Eunice and now, I am sure, lives in you" (1:5 NRSV).

Often this legacy is passed on most effectively in those ordinary—and perhaps sometimes mundane—moments shared with a grandchild. Singing a lullaby, helping to tie a shoe, reading a book, helping with homework or a problem, driving the car, listening and talking—these are holy moments when connections between faith and life can be made, making indelible imprints on a child's soul.

Grandmothering also is a priceless gift—one that can be fully appreciated only after years of preparation (otherwise known as motherhood). I enjoyed watching my own mother receive this gift not one, but four times. Though each grandchild was every bit as precious to her as the one before, it was as if she appreciated the gift of new life a little more deeply each time. Her excitement and joy only multiplied as the family grew. And, oh, how she enjoyed her precious "treasures"—her gifts of God! Though my youngest was only five when "B" (short for Betty) passed away, even she remembers B's exuberant joy in simply being with her grandchildren—despite her physical challenges and pain. There's no doubt that she recognized and cherished the incredible gift of grandmothering.

Six Christian writers who likewise recognize and cherish the gift of grandmothering have come together in this book to share personal stories, biblical guidance, and words of encouragement for the joys and challenges of grandmothering. Though they write in a variety of styles and draw from a multitude of experiences, they have a common purpose: to remind you that your role as grandmother is both an awesome opportunity and a priceless gift—one that will impact not only your grandchildren but also generations to come.

Whether you are a grandmother early or late in life; whether you have one or many grandchildren; whether you are with your grandchildren on a daily or an occasional basis—you will find that these devotions "ring true" because they are written by grandmothers who share a common faith and who have experienced universal challenges, questions, needs, and joys. You may begin using the book at any time of the year, making your way through the months until you've completed a year's cycle. It is my hope that, in the process, you will come to have an even deeper appreciation for the awesome opportunity and priceless gift of grandmothering!

Sally D. Sharpe, Editor

About the Writers

Sylvia M. Corbin Berry (NOVEMBER–DECEMBER) is married and has three children and six grandchildren. She returned to school and graduated cum laude from the Samuel DeWitt Proctor School of Theology with a Master of Divinity, emphasis in Christian Education. She pastors a small church in King and Queen County, Virginia. She also enjoys working with youth and has a passion for writing, drama, and puppetry. Currently she is writing a vacation Bible school script and curriculum. Her love for ministry and family are her greatest inspiration.

Martha Chamberlain (MARCH–APRIL) devotes her energy to family, writing/editing, and service. After a career in nursing and publishing her first three books and numerous articles, she developed a workshop for writers. Martha volunteers in mission, teaches "Tell Your Story" workshops, and facilitates a covenant group of women who keep journals. Working on her next book, she lives in Virginia with her clergy husband.

Ellen Groseclose (JULY–AUGUST) lives in Wenatchee, Washington. She and her husband, Kel, are blessed with six children and twelve grandchildren. Ellen enjoys making quilts for each family member, reading mysteries, cross-stitching, and keeping their home ready for their grandchildren's frequent visits.

Georgia B. Hill (MAY–JUNE) is the author of four published books, including *Our Christian Wedding* and *Our Baby, A Gift from God*. She also assisted her late husband, Dr. Bob Hill, in writing more than sixty books. A graduate of Belmont University, Nashville, Tennessee, Georgia has served in leadership roles in Christian women's clubs and various women's organizations. She enjoys painting, cross-stitching, and reading. She also enjoys sewing for the little girls among her sixteen grandchildren and four great-grands.

Nell W. Mohney (JANUARY–FEBRUARY) is a motivational author and speaker who leads seminars for professional groups, spiritual-life retreats, and church gatherings nationwide. She writes a weekly feature for *The Chattanooga Times Free Press* and is the author of ten books, including her latest release, *Running the Marathon of Life*. She is married to Dr. Ralph Mohney, a retired United Methodist minister and former college president. Their son and daughter-in-law, Ralph and Jackie, live in Chattanooga. Their granddaughter, Ellen, is a youth director, and their grandson is a junior at the University of Georgia. The roles Nell likes best are wife, mother, and grandmother.

Helen C. Scott-Carter (SEPTEMBER–OCTOBER) is Director of Children's Ministry of the A.M.E. Zion Church. She is the author of several children's books, including *History of the A.M.E. Zion Church for Children*, and she writes curriculum and teacher tips for the church school literature department of the A.M.E. Zion Church. Helen taught in the D.C. public schools for thirty-seven years, six of these as an assistant principal. In 2004, she was named *Woman of the Year* by the Century Club of the Business and Professional Women's Clubs in Washington, D.C. She and her pastor husband, Manford Carter, have four children and sixteen grandchildren—the joys of her life.

January

The Incredible Experiences of Grandmothering

NELL W. MOHNEY

JANUARY 1 NEW BEGINNINGS

"See, I am doing a new thing!... Do you not perceive it?"
(Isaiah 43:19 NIV)

On January 1 each year, I think of the words of Louise Fletcher Tarkington:

I wish there were some wonderful place,
Called the land of beginning again.

In a real sense, there are two such places: the gift of a brand-new year, and the gift of a brand-new grandchild.

There is something of the same feeling when your own children arrive, although that experience is laced with fears about your inadequacy as a parent and concerns about practical matters such as diaper changing and 2:00 a.m. feedings. With a grandchild, the feeling is pure joy. It is the mixture of all that God is planning for a new human being, of excitement about the possibility wrapped up in that tiny life, and of gratitude for being a part of the process.

For the next two months, I will share some of the funny, poignant, and life-changing experiences of being a grandmother. I encourage you to keep a journal, detailing how God is blessing your own life through the incredible experiences of grandmothering.

Loving God, thank you for providing continuity of life and the opportunity for new beginnings and second chances. Amen.

JANUARY 2   THE MIRACLE OF NEW LIFE

You created my inmost being; you knit me together in my mother's womb. I praise you because I am fearfully and wonderfully made.   *(Psalm 139:13-14 NIV)*

It was 10:00 p.m. when the call came. My husband, Ralph, and I were entertaining for dessert the fifteen speakers who had just participated in an evening meeting at our church. With coffee server still in hand, I answered the telephone hurriedly to hear our son's excited voice say, "We have just checked into the hospital. You should have a grandchild by morning."

Because we lived two hundred miles away, and knew that our daughter-in-law's parents would be with them, I said, "We'll leave early in the morning." I was ecstatic!

It was a little past midnight when she was born—a beautiful, healthy, perfectly formed seven-and-a-half-pound baby. When I held her in my arms for the first time, it was awesome! God had allowed our son and daughter-in-law to become cocreators with him to bring this new life into the world. As I examined the perfectly formed body and tiny ears and nose and toes, I realized anew the miracle that occurs in physical birth.

Eternal God, thank you for your wonderful gifts of physical and spiritual birth. Help us to grow in wisdom, in stature, and in favor with God and others. Amen.

JANUARY 3   THE POWER OF A NAME

For this reason I kneel before the Father, from whom his whole family in heaven and on earth derives its name.
                                        (Ephesians 3:14-15 NIV)

In his epochal book *Roots*, Alex Haley describes a memorable scene. The son of Binta and Omoro had just been born in Gambia,

West Africa. Omoro took the newborn outside, held him high toward the heavens, and declared, "You are unique. You are special. You are created in the image of God. Your name is Kunte Kinte."

Psychologists tell us there is no more beautiful sound to a person than that of his or her own name. As grandmothers, we have a special opportunity to speak the name of a grandchild with respect and honor—never in derision.

One of our fun projects for grandchildren was a "This Is Your Life" book including facts about where the child was born, names of friends, awards, and pictures. They never tired of looking at their books. There was always a page called "This Is Your Name," which tells about the person for whom the child was named.

Helping grandchildren have a sense of extended family provides security and acceptance, and adds to their self-esteem.

Everlasting God, thank you for loving us in all circumstances of life. Enable us to carry the name "Christian" with honor and pride. Amen.

JANUARY 4   LIVING UP TO YOUR NAME

"And I tell you that you are Peter, and on this rock I will build my church, and the gates of Hades will not overcome it."
(Matthew 16:18 NIV)

I shall never forget the moment I learned our grandson's name. The night before he was scheduled to be born, I telephoned my son's home. My granddaughter, Ellen, answered and said, "Mommy and Daddy have gone to the hospital to get our new baby."

At the hospital, our son took us to the nursery window for our first look at our plump, bright-eyed grandson, and quietly said, "His name is Richard Wesley Mohney. We named him for Rick." It was a moment of great emotion for me. Our son Rick had died following an accident when he was twenty.

Now, suddenly, we were given the opportunity to love another little boy named Richard, and to help him know the God who so graciously gives each of us a second chance. In Matthew 26:69-75,

Peter denied that he even knew Jesus, yet Jesus' prayer on the cross included Peter. Peter accepted the second chance and became the "rock" that Jesus envisioned.

Let's accept our second chances to be all that God created us to be.

Thank you, Lord, for not giving up on us—for giving us second and third chances to fulfill your purposes. Amen.

JANUARY 5   TURNING LOOSE OLD HABITS

Jesus grew in wisdom and stature, and in favor with God and men.   (Luke 2:52 NIV)

Our ten-month-old granddaughter and her parents had been with us for a late-summer visit. She was pulling up at every small table in our house. Holding on, she walked confidently around the coffee table in the living room. Yet, we couldn't entice her to turn loose and "solo." It was two days after they returned home that we received the exciting news: "Ellen took her first steps alone today."

"Did she fall?" I asked apprehensively. "Yes, but she got right up and started again." By the time we saw her a month later, she was walking nonstop.

I wonder how often I must look like a baby Christian to God. I hold on to old, familiar ways when God is calling me to turn loose, take risks, and take new steps for his purposes. God wants me to trust in my own God-given abilities. Even when I fall, I need to get up and try again, knowing that one day I will be running God's race as a more mature Christian.

Patient and loving God, help us to grow in grace and in the knowledge of our Lord and Savior, Jesus Christ. Amen.

JANUARY 6   GOD LOVES ALL CHILDREN

"Just as you did it to one of the least of these who are members of my family, you did it to me."   (Matthew 25:40 NRSV)

Recently I watched a television documentary of starving children in Ethiopia. There was a seven-year-old who looked as if he might be three because of malnutrition. A dollar a day given to a reputable overseas relief program will feed and educate such a child. Let's hear again Jesus' words: "Just as you did it to one of the least of these...you did it to me."

Then I thought of my friend whose only grandchild was born with brain damage. She loves that grandchild as much as I love mine. Yet, she won't see the child achieve normal mental development. Her grandchild will never lack food, physical care, or love, but the child and his parents will need friends who are sensitive to their needs. A church in my community demonstrates that kind of sensitivity by teaching young people to care for mentally challenged children. One evening a month, these young people allow parents of these children to have an evening out.

We all are called to meet, through Christian love, the needs of God's children.

Lord, help us to remember how you care for each of your lambs. Enable us to see all children through your eyes. Amen.

JANUARY 7   CONNECTED THROUGH PRAYER

"I pray for them ... for those you have given me, for they are yours."   *(John 17:9 NIV)*

Living in a different city from our grandchildren when they were young made it more difficult to find creative ways to communicate with them. During my childhood, we saw both sets of grandparents weekly. I longed for that kind of physical closeness, but Ralph was a busy pastor, and I was on the church staff, so there were no free weekends and little time in between.

Of course, we prayed for each of them daily and talked with them by telephone each Sunday afternoon. We always tried to have a short anecdote or funny story to tell—about the puppy that appeared on our doorstep, or the kitten that climbed our tree but was afraid to come down. Always we ended the conversation with,

"We love you." Our one-year-old grandson would parrot it back, "Love oo." I never finished the conversation without feeling connected in love.

Let's remember that we can stay connected to God through prayer, and thus communicate God's love to our grandchildren.

Eternal God, enable me to clear my channels to receive your guidance and to stay connected with my grandchildren. Amen.

JANUARY 8   THE LIVING WATER

Jesus answered her, "If you knew the gift of God and who it is that asks you for a drink, you would have asked him and he would have given you living water."   *(John 4:10 NIV)*

It had been one of those days! Ralph left early for a two-day out-of-town conference. Our two-and-a-half-year-old granddaughter was visiting us for a week. In order to accomplish some necessary errands, I had taken Ellen by the church's preschool program for the morning. Following her afternoon nap, we went to the playground, then swimming, out to dinner, and finally to the grocery store. It had been a long day—especially for a two-year-old. As her plump little legs walked ahead of me on our stairs, she turned and said, "Gran, my wegs are tired. Are your wegs tired?"

"Yes, Ellen, my legs are tired," I said, "but my heart is happy because you have come to visit us."

Being a parent or grandparent is physically tiring, but it's an investment in developing a strong Christian personality. Our fatigue reminds us of the sacrifice Christ made that we might be whole. Our investment is one that will pay huge dividends for them and for us.

Eternal God, when we are weary and our spirits are parched, let us drink of the living water you offer. Amen.

JANUARY 9   LOVING EACH OTHER

"My command is this: Love each other as I have loved you."
(John 15:12 NIV)

My father taught us three children about God's unconditional love by asking us often, "How much do I love you?" Holding his hands twelve inches apart, he would ask, "This much?" When we shook our heads vigorously, he would ask, "Then how much?" Opening our arms widely, we replied, "You love us this much, no matter what."

"Suppose I have to discipline you. How much do I love you then?" Smiling gleefully because we knew the answer, we spread our arms wide and replied again, "You love us this much, no matter what." Reminding us that our outstretched arms formed a cross, he told us that that is how much God loves us.

On our bedside table is a picture of our college-age grandchildren. When we push a button on the frame, we hear them declare, "Hi, Gran and Granddad, we love you this much." Rituals passed on from several generations teach eternal lessons. Our grandchildren delighted in this same ritual and close their e-mails and letters with those words.

O God, keep us ever mindful of your loving gift of salvation, and enable us to pass on your love to our grandchildren. Amen.

JANUARY 10   THE LISTENERS

Then he went upstairs again and broke bread and ate. After talking until daylight, [Paul] left.   *(Acts 20:11 NIV)*

When our grandchildren were ages six and three, we moved back to the city where our son and his family lived. Ralph and I began the practice of having the children spend every Friday night with us when we were in town. It was a wonderful time to get to know them individually.

After we had dinner and some fun activities like bike rides, swimming, popping popcorn, or watching children's movies, Ellen would sleep with me in the master bedroom and Ralph would take Wes upstairs to the guest bedroom.

One night our energetic grandson bounced on the bed for almost an hour, talking nonstop as he jumped. Suddenly, he sat down and said, "Granddad, do you know why I like to come to your house?" Without waiting for an answer, he said, "Because I can talk as much as I want to."

Just as God is the "Listener" for us, so grandparents can become "the listeners" for our grandchildren.

Lord, give us patience to listen to our grandchildren and encourage them to articulate their questions and fears. Amen.

JANUARY 11   NURTURING RELATIONSHIPS

Then he got into the boat and his disciples followed him.
(Matthew 8:23 NIV)

Jesus and his disciples bonded into a closely knit group not only because of their love for one another and their desire to do God's will but also because they did so many things together—traveling, eating, fishing. They were together when Jesus taught and healed and performed the miracles. Their togetherness allowed them to see one another's strengths and weaknesses—Peter's impulsiveness, James and John's ambition, Thomas's doubt, and Judas's betrayal.

Going places with grandchildren—such as school and church plays, family reunions, the circus, and water park—makes for natural conversation. It also allows us to see one another's strengths and weaknesses.

Sometimes, it is those grandparents who live near their grandchildren who most need to make time for them—for spend-the-night or vacation invitations, as well as for school and church events. As we learn from Jesus' example, only as we spend time together can we nurture relationships with our grandchildren.

O God of wisdom, may our relationships with grandchildren be loving and constructive—never judgmental or "preachy." Amen.

JANUARY 12   MAKING DISCIPLES

"Therefore go and make disciples of all nations, baptizing them in the name of the Father and of the Son and of the Holy Spirit, and teaching them to obey everything I have commanded you. And surely I am with you always, to the very end of the age."
(Matthew 28:19-20 NIV)

Power and control come from discipline, and the root word for discipline means "to teach," not to punish. At every opportunity, Jesus taught his disciples about the nature of God and the kingdom of God in everyday living and the world beyond. He taught through familiar illustrations—a lost coin, a lost sheep, a lost son—and through the use of stories or parables.

One of the privileges of being a grandparent is having more time to teach values in creative ways. There are some values that seem significant from one generation to the next: self-esteem, love, faith, creativity, responsibility, leadership, communication skills, and cheerfulness.

Of the various ways of teaching these, none is more significant than example. Ralph Waldo Emerson is credited as having once said, "What you are, speaks so loudly, I can't hear what you say." Let us personify the values that Jesus taught.

Eternal God, help us to incorporate your values into our lives so that we can teach them authentically to our grandchildren. Amen.

JANUARY 13   LOVE IS NOT PERMISSIVE

Love does not delight in evil but rejoices with the truth.
(1 Corinthians 13:6 NIV)

When our grandson, Wes, was young, he was bright and loveable but didn't like to be told "no." When he was four, Ralph was grandson-sitting while our daughter-in-law attended a meeting. Wes arrived with a small football, which he and his granddad passed outside before coming in to build a LEGO ship.

Ralph's one rule was that Wes could play with the ball in the den, but he couldn't throw it from the upstairs balcony to the downstairs entrance hall. If that happened, the football would be put away until Wes's next visit. Sometime in the late afternoon, Wes had an overwhelming desire to test the limits. The ball was thrown downstairs, and Ralph put it away.

Our grandson left our house unhappy, but on a return visit, Wes and his granddad had a long talk about what had occurred. Today they are great buddies, but there is no doubt that Granddad means what he says. Love is not permissive.

Help us, O God, to love our grandchildren unconditionally, but give us wisdom to differentiate between love and permissiveness. Amen.

JANUARY 14   THE SEASON OF GRANDPARENTING

There is a time for everything, and a season for every activity under heaven.   *(Ecclesiastes 3:1 NIV)*

It had been a long afternoon and evening at the amusement park. Actually, we had taken our grandchildren for what we expected to be a couple of hours. Imagine our surprise to learn that on that special day you simply had your hand stamped and could ride on as many rides as you liked.

We ate fast food on the grounds and stayed until the park closed. We were exhausted! Once in the car, I was trying to keep the children awake until we got home and they could have a quick bath and go to bed. So I asked, "What did you like best about our trip today?" Ellen answered, "I liked the Tilt-A-Whirl." Wes said, "I liked the giant slide." Looking over at my fatigued husband, I asked, "What did you like best?" Without hesitation he replied, "Going home." Later as I laughed about my husband's honest reply, I gave thanks that young adults have the children. That season is past for us, and now we are in the wonderful season of grandparenting.

Lord, thank you for your plan for families. Thank you for young parents who are struggling to rear whole Christian per-

sons in a secular world. Let us be willing to be strong support for these families. Amen.

JANUARY 15   GRANDPARENTS WHO REAR
                                         GRANDCHILDREN

He was pierced for our transgressions, he was crushed for our iniquities. **(Isaiah 53:5 NIV)**

The caller ID read "Chattanooga Police Department." My immediate thought was, "My goodness, what have we done?" So far as I knew, we didn't have any overdue parking tickets. The call turned out to be an invitation for me to speak at a police-sponsored community outreach luncheon for grandparents rearing grandchildren.

Yesterday I wrote of the "seasons of life" and how great it is that young adults have the day-to-day responsibilities of child rearing. Then, I realized that some grandparents never lose the parenting role.

I accepted the invitation, and I learned that the 150 people who were present that day are only a few of the courageous people who have put their lives on hold during what were to have been their retirement years. They did it so that their grandchildren might have a chance at life.

I've never spoken to an audience for whom I had more respect. There was great heartache in the room, and yet such courage. Because of their sacrifices and gifts of unconditional love, young people are given a chance.

Merciful Father, thank you for all grandparents who are willing instruments of your love to enable your purposes to be fulfilled in their grandchildren. Amen.

JANUARY 16   PASSING ON VALUES

"But if anyone causes one of these little ones who believe in me to sin, it would be better for him to have a large millstone hung

around his neck and to be drowned in the depths of the sea."
(Matthew 18:6 NIV)

I felt chilled to the bone as I folded the newspaper. In that one issue, I read that a thirteen-year-old son had shot and killed his mother, who refused to buy him some new stereo equipment; that 150,000 students carry weapons to school in America each day; and that the leading killer of youth is motor vehicle accidents (82 percent of which are caused by intoxication or drugs). Statistically speaking, suicide ranks second and homicide ranks third as the cause of death for young people.

What can grandparents do? We need to know what is happening and educate ourselves about drugs. When we are with our grandchildren, we can speak about our values in a nonthreatening, matter-of-fact, "non-preachy" manner. We can make our family gatherings fun and allow them to reflect the values of our extended family.

In a broader perspective, we can support legislation concerning family values, participate in some form of youth work, and, most important, be good role models—grandmothers who radiate love, laughter, hope, and deep faith.

Eternal God, enable us, in the name of your Son, to do the best things in what seems to be the worst of family times. Amen.

JANUARY 17   A DIFFERENT KIND OF GIFT

"Which of you, if his son asks for bread, will give him a stone?"
(Matthew 7:9 NIV)

We won't soon forget Christmas Eve 1991! Honoring our six-year-old Wes's request for a hamster, we bought him one—along with a wire cage with food dish, exercise wheels, and hamster wheel. Since our grandchildren were in and out of our house, the pet shop owner agreed to keep the hamster until two days before Christmas.

The furry creature seemed delighted with his new home. He raced around the exercise equipment for eight hours. We know because the wheel had a squeak, and eight hours of listening to that nearly drove us crazy. On Christmas Eve morning, the hamster looked sick. He wouldn't eat, exercise, or even drink water.

After being told to bring him back to the pet shop, Ralph placed him in a heavy paper sack and secured the top. On the drive, Ralph could hear the rodent scratching on the sack. After parking, Ralph picked up the sack to find it empty. Then the furry creature darted from the back seat and scurried under the dashboard.

To be continued tomorrow...

O God, thank you that nothing that concerns us is trivial to you. Teach us how to give as you give to us. Amen.

JANUARY 18   A GRANDCHILD'S DELIGHT

"If you, then, ... know how to give good gifts to your children, how much more will your Father in heaven give good gifts to those who ask him!"   (Matthew 7:11 NIV)

My husband had no time to coax the hamster out from under the dashboard. It was time for the pet shop to close. Fortunately, there was one hamster left, so we purchased him and placed him securely in the wire cage. By then it was time to attend our church's 6:00 p.m. Communion service. I wanted our furry friend to come out of hiding—but not while I was in the car! Later, as I put finishing touches on our Christmas Eve dinner, Ralph took some hamster food and sprinkled it on the floorboard of the car and waited patiently. Enticed by the smell of food, the hamster soon appeared, and Ralph caught him in a viselike grip.

That evening we ate our dinner in relaxation, and the following day we delivered two hamsters solidly sealed in their cage. Our grandson was overjoyed! The hamsters, named Chip and Dale by Wes's older sister, provided much amusement and good conversation throughout the day and for months to come.

O God, the giver of good gifts to all who ask, enable us to seek your gifts and receive them joyfully. Amen.

JANUARY 19   AN EXTRA CUSHION OF LOVE

I have been reminded of your sincere faith, which first lived in your grandmother Lois and in your mother Eunice and, I am persuaded, now lives in you also.   *(2 Timothy 1:5 NIV)*

It was President Jimmy Carter who, in 1978, declared the first Sunday after Labor Day as Grandparents Day. His purpose was to recognize the active role of grandparenting.

Recently, a newspaper article by a first-grade teacher reinforced this. She said that she could always tell which children had grandparents who were engaged in their lives. These students, she said, were much more confident and got along better with other children. She wrote, "They have more energy, participate more easily in interactive experiences, and the extra cushion of love provided by grandparents makes them feel secure." All of this is a part of God's great plan in which values and faith pass from generation to generation.

Recently, I had the cherished privilege of praying the dedicatory prayer for our granddaughter, Ellen, as she was dedicated as youth director in a church in Signal Mountain, Tennessee. When I laid my hands on her head, I felt an overwhelming sense of God's awesome plan and my privilege to be a participant in that plan.

Loving God, thank you for your plan for families, and for allowing grandparents to have an active role in this plan. Amen.

JANUARY 20   OLDER CHRISTIAN WOMEN ARE
                                             TEACHERS

Likewise, teach the older women to be reverent in the way they live, not to be slanderers or addicted to much wine, but to teach what is good. Then they can train the younger women.   *(Titus 2:3-4a NIV)*

It was a grocery store experience that stunned me. Waiting in line at the checkout counter, I overheard one woman tell another that she was moving out of town so that she wouldn't have to baby-sit for her first and recently born grandchild. I couldn't believe my ears. When I glanced around, I saw a gorgeous, well-toned body and an unsmiling face with eyes that were unkind. She obviously was a self-absorbed woman who was going to miss one of life's greatest blessings.

Ralph and I chose to return to Chattanooga when our grandchildren were quite young. What a privilege it has been! Grandparenting gives us a second chance at life. This time around I could be more relaxed and really enjoy our grandchildren. Because I like to be organized, I was too structured when our children were growing up. Now I have learned to seize the moment. When grandchildren want to talk or go on a picnic, Ralph and I have practiced neglect of other things in order to make memories.

Creator God, help us to understand that we can continue to be cocreators with you when we joyfully pass on your love and purposes to our children and grandchildren. Amen.

JANUARY 21   THE ART OF UNDERSTANDING

"I will give you a wise and discerning heart." (1 Kings 3:12 NIV)

My friend Martha has a wise and discerning heart. One day when her beautiful and talented granddaughter, Millie, a college junior, appeared at Martha's door as an inconsolable child, Martha's wisdom was evident. She suspected the reason for Millie's tears and held her close until the sobs subsided. Then Martha led her granddaughter to the sofa and held her hand as Millie poured out her pain. Her parents had just told their daughter of their plans to divorce, and she was devastated. Her grandmother is the person to whom she turned for comfort and understanding.

This was no time for using clichés, such as "You'll feel better about this in a few months," or for trying to help her granddaughter see her parents' point of view. Right then, Millie needed a safe place—or a tranquility zone, as Alvin Toffler describes it in his book, *Future Shock*—to express her feelings. She needed someone to listen and understand and love. After all, to listen is to love.

O Christ, who identified so easily with the pain of others, give us the gift of an understanding and discerning heart—particularly as it applies to our grandchildren. Amen.

JANUARY 22   BE A STABILITY ZONE FOR OTHERS

"'Love the Lord your God with all your heart and with all your soul and with all your strength and with all your mind'; and, 'Love your neighbor as yourself.'"   *(Luke 10:27 NIV)*

In the book *Future Shock*, Alvin M. Toffler speaks of the need for "stability zones" in a world of chaotic change. It seems to me that Christian grandparents can provide just such a stability zone. This kind of relationship doesn't just happen when a grandchild is in high school or college. It requires a bonding that is cultivated through the years. The bonding occurs through showing love, respect, and thoughtfulness; being nonjudgmental; and making happy memories.

Yesterday I wrote of my friend Martha and her granddaughter, Millie. Millie never would have sought her grandmother for comfort if, through the years, she had not felt loved and respected by her grandmother.

In that kind of setting, Martha was able to help her granddaughter work through her feelings and not bog down in bitterness. Only then could Millie see something of the problems with which her parents were dealing, and only then could she see some options for her own life.

O God, enable us to love you with our entire being so that we may be "stability zones" for our grandchildren and others. Amen.

JANUARY 23   GIVE JOY TO OTHERS

"I have told you this so that my joy may be in you and that your joy may be complete."   *(John 15:11 NIV)*

We have only to read the newspapers or watch television newscasts to realize that many children have little joy in their lives. Abuse, neglect, divorce, violence in the streets and in their homes—all these are prevalent in our society. As a result, many children miss the joy of childhood. Oftentimes, grandparents have the privilege of making happy memories for these grandchildren.

Jesus spoke often about joy: "Be of good cheer" (John 16:33 NKJV); "Let not your heart be troubled" (John 14:1 NKJV). In today's scripture, Jesus is preparing his disciples for his death, but he asks them to remember his teachings that his joy might be in them.

Far more important than silver, china, furniture, or money that we can leave grandchildren are ideas, ideals, and happy memories. When grandchildren are with us, our major task is not correcting grammar or insisting on clean rooms, though we can find creative ways to encourage these things. Our major task is to provide happy memories that will also encourage good self-esteem, consideration for others, and faith in God.

Eternal God, help us to receive your joy and to pass it on to our grandchildren. Amen.

JANUARY 24   TRUST IN GOD'S PROMPTINGS

Trust in the LORD with all your heart and lean not on your own understanding; in all your ways acknowledge him, and he will make your paths straight.   *(Proverbs 3:5-6 NIV)*

Jimmy, eighteen, was a high school football player who moved with the grace of a natural athlete. His academic achievements equaled those on the athletic field. Lately, however, his mother, a single parent of three, was concerned that Jimmy's grades were slipping, and he seemed introspective, even secretive at times. There was no evidence of it, but she wondered if he was using drugs.

Nadine, Jimmy's grandmother, knew the power of prayer. Each day she set aside a specific time to pray that God's best would be accomplished in Jimmy, and that she could be used as an instrument.

Gradually, opportunities opened. She found an article about one of Jimmy's athletic heroes and sent it to him. Another time, she wrote, "On Friday, I'm making chocolate chip cookies. If you have time, stop by for a 'care package'." He did, and gradually he began to stop by more often. Nadine became convinced that Jimmy's problem was depression and anger over his father's death. After talking with a Christian counselor, Jimmy today is a well-adjusted college graduate.

Eternal God, enable us to be persistent in prayer so that we may hear your promptings for our grandchildren. Amen.

JANUARY 25   THE POWER OF PRAYER

I will not take my love from him, nor will I ever betray my faithfulness.   *(Psalm 89:33 NIV)*

Most of the grandchildren I've mentioned have had happy resolutions to their problems. What if your grandchild has a drug problem, or is in trouble with the law, or is sexually promiscuous? Annagene had such a grandchild. At a spiritual life retreat I led, I sensed the heaviness of her spirit even before we talked. Her grandson, Sam, is only sixteen, but he had been using drugs since he was thirteen. He was openly rebellious with his parents, and he kept the household in a constant uproar.

Annagene's suggestions about drug rehab and counseling had been ignored. What could she do? I suggested that she pray daily for him—always seeing him well and whole—and for her son and daughter-in-law, looking for ways to show love instead of offering advice. And for her own peace of mind, I recommended that she affirm daily God's promise in Psalm 89:33: "I will not take my love from [you], nor will I ever betray my faithfulness" (NIV). This is a promise all of us can affirm daily!

Merciful God, thank you that we can count on your faithfulness even in the midst of our pain and sorrow. Amen.

JANUARY 26   THE MAGIC OF WORDS

In every matter of wisdom and understanding about which the king questioned them, he found them ten times better than all the magicians and enchanters in his whole kingdom.
(Daniel 1:20 NIV)

One day I was icing a chocolate cake when our five-year-old son rushed into the kitchen. Excitedly he told me of a television magic show he had just seen where a man said some magic words and a rabbit disappeared. Somewhat disturbed, he said, "I don't believe in magic words, do you?"

Seeing an opportunity for an object lesson about kindness and courtesy, I replied, "Yes, I do." Eagerly he asked, "What are they?" When I told him, "please" and "thank you," he was obviously skeptical.

"Well, let's try them," I said. "You like this cake, don't you?"

Dancing around the table he replied, "It's yummy."

"Well, if you can say 'please' before and 'thank you' afterward, you are much more likely to get a piece."

Quickly he asked, "May I please have a piece of cake right now?" Ruffling his hair, I promised, "You may have it right after lunch."

As I have watched grandchildren use words of kindness and courtesy, I realize that these are indeed magical words.

Gracious God, help us to incorporate your wisdom and loving-kindness into our lives so that we can relate to others in courtesy and love. Amen.

JANUARY 27   KEEP YOUR FOCUS ON CHRIST

Never be lacking in zeal, but keep your spiritual fervor, serving the Lord.
(Romans 12:11 NIV)

As wonderful as the gift of grandchildren is, they can't be the center of the universe. In the first place, it wouldn't be good for them and, second, it would make us insensitive to the needs of others—especially those who want to be grandparents and aren't, and those whose relationships with children and grandchildren are strained because of divorce or conflict. We grandmothers need to keep our focus on Christ in order to keep our perspective.

I love the story of the man boarding a discount airline where no seats were assigned. As he made his way down the aisle, he asked each seated passenger, "Do you have grandchildren?" If they said, "Yes," he moved on down the aisle until he found a seatmate who had no grandchildren.

He either didn't want to be bored by a bragging grandparent, he wanted to talk about his own, or he was one of those hurt persons mentioned previously. We need to keep our focus on Christ so that we can serve others with sensitivity.

Help us, Lord, to stay focused on you and sensitive to all those with whom we come in contact. Amen.

JANUARY 28   WILLING TO BE A WITNESS

The LORD is great and greatly to be praised.
(Psalm 96:4 NKJV)

Once I heard Dr. Norman Vincent Peale tell a story of renowned singer Ethel Waters. She sat beside a drunk man on a three-hour flight. Some people would have moved immediately, or ignored the offensive man. Instead, Waters encouraged him to eat his food to soak up the liquor he had been drinking.

Then, she said, "Tell me what's troubling you?" The man said that his beautiful granddaughter was a talented musician and had called and asked him to attend her concert. Instead, he stayed home and played golf. Now he was going to her funeral.

Waters said, "Drinking won't help you in this situation, but God loves you and is going to help you." The message seemed to get through the man's alcohol-soaked brain. He slept for the remainder of the flight. When the plane landed, he looked soberly into her eyes and said, "I thank you so very much."

"Honey, it's the Lord you need to thank," she replied. "He's with you now and will be with you forever."

Father, thank you for your ever-present love. May we receive it fully and pass it on to our grandchildren. Amen.

JANUARY 29   THE PORTRAIT OF A
                                                    GRANDMOTHER

She is clothed with strength and dignity; she can laugh at the days to come.   *(Proverbs 31:25 NIV)*

A friend gave me a copy of an essay written by a third-grade student. Here is my own abbreviated and paraphrased version of it: Grandmothers have nothing to do but "be there." They take their grandchildren to the grocery where the "pretend horses" are, and they have lots of quarters. Sometimes they take them on walks and slow down to look at pretty leaves and caterpillars and other neat stuff. They never say, "Hurry up."

Some grandmothers are skinny and some are fat, but they're never too fat to tie a grandchild's shoe. Grandmothers wear funny-looking glasses and underwear, and they can even take their teeth out. When they read a story, they never skip words; and they don't mind reading the same story again and again.

You should have a grandmother of your own, especially if you don't have a TV, because grandmothers are the only grown-ups who have time for you.

Our grandchildren need our love and our time.

Eternal God, help us to remember it is a privilege to be a connective link of faith and love in the life of a grandchild. Help us to be virtuous grandmothers. Amen.

JANUARY 30   CHRIST'S CLAIM ON LITTLE
                                                         CHILDREN

Jesus said, "Let the little children come to me, and do not hinder them, for the kingdom of heaven belongs to such as these."
(Matthew 19:14 NIV)

Most of our houseguests make their beds and keep their things somewhat orderly. Not this lady! She never offered to make her bed, and her belongings were scattered all over the house. We took her to a lovely restaurant, but she seemed unimpressed by the excellent food and was noisier than anyone at surrounding tables. At the close of her visit, she left without even so much as a "thank you."

You are probably thinking that we will never invite her to our home again. You are wrong! That guest was our nine-month-old granddaughter, whom we would like to have visit us every week.

It is true that she didn't say "thank you" for all our efforts, but she hadn't learned those words yet. Our thanks, however, came every morning when we walked into her bedroom. The moment she saw us, a smile enveloped her face with the glory of a sunrise at the Grand Canyon. When she reached out her arms for us, it was all the thanks that grandparents could ever hope for!

God of provision and joy, my heart is filled to overflowing when I think of the gift of grandchildren. Help me always to be worthy of the trust. Amen.

JANUARY 31   A NEW BEGINNING

"See, I am doing a new thing! . . . Do you not perceive it?"
(Isaiah 43:19 NIV)

We began this month with the wistful words of Louise Fletcher Tarkington:

> I wish there were some wonderful place,
> Called the land of beginning again.

How many times have you wished that you could go back and do some things differently with your children? We all have twenty-twenty hindsight!

The glorious truth is that there is a land of beginning again in the experience of grandparenting. If we wish that we had been more patient with our children, we can be more patient with our grandchildren; if we wish we had given more of our time, we can do it now; if we wish we had exemplified faith more effectively—spoken of it more convincingly—we can do it now with our grandchildren.

A new beginning means leaving behind some excess baggage—old ideas that make us rigid in our thinking; old habits that are destructive and enslaving; old fears and ideas that keep us from taking bold, new steps for God; old grudges that make us weary and old in spirit. Like barnacles covering a ship, these old things make us unworthy vessels on the sea of life.

Lord, help us recognize the new beginnings you offer in the role of grandparenting. May we seize the opportunity and make it eternally significant. Amen.

February

The Incredible Experiences of Grandmothering (Continued)

NELL W. MOHNEY

FEBRUARY 1   CELEBRATING OUR UNIQUENESS

"For I know the plans I have for you," declares the LORD, "plans to prosper you and not to harm you, plans to give you hope and a future."   *(Jeremiah 29:11 NIV)*

Today is our grandson's birthday. He is a handsome, confident, well-built college student with plans to be a landscape architect. When he was eight, however, he was not feeling very good about himself. He wasn't as tall as he wanted to be, and his motor skills had not yet developed enough to be as good in sports as his eleven-year-old sister was.

Wes's birthday seemed a perfect time to help him feel special, so I planned a "Very Important Person" theme dinner for him. We had VIP invitations and placecards, and we all wore red, white, and blue. A poster over the mantel had pictures of George Washington, Abraham Lincoln, and Wes Mohney.

Just before Wes received his gifts, we each told him what we most liked about him. Those accolades seemed to give him a shot of self-confidence. In fact, it was so special that we have done that at every family birthday since.

As grandmothers, we have many opportunities to help grandchildren grow in self-confidence and in love.

Help us, O God, to see the uniqueness of each of our grandchildren, and to celebrate their God-given talents. Amen.

FEBRUARY 2   THE TYRANNY OF INGRATITUDE

Nor should there be obscenity, foolish talk or coarse joking, which are out of place, but rather thanksgiving.   *(Ephesians 5:4 NIV)*

I once witnessed a terrible scene during the noon hour in a department store. A woman in her midsixties rushed in to meet a girl who appeared to be her granddaughter. Later I learned that the woman was a widowed grandmother taking care of three grandchildren whose divorced mother had left town with a traveling sales representative.

The teenage granddaughter modeled a beautiful white prom dress, declaring, "I've decided on this one." After looking at the price tag, the grandmother said, "It's beautiful, but I'm not sure we can afford it." After the granddaughter pleaded, the grandmother finally said, "All right. We'll manage somehow."

Instead of thanking her grandmother, the teenager went to the back and brought out several other expensive items. When the grandmother said, "We'll talk about those later," the girl exploded in anger. The tearful grandmother left humiliated. A hug and a sincere "thank you" could have sent her out rejoicing.

As grandmothers, we must take every opportunity to teach our grandchildren the importance of gratitude and how ingratitude hurts others.

Loving God, help us to model a spirit of gratitude for all our grandchildren. Amen.

FEBRUARY 3   WELCOME YOUR GRANDCHILDREN

"And whoever welcomes a little child like this in my name welcomes me."   *(Matthew 18:5 NIV)*

Why do grandparents act so strangely exuberant? The moment I learned about our first grandchild's birth, a strange transformation took place in my life. Through the years, I have watched in amusement as otherwise intelligent people have become maudlin, talkative, and even a little crazy when they become grandparents.

In the past, I'd been guilty of going in the opposite direction when someone started toward me with a grandparent's book of pictures. Now I not only understand their actions, I have joyfully joined their ranks. A part of the reason for this strange behavior is that we recognize now, from the perspective of years, how great a miracle human birth really is.

When my husband, Ralph, and I held our first grandchild, we remembered the feelings we experienced when holding our own firstborn. It's awesome and wonderful to realize that children are gifts from God to be cherished, not possessions to be owned.

God of all generations, enable us to show gracious hospitality to the grandchildren born into our family. Help us to value, respect, and love them. Amen.

FEBRUARY 4   COCOON LIVING

"Then you will know the truth, and the truth will set you free."
(John 8:32 NIV)

It was on this day in 1987, when our grandchildren were six and three years of age, that we received an Easter garden we had ordered. The garden contained five tiny caterpillars that were to become five beautiful butterflies by Easter. It seemed a wonderful symbol of the season. The caterpillars represented Jesus wrapped in grave clothes, and the butterflies portrayed the beauty and freedom of resurrection.

Our grandchildren reported regularly on the transformation taking place, and Easter that year was especially significant for us all. In addition, I thought how easy it is for us to settle into cocoon living. It's safe, comfortable, and nonrisky—but deadening.

When Wes didn't like to see caterpillars struggle, we told him about another little boy who cut the cocoon to free the butterfly more quickly. Instead, there emerged a misshapen butterfly that was too weak to fly. We reminded Ellen and Wes that God's plan is for us to become mature through struggling to do the hard things, knowing that God is there to help us.

Eternal God, set us free from rigid cocoon living of fear, worry, perfectionism, and resentment. Help us to model Christian wholeness for our grandchildren. Amen.

FEBRUARY 5   GRANDPARENTS DAY AT SCHOOL

Teach us to number our days aright, that we may gain a heart of wisdom.   *(Psalm 90:12 NIV)*

From the time our grandchildren were in preschool, Ralph and I made every effort to attend their programs. When they were in middle and high school (all on the same campus), the school had a Grandparents Day.

Grandparents came from as far away as California and New York. We arrived on campus at 8:30 a.m. and were taken by van to the cafeteria where our grandchildren met us for breakfast. We watched with appreciation (and sometimes with amazement) as our grandchildren demonstrated their social skills in introducing us to their teachers and friends. After moving from class to class (twenty minutes in each), we had our pictures made with our grandchildren and were later sent complimentary copies.

The final event was a program presented by a group from the glee club, band, dance, or drama group. Everybody wins on Grandparents Day. Grandparents get to spend time with grand-children, and the young people like shorter classes and taking the afternoon classes off. I'm grateful to all schools that celebrate Grandparents Day and affirm the value of the extended family.

O God of the past, present, and future, teach us to number our days aright that we may gain a heart of wisdom. Amen.

FEBRUARY 6   YOU FORGOT TO SAY "THANK YOU"

Jesus asked, "Were not all ten cleansed? Where are the other nine? Was no one found to return and give praise to God except this foreigner?"   *(Luke 17:17-18 NIV)*

Recently I read of a Holocaust victim who had survived the horrors of a German concentration camp. While there, her husband and only son were killed simply because they were Jewish.

The experience so traumatized the woman that she had what psychiatrists called "an emotional shutdown." She could no longer feel pain or experience love or joy. She could only function as a robot. Her breakthrough came when a neighbor brought the sad woman a casserole. The neighbor's three-year-old grandson observed the proceedings and then said, "You forgot to say 'thank you'."

Suddenly the woman remembered her own son as a child and thought of the many times she had said those very words to him. A smile enveloped her face as she stooped down, hugged the child, and expressed gratitude to his grandmother. The emotional logjam was broken. That day her heart began to open to life, to God, and to others.

Jesus must have said in effect, "You forgot to say 'thank you'" when nine lepers failed to express appreciation for their cleansing.

Merciful God, help us never to forget to say "thank you," and enable us to teach our grandchildren the effect of gratitude on human personality. Amen.

FEBRUARY 7   THE ATTITUDE OF GRATITUDE

Give thanks in all circumstances, for this is God's will for you in Christ Jesus.   *(1 Thessalonians 5:18 NIV)*

One bleak, November day, two weeks after the accident that took the life of our college-age son, I was observing my quiet time—both out of habit and out of need. Suddenly the words of 1 Thessalonians 5:18 seemed to explode into my grief-soaked brain: "Give thanks in all circumstances...."

I put down my Bible and asked aloud, "In *all* circumstances?" As I read again the fifth chapter, I understood anew that Paul was not saying, "Give thanks *for* the death of your son." Instead he was saying, "Change your focus—not on what you have lost, but on what you have left." I began to give thanks for a husband who loves me; for another son; for having Rick for twenty years; for friends and family; for Christ and his church, and for the Holy Spirit who brings us comfort. It was gratitude that opened my heart and caused my grief to lift.

If misfortune or tragedy touches our lives, we may find relief by remembering to "give thanks in all circumstances."

Eternal God, help us to remember that genuine appreciation warms hearts and overcomes grief and depression. Amen.

FEBRUARY 8   THE POWER OF PRAISE

"So in everything, do to others what you would have them do to you, for this sums up the Law and the Prophets."
(Matthew 7:12 NIV)

When I was in the fifth grade, a local bank sponsored an essay contest, and I was lucky enough to win the ten dollar prize. The award was to be presented at school, and I expressed appreciation for it. My father suggested that I write a "thank you" note to the president of the bank. That didn't seem necessary to me, but I did it.

To my amazement, I received a letter from the bank president saying that they had sponsored the contest for a number of years and that mine was the first letter of appreciation they had ever received. That day I learned that even a small amount of gratitude warms human hearts.

The late Harvard psychologist William James wrote, "Everyone you meet is wearing an invisible sign which reads, 'I want to feel genuinely appreciated'." This sign, however, doesn't say, "I want to be flattered or insincerely praised."

If we can help grandchildren grasp this truth, we have given them one of Christ's true secrets of success as expressed in the Golden Rule.

O God of encouragement and love, enable us to teach our grandchildren to spread your love through appreciation. Amen.

FEBRUARY 9   WE ARE CHRISTIANS UNDER
                                              CONSTRUCTION

He who began a good work in you will carry it on to completion until the day of Christ Jesus.   (Philippians 1:6 NIV)

Marjorie Scholtz, a Bostonian, experienced two major tragedies. Her physician husband died of cancer, and their four-year-old daughter died a few years later. After working through her grief, Marjorie was convinced that Christians shouldn't waste their tragedies. She chose to volunteer in two children's hospitals, one of which was a psychiatric facility.

It was in the latter that she met "little Annie," who was believed to be hopelessly insane and was confined to a cage at the end of a hospital corridor. Annie was aggressively hostile, and she had not spoken a word since coming to the facility.

Little Annie didn't respond to Marjorie's stories or loving words. On a hunch, Marjorie decided to make brownies for the child. No response. But the following day, the brownies were gone, and as Marjorie walked down the hall, she heard a tiny voice call out, "Thank you." It was the breakthrough that led to little Annie's healing. Today we know her as Anne Sullivan, who taught Helen Keller and blessed us all in the process.

O God, bring each of us to wholeness, and let us be used to bring your wholeness to our grandchildren. Amen.

FEBRUARY 10   LET'S ENCOURAGE OUR
                                              GRANDCHILDREN

Joseph, a Levite from Cyprus, whom the apostles called Barnabas (which means Son of Encouragement)...   (Acts 4:36 NIV)

Randy was a hyperactive four-year-old who seemed to be constantly in trouble. His grandmother told me that he was not hostile or malicious; he was a bright, energetic, and mischievous boy. Even so, his playmates were often in tears when they were with him, and his siblings complained that he was constantly into their things. When his mother put him to bed at night, she would often say, "Randy, do you need to ask God to forgive you for something you have done today?"

Once during his grandmother's visit, Randy had been unusually well behaved, so his mother didn't mention forgiveness. On her way downstairs she heard a plaintive voice ask, "Haven't I been pretty good today?"

Suddenly she realized that she had been quick to point out his faults, but slow to give praise. She needed to be more like Barnabas: a son—or daughter—of encouragement. We need to remember that encouragement is as necessary to the greening of the human spirit as breathing is to the life of the body.

Gracious God, help us to stay close to you so that we can be encouragers to our grandchildren. Amen.

FEBRUARY 11   BUILDING BLOCKS FOR
                                                      WHOLENESS

But we have this treasure in jars of clay to show that this all-surpassing power is from God and not from us.
(2 Corinthians 4:7 NIV)

It is not easy to be caring, faithful parents and grandparents in the milieu of today's world. Yet we have no alternative if our children are to be whole.

My own parents were far from perfect, but they gave me the foundation for wholeness. These are the building blocks I am trying to pass on to my grandchildren. First is unconditional love. I knew exactly what my parents expected, but even when I didn't measure up, I knew they loved me.

Second, they stressed the importance of education. Though my parents married early and limited their own educational opportunities, they seemed to know instinctively and sensibly the importance of education for their three children.

Third, they never compared us with one another or others. Though our personalities and talents were different, they helped each of us discover our own treasures and to respect those of others.

It was not until I had children of my own that I realized the difficulty of these things. As a grandmother, I am even more aware of their importance.

Gracious God, thank you for the values passed on from parents and others. May we lovingly reinforce these values in our grandchildren. Amen.

FEBRUARY 12   TWO MORE BUILDING BLOCKS

It is for freedom that Christ has set us free. Stand firm, then, and do not let yourselves be burdened again by a yoke of slavery. *(Galatians 5:1 NIV)*

My parents used two other building blocks in our foundation for wholeness. First, they instilled in me a belief that living in our great land carries responsibilities. As they seared in my mind a respect for work, dignity, and the importance of a productive life, they often said, "There are no free lunches."

Also, no integration of personality is complete without a solid sense of values that serve as an inner gyroscope. In my family, these values came from the Christian faith. During my college years, I sometimes rebelled against what I considered the restraints of religion. Only later did I discover that Christ didn't come to punish or limit us, but came to set us free to be what God created us to be. He came to show us God's immeasurable love and give us the Magna Carta of real freedom as suggested in Galatians 5:1.

I thank God today for parents and grandparents who are helping children become responsible citizens and faithful disciples of Jesus Christ.

Thank you, Lord, for the strong values we have received. Help us to model them and joyfully pass them on. Amen.

FEBRUARY 13   MY MODEL OF FAITH

I rejoiced with those who said to me, "Let us go to the house of the LORD."   *(Psalm 122:1 NIV)*

Perhaps more than any other person, my paternal grandmother, Maria Webb, sowed the seeds of strong faith in my life. I never think of her without recalling her credo: "God always answers prayer. Sometimes the answer is 'yes'; sometimes 'no'; sometimes 'wait'." She believed that credo with every ounce of her five-foot-two-inch being. To understand the intensity of her belief, you need to know something of the life and principles of that godly woman.

There was not an ounce of pretense about her. She was full of fun, and I always felt joyful after being around her. One especially joyful memory is of our Saturday night preparations for Sunday. She consistently said with a lilt in her voice, "Tomorrow is Sunday, and we are going to Sunday school and church."

She never implied that it was a chore. Rather, it was a marvelous privilege, and we could expect good things to happen. Even today, I go to worship expecting something good to happen to me personally, and it usually does.

Gracious God, help us as grandmothers to remember that faith is more caught than taught. Amen.

FEBRUARY 14   STEWARDS OF GOD'S CREATION

The earth is the LORD's, and everything in it, the world, and all who live in it.   *(Psalm 24:1 NIV)*

Yesterday I mentioned the powerful influence of my grandmother in sowing seeds of faith in my life. Coexistant with her faith was a sense of expectancy. At her home, we would awaken to the smell of freshly cooked bacon, eggs, and baked bread and my grandmother saying, "Let's see what God is up to today."

After our chores, she would take us on walks to find wildflowers or birds' nests, or to wade in the creek. Always she spoke of God's good earth and our need to care for it. I had never heard the word "environmentalist," but that is what my grandmother was. She gave all of her grandchildren the belief that we are stewards of God's creation.

One scene is indelibly imprinted in my mind. We had had such fun on our hike and were seated on a log, dangling our feet in the water. It was a peaceful, happy scene when she said, "Children, each of us should leave the world a more beautiful place than when we found it."

Eternal God, help us to teach our grandchildren that the earth is the Lord's and that we are stewards of God's earth. Amen.

FEBRUARY 15   PRELUDE TO TRAUMA

"What I feared has come upon me; what I dreaded has happened to me."   *(Job 3:25 NIV)*

The day began with the usual warmth I feel when I visit in our son and daughter-in-law's home. Following dinner, I had a delightful playtime with our three-year-old granddaughter, Ellen.

Early the next morning, Ellen was in my room, bouncing on my bed and telling me of her plans for the day. She waited patiently while I had a bath. Then she said excitedly, "Gran, let's make a mess." That was our secret code for getting all my makeup out on the bathroom counter. While I put on makeup, she experimented with lipstick, blush, and eye shadow.

When I opened my garment bag, I realized that my dress needed pressing. Ellen went with me to the ironing board in the basement. While the iron was heating, my daughter-in-law called to say that coffee was ready. Wearing a robe and house shoes, I left Ellen in the basement and went up to get a cup of coffee. I in no way envisioned the trauma that awaited me.

To be continued tomorrow...

Ever-loving God, help us to remember that you are always with us and that we can call upon you when life's traumas come. Amen.

FEBRUARY 16   THE POWER OF FORGIVENESS

Be kind and compassionate to one another, forgiving each other, just as in Christ God forgave you. (Ephesians 4:32 NIV)

On my way back to the basement, I stumbled, and the coffee cup flew out of my hand. Ellen was coming upstairs to meet me, so I screamed, "Turn around, Ellen. Go back!" She did turn around, but she sat down on the steps. Some of the hot coffee landed on her right shoulder and burned her badly.

In terrible pain, Ellen began to scream. All of us ran to her. Our son put ice on her shoulder while Jackie called the pediatrician. They were told to bring her to the hospital immediately. As they were leaving, my beautiful daughter-in-law turned to where I sat dissolved in tears. Putting her arms around me, she said, "It is going to be all right, Nell. We love you." That loving gesture, plus my granddaughter's instant resuming of our warm relationship, taught me much about God's forgiveness.

While even today there is a scar on Ellen's right shoulder, I never have felt recrimination from any of them. I was unworthy of their forgiveness, but they gave it lovingly. How symbolic of God's forgiveness.

God of love and forgiveness, let us seek your forgiveness and pass it on lovingly to those who have hurt us. Amen.

FEBRUARY 17   THE AWESOME POWER OF
                                       TEACHERS

These commandments that I give you today are to be upon your hearts. Impress them on your children.
                         (Deuteronomy 6:6-7 NIV)

One evening, I was speaking at a dinner meeting of teachers. Just before dinner began, an attractive lady introduced herself as my grandson's second-grade teacher.

She said all the things a grandmother wants to hear about her grandson—good student, gets along well with others, enjoys life. Then she told of an incident that warmed my heart.

The year before, I had given the first two copies of my new book to our grandchildren because the book was dedicated to them. They both had thanked me dutifully but, as I expected for their ages of seven and ten, neither seemed to be impressed with the hard work that the book represented. My grandson's teacher said our grandson had brought the book to school for a "show-and-tell" time, and had read the dedication. Except for that teacher, I never would have known about the incident.

As I drove home that evening, I gave thanks for the men and women who have the awesome task of molding the minds of children and helping to build character.

Eternal God, thank you for the gracious influence teachers have in the lives of our grandchildren. Amen.

FEBRUARY 18   THANKS FOR OUR LIVES

For he is our God and we are the people of his pasture, the flock under his care.   ***(Psalm 95:7 NIV)***

Henry David Thoreau was one of America's greatest philosophers. A rugged individualist, he lived simply on Walden Pond near Concord, Massachusetts. There was time to contemplate and understand the meaning of life. Every time I read his book *Walden*, I feel that the dry places of my spirit are being watered.

Wisely he said that every human being ought to give thanks at least once a day for the fact that he or she was born. Thoreau said he himself did that. Think what we would have missed if we hadn't been born! For one thing, we would have missed the world's beauty. When the leaves turn each fall, I think it is my favorite season— that is, until the first snow falls in winter, or the flowers bloom in the spring, or the grass is green in the summer. Such beauty!

We also would have missed the joy of friendship and love. We would have missed the thrill of marriage; the excitement of seeing our children grow and develop; and the unspeakable joy of having grandchildren!

Thank you, O God, for the incredible gift of life, and for your promise to be with us always. Amen.

FEBRUARY 19   COMPASSIONATE TEACHERS

Teach me your way, O LORD; lead me in a straight path.
                                        (Psalm 27:11 NIV)

There was an aliveness about Kathy. She exuded energy and
interest, joy in being alive, and openness to others. Though I had
heard we all radiate our character and personality, I'd never before
seen it as vividly as I did that day.

Later, over dinner, I learned that Kathy had not always radiated
such wholeness. In fact, she had grown up in a dysfunctional family where she was victim of verbal abuse by her mother and physical abuse by an alcoholic father. As an only child, Kathy grew up
feeling lonely and rejected.

It was a compassionate Sunday school teacher who first
enabled Kathy to like herself and to discover her unique talents. It
was this woman who led both mother and daughter to a commitment to Christ and thus to a strong friendship with each other. The
joyful empowerment I saw in Kathy came through years of personal and spiritual growth that allowed her finally to forgive her
father. It occurred to me that we grandmothers also have the wisdom to become compassionate teachers of our grandchildren.

*Thank you, Lord, for Sunday school teachers who are able to
communicate your power and love to our grandchildren. Amen.*

FEBRUARY 20   "THANKS FOR EVERYTHING"

*Always giving thanks to God the Father for everything, in the
name of our Lord Jesus Christ.*   *(Ephesians 5:20 NIV)*

As a young person during World War II, I had the privilege of
meeting a national hero, General Dwight D. Eisenhower. Standing
in the cordoned-off area of the hotel in which I was staying, I took
advantage of an unexpected opportunity. When the general paused
in front of me, I extended my hand. He not only shook my hand
but also chatted with me. It was very exciting!

Later, when he became president, he told a reporter that when he went to bed at night he prayed something like this: "Lord, when I have thought about you today, I've made good decisions. When I have forgotten you and depended only on myself, I didn't do so well. Now, Lord, you take over and run the country while I am asleep." Then he would say, "Thanks for everything," and peacefully drop off to sleep.

When we feel pressured, help us to remember how a president of the United States, who was also a grandfather, gave thanks in everything.

Eternal God, we don't have a country to run, but help us turn to you in thanksgiving and trust. Amen.

FEBRUARY 21   FOR HEALTH AND FAMILY LOVE

Praise the LORD, O my soul; all my inmost being, praise his holy name. . . . Who forgives all your sins and heals all your diseases.
(Psalm 103:1, 3 NIV)

Yesterday as I wrote of a president's expression of gratitude, I was reminded of an especially glorious Thanksgiving in 1991. On Tuesday of that week, Dr. Portera smiled as he entered my room on his usual hospital rounds.

On March 1 of that year, he had removed a malignant ovarian tumor from my body, following which I received ten months of chemotherapy. He had then scheduled a second-look surgery for Thanksgiving week. It was on that Tuesday that the oncologist entered my room with the great news: "Reports are excellent; there is no evidence of cancer." As I expressed appreciation to him, my mind was shouting, "Cancer free! Cancer free!" And my heart sang the doxology. "Thank God," said Ralph as tears ran down my cheeks.

On Thanksgiving Eve, as Ralph and I pulled into the driveway of our home, there was a huge banner—made by our grandchildren—on the garage door. It read: "Welcome home, Gran. We love you."

Thank you, God, for the gift of physical health and family love. Help us never to take either for granted. Amen.

FEBRUARY 22 THE SINGING HASN'T STOPPED

I will sing to the LORD all my life; I will sing praise to my God as long as I live. **(Psalm 104:33 NIV)**

Our three-year-old grandson and I were standing on our back deck, and I said, "Wes, let's be quiet and see what we can hear."

"Listen," said Wes. "Listen to the birds sing."

"Isn't it beautiful?" I replied.

The next morning I heard a distressed cry from the deck. Rushing outside, I heard my grandson say sadly, "Gran, the singing has stopped."

I swept him into my arms and said, "Oh no, Wes, the singing hasn't stopped; the birds moved to another place."

That afternoon, I dissolved in tears in hearing of the death of a dear friend whose magnificent soprano voice rang from our church's choir loft every Sunday. "It's hard to realize that I won't hear her sing again," I said to my husband.

A tug at my dress caused me to look down and hear Wes say, "Singing moved, not stopped." As I stooped to hug him, I realized that he had given me an eternal truth. The singing hadn't stopped, but my friend was now singing in the heavenly choir.

Eternal God, may we hear your messages from the Bible, from preachers and teachers, and, sometimes, from our grandchildren. Amen.

FEBRUARY 23 PRAY FOR YOUR GRANDCHILDREN

"I have revealed you to those whom you gave me."
(John 17:6a NIV)

In a Sunday morning worship service, our minister asked us to pray for the persons on our right and left. On the drive home from church, I said to our ten-year-old granddaughter, "Ellen, when the pastor asked us to pray for the people seated next to us, I prayed for you and the man you will someday marry."

Quick as a flash she asked, "What does he look like?

"I don't know that, but he will be a strong Christian, love you deeply, and enjoy his work."

We laughed and talked a little about that and then had lunch with her brother and their granddad. In the afternoon we all went swimming. Once as she swam past me, she asked, "Is he rich?" Forgetting completely our earlier conversation, I asked, "Is who rich?" Grinning, Ellen replied, "That man I'm going to marry."

"Well, if he's a Christian, loves you, and sees his job as God's calling, he will be rich," I replied.

As grandparents, we have the privilege of praying for our grandchildren.

O God, help us to realize the power you have given us to pray for our grandchildren. Enable us to tap into that power joyfully. Amen.

FEBRUARY 24   A GRANDDAD-GRANDSON
                                         RELATIONSHIP

To Timothy my true son in the faith.   *(1 Timothy 1:2 NIV)*

The telephone rang at 10:30 p.m. When Ralph answered, I heard him say, "Slow down, Wes. Take three deep breaths." After that, my husband listened, only asking an occasional question. When our grandson had poured out the entire story of a disagreement with his parents, my husband wisely recognized that our grandson's tears were not from anger but from frustration that his point of view had not been completely understood.

After Wes had become calm, his granddad began to help him look at the situation objectively. Though a bond had developed between them during Wes's early childhood years, regular spend-the-night parties at our house, and our attendance at school programs and athletic events, that night the bond was cemented.

They became prayer partners and ate lunch together frequently during Wes's high school years. As I observed this intergenerational friendship, I said to my husband, "You have had a great ministry—minister in large churches, district superintendent, and college president—but mentoring your grandson may be your finest ministry, and I thank God for it."

Loving God, help us to be available to listen and care and help our grandchildren, in your name. Amen.

FEBRUARY 25   MORNING DEVOTIONS

Jesus said, "Let the little children come to me, and do not hinder them, for the kingdom of heaven belongs to such as these."
(Matthew 19:14 NIV)

When our twenty-one-year-old granddaughter, now a youth director, visited us recently, I had to interrupt her morning quiet time with an important telephone message. As I left her room, I remembered our breakfast-time devotions when Ellen and her brother were young and spent almost every Friday night with us.

Of all the devotional books we used, the one they liked best was *This Is the Day* by Carol Rees and R. David Holloway. The subjects they most enjoyed were "God's Plans for Families," "When Brothers and Sisters Fight," "How to Help Others When They Are Sad," and "Learning to Say 'I'm Sorry'."

Devotional times give us opportunities to teach God's word and help grandchildren see God in everyday life. Children's devotional books make it an easy and fun time to discuss what may be bothering a grandchild. Children also have much to teach us about the kingdom of God. I'm convinced that the best learning about God takes place in the daily events of life that are common to us all.

Loving God, help us to teach our grandchildren to find your presence in the most ordinary daily experiences, and to learn from your word. Amen.

FEBRUARY 26   CHRIST, OUR NORTH STAR

"But you remain the same, and your years will never end."
(Hebrews 1:12b NIV)

The Alaska flag includes stars representing the Big Dipper and the North Star. The North Star depicts a compass to keep our lives on course. As Christian grandmothers, our North Star is Jesus, Son of God and our Savior. The quality of his life—love, service, forgiveness, faith, joy, hope—shines like a North Star.

When we invite Christ to become Lord of our lives, he lives in us through his Holy Spirit. This doesn't involve a problem-free life—only that we will never walk alone; we'll be empowered for living on planet earth and assured of life after death.

Last Christmas, three generations attended our extended family dinner. As we lighted the Advent candle, I prayed that each generation would pass on the torch lighted from the North Star—the Star of Bethlehem.

Thank you, Lord, that you are our compass, our unchanging North Star to enable us to chart our courses. Amen.

FEBRUARY 27   SEASONS OF GRANDPARENTING

There is a time for everything, and a season for every activity under heaven. ***(Ecclesiastes 3:1 NIV)***

Just as there are life seasons, so also there are seasons in grandparenting. In the early years, we are very "hands-on" grandparents—babysitting, enjoying overnight visits, planning fun activities for bonding and making memories. We are able to contribute faith values to the life foundation of our grandchildren.

By their middle-school years, their lives become so full of activities that we are no longer hands-on but supporters of their interests. My husband and I discovered that we, their parents, and our grandchildren could make memories by taking long weekend trips over the Thanksgiving holiday. Our daughter-in-law has kept scrapbooks of these trips. Some activities have stretched me beyond my comfort zone—parasailing in Mexico, hiking in the snow in Yosemite, and standing in the rain at Macy's Thanksgiving Day parade. Yet, we are seldom together now without someone mentioning a Thanksgiving memory.

More important than furniture or crystal that we can pass on to Ellen and Wes are memories, ideas, and faith. In the words of the timeless Nike ad, we must "just do it."

During all the seasons of grandparenting, O God, help us to enable our grandchildren to become faithful disciples of Jesus Christ. Amen.

FEBRUARY 28   SUNRISE, SUNSET

Praise him from sunrise to sunset!   ***(Psalm 113:3 TLB)***

Did you ever look into the mirror and ask, "Where did all the years go?" You may have even thought, "I feel the same as when I was in college, so who is this older person looking back at me in the mirror?"

In the musical *Fiddler on the Roof*, Tevye and Golde express the same sentiment in the song "Sunrise, Sunset."

Sunrise, sunset, swiftly fly the years.
One season following another, laden with happiness and tears.

When our granddaughter left for college, I knew that we were entering another stage. Then, three years later, our grandson graduated from high school. It was obvious that Ellen and Wes will never be far from our hearts, but our days of hands-on grandparenting have come to an end. Yet, as Robert Browning said, "Our times are in his hand." We can trust God for the future of those we love more than life. What an awesome God we serve!

Eternal God, help us to trust you in the sunrises and sunsets of our lives. Amen.

March

Questions

MARTHA CHAMBERLAIN

The child Jesus stayed behind in Jerusalem. . . . [The parents] found him in the Temple seated among the teachers, listening to them and asking questions.   **(Luke 2:43, 46 Message)**

Jesus knew from childhood that questions are more valuable than answers; questions engage both cerebral and emotional responses. Jesus asked more questions than he answered. He frequently taught by the rabbinical method of asking a question to answer a question. This month we'll reflect on some questions that may lead to more questions.

We grandmothers have played the exasperating "why game." Initially, the process helps clarify our answers, but by the tenth "why," our patience and knowledge crumble.

"Nana, why do birds fly?"

"Because they have wings, dear."

"Why?"

"Well, God created them to fly."

"Why?"

"Because God wanted creatures in sky, sea, and earth."

"Why?"

And what about a ten-year-old's question: "Why do I have cancer?"

Our questions never exhaust divine patience or omniscient knowledge. God neither plays games with our deepest questions nor shames slow learners. Still, "listening" as none other can, God may continue answering question with question. Think of it as interactive learning. Don't despair. Just keep asking. God is listening—with questions.

Are we listening?

O divine Teacher, may we truly listen—not only for answers, but for your questions that prod us to keep searching. Amen.

MARCH 2   AGHAST AT THE IMAGE

[Jesus] told his next story to some who were complacently pleased with themselves over their moral performance . . . : "Two men went up to the Temple to pray. . . . The Pharisee posed and prayed like this: 'Oh, God, I thank you that I am not like other people.' "   *(Luke 18:9-11 Message)*

Our thirteen-year-old foster daughter, Jenny, stretched me like a rubber band. I was a good mom, a respected church leader, a strong social activist. But Jenny tested my patience—even running away and cursing me.

When she boarded the school bus, I sighed with relief—until the principal called, asking me yet again not to allow Jenny to wear such short skirts, which she had pinned up every day on the school bus.

Whenever I confronted Jenny with her inappropriate behavior, she tried all the harder to exasperate me. My facade was calm, unflappable; inside, I seethed. After one stormy episode, she hissed, "Don't say you're 'upset' with me. Tell the truth. You're mad as hell—just like me!"

Just like her? Jenny—of all people—had held up a mirror that reflected my anger and dishonesty. I was aghast.

Today Jenny is an outstanding woman and close friend—both a mother and grandmother. But other "testers" keep me alert, including grandson Connor, who blurted out publicly, "Nana, you need a breath mint!"

Who holds the mirror that reflects the real me?

O God, grant me humility to learn from someone unlike me— even a child. Amen.

MARCH 3   COOKING BY MOUTH

[God fed] you with manna, a food previously unknown to both you and your ancestors. [God] did it to help you realize that food isn't everything, and that real life comes by obeying every command of God.   *(Deuteronomy 8:3 TLB)*

In the darkness, the women whispered among themselves. Captured and interned in the concentration camp at Terezin, these Jewish mothers and grandmothers plucked memories of feasts with their families. They ate what was thrown into their damp, crowded cell, but, as one woman expressed it, their real food was whatever their memories created. They called it "cooking by mouth."

After a day of hard labor, they secretly planned a Shabbat celebration or recalled a faraway Seder meal. They argued quietly about the recipes as each remembered her particular tradition, ingredients, amounts, and methods of cooking.

Then someone wrote that day's recipe(s) in minuscule script on whatever scraps of paper they had salvaged that day.

Years after these women of Terezin had been killed by their captors, a tiny package arrived in New York. A woman opened the unexpected treasure. A stranger had discovered the "cookbook," smuggled it out of the camp, and finally found the granddaughter of one of the cookbook's authors.

In your darkest hours, who feeds you?

Bread of heaven, help me find and feed upon undiscovered manna in your gifts of imagination and memory, beauty and relationships, scripture and great hymns. May my grandchildren learn to feast on heavenly food regardless of circumstances. Amen.

MARCH 4   AUDACIOUS HOSPITALITY

Be ready with a meal or a bed when it's needed. Why, some have extended hospitality to angels without ever knowing it! ... God takes particular pleasure in acts of worship ... that take place in kitchen and workplace and on the streets.

(Hebrews 13:2, 16 Message)

I gazed from our front door at cows in a field. How would I, a transplanted city girl, adjust to this rural community? Where would I find friendship?

What I didn't know was that nearly two miles away, an old grandmother had gathered four steaming sweet potatoes from her wood stove. Beads of juice oozed into the worn threads of her bib apron.

Past a sagging gray outhouse, she trudged her rutted dirt road splashed with autumn color. Her cloudy cataract-covered eyes stared beyond the little white church to a familiar gravestone. Trudging on, she turned south onto the paved road.

At last, she knocked on my door. A smile crinkled her parchment skin as she gave away her potato gift. The mystery of joy galloped between us, spanning generations and ignoring the culture separating us. More than thirty-five years later, I still wonder at her toothless beauty and audacious hospitality.

Who waits for my expression of simple hospitality?

O God, open my eyes to the ways of simple hospitality—to the stranger, to the unloved, to the rejected, and yes, to my dearly loved family. Amen.

MARCH 5   LIVING THE PRAYERS

When these birthday parties ended ... Job would summon his children to him and sanctify them, getting up early in the morning and offering a burnt offering for each of them. For Job said, "Perhaps my sons have sinned and turned away from God in their hearts." This was Job's regular practice.   *(Job 1:5 TLB)*

We cannot help respecting Job for his consistent—insistent—prayer life for his children. Imagine! He prepared a burnt offering for each of the ten. Add to that their spouses and children and that sounds like a full-time prayer life, does it not?

Unique is the word for the Grandmother Journey. Preceded by innumerable choices, we have no choice in what ultimately makes us grandmothers. Sometimes it's a surprise package, or an answer to prayer. Sometimes it's a medical miracle, or a wide-eyed toddler from a faraway land. Sometimes it's a mentally challenged, drug-addicted, or chronically ill child of God. Sometimes it's a child whose parents are irreconcilably separated by disease, divorce, or death.

However the grandchild comes, we proudly admit ownership. However challenging—or fulfilling—our role may be, we pray. Recalling our own mistakes, we humbly lift up these precious ones of any age, color, race, or condition, giving thanks for the privilege.

In what way do we, like Job, offer daily "sacrifices" for these treasured ones?

Loving heavenly Father, keep us mindful of our awesome responsibility for our grandchildren—some of whom live in our homes; all of whom live in our hearts. Amen.

MARCH 6   IF THIS TREE COULD SPEAK

Sing, O heavens, for the Lord has done this wondrous thing. Shout, O earth; break forth into song, O mountains and forests, yes, and every tree.   (Isaiah 44:23 TLB)

"If this tree could speak..." A neighbor expressed dismay over the planned demise of the tree to accommodate urban sprawl. This chinquapin oak—estimated to be two hundred years old—may have sheltered soldiers in the Civil War in this historically rich Shenandoah Valley.

But the tree *does* speak. Powerfully, it articulates the majesty of a Creator God. It gives unconditionally its beauty and shade while providing a home for wildlife.

Our teenage grandsons also appreciated the beauty and history of the oak. In fact, when they visited, we drove to the site of the magnificent oak. Even at age seven, Connor seemed to realize the majesty of trees and had, in fact, written a letter to their newspaper editor: "Who sent the tree choppers to rip up these good trees?... They killed two dogwood trees next to my driveway and I'm mad...."

Our African friends also displayed a practical application of reverence for creation. In times past, when necessity demanded cutting down a tree, they approached the tree apologetically and cut the tree reverently, a few chops at intervals, until it finally toppled.

Do my actions support my ideals?

Creator God, how awesome are the works of your hands! Teach me how to show my respect and gratitude for your gift of life and living things. Amen.

MARCH 7   RECOGNIZING THE WORD

I have thought much about your words, and stored them in my heart so that they would hold me back from sin. Blessed Lord, teach me your rules. I have recited your laws, and rejoiced in them more than riches.   *(Psalm 119:11-14 TLB)*

When the parents of our fourteen-month-old granddaughter, Pearl, quote a line from any of her books, she runs to find the book. Miraculously, the simple sentences spark recognition. This results in action that leads her to the book—and to hearing the story while cuddled in a parent's arms.

A Cambodian man was given a Bible. One by one, he tore out pages in which he rolled cigarettes. One day his eyes focused on one verse: "For God so loved the world...." God? Loves? He read on. The power of the Word opened the door to searching and discovery that led him and his family to embrace Christianity.

I want my grandchildren to "recognize the word" that will lead them ultimately to a vital relationship with their heavenly Father. For some this is a long, slow process that begins in childhood. For others, the power of the Word intercepts a lifestyle with its powerful message in an unexpected encounter.

Will my family recognize the words that can lead them to the Word?

May our grandchildren "recognize the Word" as they see it lived, quoted, or read. Amen.

MARCH 8   CATERPILLAR CRAWL

We don't yet see things clearly. We're squinting in a fog, peering through a mist. But it won't be long before the weather clears and the sun shines bright! We'll see it all then, see it all as clearly as God sees us.   *(1 Corinthians 13:12 Message)*

Merely existing while tethered to schedule and expectation is distinct from living in the present. Lest we be thought of as peculiar, we live earthbound lives. We usually forget dreams on waking. We ignore inner promptings or any suggestion of prescience. Like the myopic caterpillar, we crawl along unmindful of all but the scenery around us, never imagining "new life."

I could tell you stories of Dad's experience after Mother died, or of my second mother's vision when she married Dad, or of Mike's presence in the kitchen after he disappeared. But I won't. I only know that at times God allows us a glimpse into *kairos*, assuring us that although we see dimly, another world exists even now, flooding us with hope.

Most grandparents have more time for reflecting, praying, writing, nurturing nature, reading, studying scripture, and tending friendships. Such activities help split the cocoon of the caterpillar, offering a glimpse into another world of the butterfly.

While my grandsons may relish mystery and strange phenomena, are my own eyes wide open to "seeing" beyond the present?

All-seeing God, open my eyes to a world so much greater than I can imagine in my caterpillar-crawl or cocoon-house. Amen.

MARCH 9   THE RIGHT DIRECTION

Point your kids in the right direction—when they're old they won't be lost.   (Proverbs 22:6 Message)

Memories of both my own and my children's growing-up years still bring joy. Homespun rituals such as bedtime prayers ("Now I lay me down to sleep ..."), and snacks (such as bread and milk), and story-time (Uncle Wiggly) affect us for life.

When I moved from a crib to make room for a baby brother, my parents bought a youth bed with its two carved squirrels facing each other on the footboard. Each morning I hung my nightgown on a hook screwed into the back of the headboard.

One morning after my youngest daughter moved into the "squirrel bed," I straightened her bedclothes, picked up her nightgown, and reached, without looking, behind the headboard to hang it. It fell to the floor.

I gasped when I realized I had enacted a childhood habit. The hook was gone, but the hole in the back of the headboard assured me that it had once held my nightclothes.

How indelibly these rituals and habits of childhood can impress our psyche!

What rituals will not only hold me steady, but also influence my grandchildren?

We thank you, God, for bringing to memory these precious connections to our past. Help us to instill rituals and habits into our grandchildren that will lead them into your presence. Amen.

MARCH 10   IF ONLY THEY HAD WRITTEN

I'm chewing on the morsel of a proverb; I'll let you in on the sweet old truths, Stories we heard from our fathers, counsel we learned at our mother's knee.... We're passing it along to the next generation.   *(Psalm 78:2-4 Message)*

A child once said, "Stories make the world." Richard Leakey suggested that rather than our being called *homo sapiens*, we might instead be named *homo narrans*, since we are uniquely created to remember and pass on our stories.

I was blessed with two precious mothers. My birth mother died when I was six years old. I still dream of finding a journal, perhaps with prayers for her two young children, or feelings about her impending death.

When my second mother was dying of cancer, I gave her a lovely padded journal, asking her to write some of her stories that I loved, or anything, on its empty pages. After her death, I found the journal and opened it with trembling fingers. Its pages were empty. She was always modest, often saying, "I just don't have anything interesting to write."

If only they had written! Excuses abound, but we grandmothers can leave a rich legacy for our grandchildren, expressing our love and our story for them to treasure.

What are your reasons for not telling *your* story?

O God, help me to carry out the divine mandate to tell my story—by whatever means I can.

MARCH 11   THROWING OUT BABY WITH THE
                                    BATHWATER

When the disciples heard [God's voice], they fell flat on their faces.... But Jesus came over and touched them. "Don't be afraid." When they opened their eyes and looked around all they saw was Jesus, only Jesus. **(Matthew 17:6-8 Message)**

The late Greek Orthodox Archbishop Iakomos was revered for courageous social activism. As Martin Luther King prepared for the Selma march, friends of Bishop Iakomos urged him not to get involved, as threats on his life had surfaced. Listening respectfully, he then asked again about the march, "When do we start?"

Hearing this, I remembered earlier news of a clergyperson whose credentials were surrendered for inappropriate sexual behavior, and I recalled my daughter's "Christian" roommate who habitually treated others with contempt. While difficult to ignore those who smear the Christian witness by their behavior, I urged my daughter not to throw out the baby with the bathwater. As the beautiful old hymn reminds us, we must focus on the right person:

Turn your eyes upon Jesus; Look full in his wonderful face,
And the things of earth will grow strangely dim.

One day when bearded Bishop Iakomos walked in the park, a young child ran to embrace him. "Mommy!" the boy cried, "It's Jesus!"

"No son, I'm not Jesus," the bishop replied. "I just work for him."

Would anyone mistake me for Jesus?

O loving God, protect our children and grandchildren from cynicism as they learn of human failure. May we live before them as transparent conduits of your love and purity. Amen.

MARCH 12   TIMELY PRAYERS

The Holy Spirit helps us with our daily problems and in our praying. For we don't even know what we should pray for, nor how to pray as we should; but the Holy Spirit prays for us with such feeling that it cannot be expressed in words.
(Romans 8:26 TLB)

I remember Dad's morning ritual. Standing at the sink to shave, he'd whisper softly, "Holy Spirit . . ." Dad was a godly man. Prayer was food for the spirit. Our parents prayed for all of us every day— but suddenly our children and grandchildren have only us to pray for them.

When my husband's parents visited one of their churches on the mission field in Jamaica, the children spent the night alone. About 1:00 a.m., the parents were awakened with an intense desire to pray for their children. After arriving home the next day, the parents asked whether anything strange had happened.

Sure enough, the children told about someone who had shaken the gate about 1:00 a.m., shouting, "Open the gate! Open the gate!" The police discovered that the gate was indeed unlocked. But the man insisted that someone stood guard and would not admit him. His machete and knives portended tragic consequences.

Will my grandchildren experience faith in the power of prayer that our parents modeled for us?

God, you pray for us when we don't know how to pray. And you will pray for our grandchildren when our faith is weak or our knowledge is inadequate. Alert us to your promptings to pray. Amen.

MARCH 13   WOODPECKER APARTMENTS AVAILABLE

Shout, O earth; break forth into song, O mountains and forests, yes, and every tree.   *(Isaiah 44:23 TLB)*

Springtime in the northern hemisphere paints a spectacular picture. Even the distant hills look fuzzy with new growth. "Color bursts like a sweet, fresh flavor," writes Cherokee author Joyce Sequichie Hifler.

My husband and I enjoy walking on the protected wetlands path. In autumn the geese zoom overhead in formation, communicating with loud honks. Stark, undressed trees press in sharp relief against gray skies in winter. In springtime at dusk, the remarkable cacophony of swamp sounds call to me. And in summer, the water seeps into every low spot, and trees burst with every shade of green.

One tall tree trunk, obviously old and long dead, looked useless amid the youthful signs of spring. But then I noticed scores of holes drilled by woodpecker contractors. Although it may take weeks of labor, woodpeckers generally build a new nest each year, thereby providing ready-made homes for species who are not builders.

Old? Useless? Our Creator God can use even us "oldies"!

In this throwaway culture, what can I salvage for pleasure or usefulness?

Encourage, Lord, those grandmothers whose health is failing, whose bodies no longer keep pace with those around them. May they see new opportunities of usefulness. Amen.

MARCH 14   HAMS ON A THREAD

When [the blind men] heard it was Jesus passing, they cried out, "Master, have mercy on us!"...Jesus stopped and called over, "What do you want from me?" They said, "Master, we want our eyes opened. We want to see!"
(Matthew 20:30, 32-33 Message)

We often laugh with our grandchildren as they learn to express themselves. My little brother, Harold, enjoyed using—unselfconsciously—what sounded to him like big, impressive words. With surprising charm, he complimented our visitor: "I like your pearls, Mrs. Reece. They break the *monocacy* of your neck." We all smiled indulgently, and she thanked him graciously.

Another time he asked to offer the blessing before our meal. With great authority, he flawlessly began, "God is great, God is good, and we thank you for our food." Then he intoned, "By your *hams*, we all are *thread. . . .*" Someone at the table giggled.

When Dad asked him later to tell us what the prayer meant, he explained, "In Grandma's smokehouse, the hams all hang on threads from the ceiling." Somehow, he conveyed to the amused family that God provides our food, just as the hams hanging in Grandma's smokehouse fed us.

Could we relax and learn from our children as they see their world through eyes unclouded by years of correction?

As our natural eyesight dims, O Lord, may we begin again to perceive with the innocence of a child. Amen.

MARCH 15   ON COMMON GROUND

Then Peter replied, "I see very clearly that the Jews are not God's only favorites! In every nation he has those who worship him and do good deeds and are acceptable to him."
(Acts 10:34-35 TLB)

My hospital roommate was confused and continually cried out for help. Because she was a Catholic, she attempted one day to pray the rosary. I'd heard the prayers often during three years of nurse's training in a Catholic hospital. Her frustration grew to a frenzy, so I called to her through the curtain drawn between our beds.

"Could we pray it together?" I asked her.

"Oh yes, please," she said.

"Hail Mary, full of grace, the Lord is with thee, blessed art thou amongst women and blessed is the fruit of thy womb, Jesus." I interjected a silent prayer of my own that my memory would carry us through.

"Pray for us sinners now and at the hour of our death."

Overwhelmed with peace as we prayed together quietly, I rejoiced in our commonality—we worshiped the same God and Mary's son, our Lord Jesus Christ.

Let's expand our acceptance to include persons of other faiths. Jesus did.

How might we build on our commonality with our children and grandchildren from babyhood through adult years?

Blessed Christ, we are so slow to learn. Help us to see our world more in tune with what you taught us to do. Amen.

MARCH 16   LIFE AS QUILT

And we know that all that happens to us is working for our good if we love God and are fitting into his plans.... What can we ever say to such wonderful things as these?... For I am convinced that nothing can ever separate us from his love.
                                        (Romans 8:28, 31, 38 TLB)

By faith we trust that "all things" work for our good, especially in hindsight. Our experiences compile a giant quilt with varying textures and colors, shapes, and sizes.

But the secret to creating a quilt rests in the hands of the one who sees beyond the pieces to the "whole." In one particularly "dark" period in which her young son died, my friend wanted to keep every piece of her son's clothing. Eventually, she was able to allow a master quilter to take those old familiar clothes to create a masterful quilt scene depicting the life he had loved.

The grandmothers who gather at Wesley House in Knoxville, Tennessee, work diligently at learning to quilt, beginning with pot holders and gradually moving to larger, more complex pieces. Listening to their conversations while they worked, I sensed they know tragedy, pain, and struggles. But they've turned over their "living quilt pieces" to the Master, who is creating stunning witnesses to God's handiwork.

What pieces of our lives do we protect, refusing forgiveness or ignoring growth opportunities?

Show us, Master Quilter, the pieces—however ugly—that we have not yet relinquished to your creative hands. You alone can work them into a thing of beauty. Amen.

MARCH 17   PITIFUL PITTANCE

But if, when you arrive in the land the Lord will give you, there are any among you who are poor, you must not shut your heart or hand against them; . . . you must lend him what he needs, and don't moan about it either!   (Deuteronomy 15:7, 10a TLB)

Natalie lived in inner-city Washington, D.C., with her mother, two siblings (both of whom were teenage single parents), and their babies. I marveled at the fortitude of that young grandmother who worked diligently for her fatherless family.

About a week before Thanksgiving, the grandmother let Natalie come for an overnight stay. Discovering the pantry with several shelves of canned goods, Natalie pranced around excitedly. "Let me take some of those cans home with me," she said.

I explained that we already had a box of goodies and a turkey for her family's Thanksgiving.

"It's not for me," she said. "My teacher told us to bring a can of food for the poor people, and I didn't have anything to take."

Natalie didn't think of herself as poor, but I'm sure she thought of us as rich. The pitiful pittance we give away still leaves bulging pantries and stuffed closets.

Really now, who are the poor?

O God, awaken us to Jesus, who became poor for us. Show us how to live more simply, more intentionally, so that we may truly "have" less so that others may "have" more. Amen.

MARCH 18   BETTER THAN SIGHT

When [Elisha's] servant got up early . . . and went outside, there were troops, horses, and chariots everywhere. "Alas, my master, what shall we do now?" . . . "Don't be afraid . . . for our army is bigger than theirs!" Then Elisha prayed, "Lord, open his eyes and let him see!"   (2 Kings 6:15-17 TLB)

A Native American woman tells about her father, who wanted to teach his child how blindness feels. Shutting her eyes tightly for a few moments didn't begin to illustrate the lesson. "Do you really want to know how blindness feels?" he asked. Then he led her gently into an experiment that affected both her physical and spiritual grasp of the wonder of sight.

For seven days and nights he did not leave her. Whether playing or sleeping, her eyes remained covered. In one frightening moment she awoke, terrified of the darkness, and tore at the blindfold. But Father sat nearby, reminding, encouraging, and gently restraining her. Once her fear subsided, she wanted to continue with the experiment, because her father was present through it all.

If we could "see" the reality of the presence of our loving heavenly Father, we could better tolerate our darkness. "Faith is being sure of what we hope for and certain of what we do not see" (Hebrews 11:1).

Do our grandchildren "see" through our example that God *is* present through all?

Open our eyes, Lord, to the reality of your presence in every situation. When the last great darkness gathers around us, may our faith lead us to the light. Amen.

MARCH 19   THE GOSPEL IN A TOTEM

It was written long ago that the Messiah must suffer and die and rise again from the dead on the third day; and that this message of salvation should be taken from Jerusalem to all the nations: **There is forgiveness of sins for all who turn to me.**
(Luke 24:46-47 TLB)

David Fison tells of experiences as a missionary to the Alaskan Tsimshian Indians. Earlier missionaries not only believed their totems were "pagan idols" but also demanded their destruction. Fison was angry with this desecration. If only the Christian missionaries had instead told Bible stories in carved relief for the Tsimshian people, they could have better understood and accepted the gospel.

In the absence of written language, the totems provided an outline for telling and retelling revered tribal stories.

While studying the culture of the people, Fison dreamed of a "strange nativity" with characters familiar to the people: Joseph as woodcarver, shepherds as keepers of the fish traps, stable as bear den, and on and on. After his "divine revelation," he carved a twelve-foot-tall yellow cedar log to tell the story of Jesus from birth to resurrection in symbols to which the Tsimshian could relate.

Fison later carved a seventeen-foot-tall red cedar Easter totem. Eventually, the Tsimshian adopted Fison into their tribe for his "translation" of the gospel—God's totems made sense to them!

How can we communicate our faith stories in the "language" of our grandchildren?

God of every tribe and nation, we give thanks for the many ways in which our global family discovers and comprehends the good news! Amen.

MARCH 20   THE POWER OF A NAME

If you must choose, take a good name rather than great riches; for to be held in loving esteem is better than silver and gold.
(Proverbs 22:1 TLB)

Naming a child connects the child to the birth family, birth experiences, or religious connotations that nurture the child throughout a lifetime. At times, God renamed an adult to mark significant milestones, such as Saul of Tarsus, the murderer, renamed Paul. After Jesus broke the bands of death, a woman heard her name spoken gently, though so powerfully that Mary must have gasped at the sound.

An African woman, having heard the gospel for the first time, began her long trek back to her village. Realizing she'd forgotten Jesus' name, she returned to the missionary, saying, "Tell me his name again!"

As the namesake of my mother Martha, who died in my early childhood, I thank God for the privilege of bearing her name. My husband carries the name of his father, now deceased, and each of my children and grandchildren is blessed with names of rich meaning. In addition, millions have been killed after admitting the name *Christian*.

Is there anything about my name that, if one recalls me, causes that person to think, "Oh, yes! She is *Christian*"?

Loving God, help me to bring honor to your name that I bear. Forgive my lapses of Christ-like behavior. Amen.

MARCH 21   PARLANCE OR PRESENCE

Keep a close watch on all you do and think. Stay true to what is right and God will bless you and use you to help others.
(1 Timothy 4:16 TLB)

We don't want to risk "turning off" our grandchildren. We work to keep communication open.

Long before we became grandparents, my husband, Ray, and I spent four years on a remote mission in Africa. When he developed a serious fungal ear infection that spread into the sinus cavities, I drove Ray and our young son to Bulawayo, Rhodesia. At times Ray crawled on the floor of the Volkswagen Kombi in intense pain.

On examination, the doctor looked alarmed. Ray was on the verge of a brain abscess and needed emergency surgery.

With his head swathed in bandages, Ray could neither hear nor speak. Suddenly, an "angel" appeared. A missionary from another denomination came daily to sit at Ray's bedside. They never conversed. They did not know each other. But he came to sit, to wait with Ray, to be present for him.

When we feel tongue-tied around our grandchildren, the most helpful response begins with our presence.

Have you ever struggled to find words to encourage, sympathize, or even reprimand your grandchildren?

Eternal God, may we sense when to speak and when to "sit," trusting you to use us to help others in appropriate ways. Amen.

MARCH 22   GROUPTHINK

Don't become so well-adjusted to your culture that you fit into it without even thinking. Instead, fix your attention on God. You'll be changed from the inside out.... Unlike the culture around you, always dragging you down to its level of immaturity, God brings the best out of you.   (Romans 12:2 Message)

Like it or not, "groupthink" affects us all. Todd Stewart, a retired Air Force general, questioned the "herd mentality" of suicide bombers loyal to "the cause"—wherever that may lead. When interviewed as a group, all of them confirmed their intention with "cultlike support for the notion that sacrificing one's life in the service of God and country was worth it."*

However, when the same young men were interviewed one-on-one without the pressure of their peers, they exposed fear, doubt, and concern about their so-called duty.

We've noticed—and criticized—our teens for their addiction to fashion and electronic media. When a popular boy shaves his head, others are sure to follow. When a granddaughter bares her midriff, her friends dress likewise.

Yet almost as likely to join the herd and succumb to groupthink are those of us who pride ourselves in finally having matured. We embrace current fashion, film, cars, recreation, diets, hairstyles, and on and on.

Is any among us free from groupthink?

O God, help us and our grandchildren as we are immersed in our culture. May we all choose wisely with your guidance. Amen.

Ladies Home Journal, March 2005, 32.

MARCH 23   A MOUTHFUL OF METAL

David shouted [to Goliath], "You come to me with a sword and a spear, but I come to you in the name of the Lord ... the very God whom you have defied.... And the whole world will know that there is a God in Israel!"   (1 Samuel 17:45-46 TLB)

Like young David, Caden already faces adversity with courage. At thirteen years of age, he's conversant and matter of fact about the network of wires that seem to connect his teeth, tongue, gums, jaws, and roof of his mouth to correct an overbite and other complex issues.

He explained the procedure that he goes through weekly, one that was initially done for him by his parents, in turn. But when they copped out—for the same reasons Caden's papa refuses even to look into his mouth—Caden alone assumed responsibility for tightening the "screws."

"You can hear the bones cracking," Caden said. "They have to break before they can be aligned," he explained.

"Doesn't it hurt?" I cringed. "Yes, but in about ten minutes, it feels better. In two years—it's over!" His youthful metallic smile shows off his determination. I pray that when evil confronts him—and it will—he continues to choose courageously.

Do you tell your grandchildren ways in which they teach you by modeling strength and courage?

Thank you, God, for the lessons in courage and perseverance that my grandchildren teach me. Amen.

MARCH 24   POSITIVE PEER PRESSURE

I know [says Paul] how much you trust the Lord, just as your mother Eunice and your grandmother Lois do; and I feel sure you are still trusting him as much as ever.... Guard well the splendid, God-given ability you received as a gift from the Holy Spirit who lives within you.   *(2 Timothy 1:5, 14 TLB)*

No, we grandmothers can't do it all, even as Lois and Eunice did not provide Timothy with all he needed. But the Holy Spirit can fill our grandchildren with what we cannot provide: "the splendid, God-given ability" for a life of service. But how blessed we are to partner with God on their behalf—we, the grandmothers!

An inner-city nurse says that most boys who come to the emergency room beaten up or shot tell her that a grandmother prays for them. She often hears, "I don't want to let her down."

One of the female guards at the Abu Ghraib prison who was accused of prisoner abuse said, "I had a choice, but I chose to do what my friends wanted me to do." Her response to negative peer pressure resulted in unbelievable atrocities.

As mothers we prayed, taught, listened, and loved, but as grandmothers, we add a dimension of strength through experience.

What tools do we possess to build inner resolve into our grandchildren to resist temptation and reject negative peer pressure?

O God, thank you for your protection and guidance for our young ones. But help us to provide all we can to keep them on the right path. Amen.

MARCH 25   REVERENCE, A LOST TREASURE

God, brilliant Lord ... I look up at your macro-skies, dark and enormous, your handmade sky-jewelry, Moon and stars mounted in their settings.... You put us in charge of your handcrafted world... Made us lords of sheep and cattle, even animals out in the wild, Birds flying and fish swimming, whales singing.
(Psalm 8:1, 3, 6-8 Message)

Our grandsons spent early years helping with shearing sheep and naming new lambs. They had many pets, but when we visited shortly after the death of Connor's pet chicken, he led me to her small grave where a stone perched precariously. He reverently knelt before it and clasped his hands in silence.

That simple act of a young child reminded me how easy it is to imperceptibly, gradually lose our reverence for the miracle of life and mystery of death. Daily news bombards us with stories of war dead, natural disasters, and inner-city tragedies until we simply can't assimilate any more. But children speak profoundly to the reality God wants us to embrace: reverence for God at work in our world.

Two of my favorite photos show one of our granddaughters bending to gaze into a pot of yellow tulips, and the other stooping to sniff yellow daffodils. We think about ways to instill reverence into children, but they—from two-year-olds to teens—model reverence for me.

In what ways do our children and grandchildren model reverence for God's gifts?

Creator God, may we gasp with delight at the artistry and music of nature. We bow before you in thanksgiving for your profound, extravagant gifts. Amen.

MARCH 26   A MOURNING DOVE

The young girls will dance for joy, and men folk—old and young—will take their part in all the fun; for I will turn their mourning into joy and I will comfort them and make them rejoice, for their captivity with all its sorrows will be behind them.   *(Jeremiah 31:13 TLB)*

Our grandsons learned about life's brevity at an early age. They met us at the funeral home after their other grandmother had died suddenly. Connor, then about eight years old, pulled me toward the casket. "I wrote a letter to Grandmommy and put it here beside her," he said. "But," Connor told us with surprisingly mature acceptance, "Grandmommy wouldn't want to stay alive because her brain got damaged. Now she's in a better place."

Now, two of our grandsons have only two grandparents. Our grandchildren experience innumerable bumps and scrapes, but we also know their journeys will intersect with deeper traumas. This startles me into a deep longing to be present for them while I can to console and encourage them.

Most of us begin learning in early childhood about death and grief. Watching us, our grandchildren will observe our sources of comfort in our losses.

How do we communicate to our grandchildren our faith in a God who will turn mourning into joy?

God, when we walk with loved ones through the "valley of the shadow" of dying—or death itself—we know you will see us through. Amen.

MARCH 27   THE PUMPKIN AND THE MONKEY

Jesus called a small child over to him and set the little fellow down among them, and said, "Unless you turn to God from your sins and become as little children, you will never get into the Kingdom of Heaven. Therefore anyone who humbles himself as this little child, is the greatest in the Kingdom of Heaven."
(Matthew 18:2-4 TLB)

Once upon a time, two toddlers fell in love. Todd gazed with fascination on his toddling playmates, especially Maya Rae.

When Maya Rae arrived daily at day care, Todd crawled as fast as his pudgy little knees and hands could propel him. Maya Rae welcomed the attention with smiles and hugs.

One Halloween morning, the parents dressed the children strangely. Todd wore a brown outfit with a furry tail. Maya Rae's mommy stuffed her into a huge, round orange ball; her arms, legs, and head protruded from its middle.

When Maya Rae arrived at school, Todd stared, but soon he recognized his sweetheart even though she looked like an orange pumpkin. As the little monkey rushed to his true love, somehow flailing arms and bulging belly collided. Both collapsed on the floor, howling in confusion.

Teacher disentangled them with laughter and hugs. "It's all right! This is still Maya Rae," Teacher said, "and this is still Todd."

And they lived happily ever after.

Has a familiar person or circumstance ever suddenly changed into an unrecognizable creature?

O God, when ordinary things and even people we love knock us down, help us to recognize what's beneath the disguise. Amen.

MARCH 28   WARNING: KIDS AT RISK

"Hard trials and temptations are bound to come, but too bad for whoever brings them on! Better to wear a millstone necklace and take a swim in the deep blue sea than give even one of these dear little ones a hard time!" (Luke 17:1-2 Message)

Unless we grannies are inattentive or on compassion overload, stories and statistics can motivate us to action. Yet the fact that thirty thousand children die every day from hunger-related causes is so overwhelming that we shake our heads in despair.

Some statistics relate to *our* kids in *our* U.S. communities: every minute a baby is born to a teen mother; every five hours a child or youth commits suicide; two of five children in fourth grade are behind a year or more in reading skills. We can make a decided difference, one child at a time.

Through **KIDS HOPE USA**, churches and schools link arms to change statistics through hands-on commitment: *one* adult connects with *one* school to tutor/support/nurture *one* child in *one* subject in which the child requires help. It's all about *one*! I can—you can—help *one*!

What a sight: *grand* mothers helping *grand* kids!

What can you do in your community?

O God, "Still the children wander homeless; Still the hungry cry for bread; Still the captives long for freedom; Still in grief [we] mourn their dead."* Help us, we pray. Amen.

*Albert F. Bayly, "Lord, Whose Love Through Humble Service," 1961. Copyright by the Hymn Society of America.

MARCH 29   OUT OF BREATH

[Jesus] told the wind to pipe down and said to the sea, "Quiet! Settle down!" The wind ran out of breath; the sea became smooth as glass. . . . [The disciples] were in absolute awe, staggered.   **(Mark 4:39, 41 Message)**

"Nana! Nana!" Caden called again. The boys were spending a few nights with me. After baths and snacks, stories and planning next-day activities, prayers and hugs—finally, I'd turned off the light and left them to drift off to sleep.

However, even with big brother Connor next to him, Caden repeatedly called out about the expected: a drink, a visit to the bathroom, too many covers, not enough light, and on and on.

Eventually, he requested the phone to talk to his parents. At last, Caden seemed sleepy.

About the time I settled into bed, a loud crack of thunder startled me, followed by a small voice yet again. I entered the boys' room quickly.

"Nana," Caden whispered, finally courageous enough to tell me the real source of his troubles. "I'm a little bit scared." That was all I needed to hear. "How about sleeping with me tonight since Papa's not home?" Within minutes we both slept soundly.

What steps do I take to quell my fears *before* I call for God's help—or do I call on God *first?*

Sometimes I'm "a little bit scared," too, Father. Teach me to voice my fear. I know you will gather me into your arms and comfort me. Amen.

MARCH 30   LIKE US AMERICANS—OUCH!

Don't fool yourself into thinking that you are a listener when you are anything but, letting the Word go in one ear and out the other. . . . Those who hear and don't act are like those who glance in the mirror, walk away, and two minutes later have no idea who they are, what they look like.   *(James 1:22-24 Message)*

Walking with my husband in the marsh, I remembered reading information about bird species building their nests in identifiable ways.

Some build a new home each springtime. Others never build their own but, instead, find a previously built empty nest in which to start their family. A third species shocks me, as they assume without shame that any nest they choose is theirs. Sometimes they lie in wait until the parent bird flies away in search of food. If eggs are present, they drop them to the ground. If fledgling birds still occupy the nest, the intruder pushes them out and sets up housekeeping. The nest is theirs; they found it.

"Can you believe that?" I asked, feeling annoyed. I wasn't sure my husband was paying attention to my monologue until he answered, "Uh-huh, just like us." Ouch! The simile stunned me. I recognized that indeed early settlers did exactly that to the Native

Americans who inhabited the territory that became the United States—and they *ain't* birds.

What are we missing with our myopic point of view?

God, may I not criticize, for my foot may catch in the trap I set for another. Amen.

MARCH 31   POOR LITTLE LAMB

Taking him by the hand, Jesus led [the blind man] out of the village. He put spit in the man's eyes, laid hands on him, and asked, "Do you see anything?" ... "I see men. They look like walking trees." So Jesus laid hands on his eyes again. The man ... realized that he had recovered perfect sight.

(Mark 8:23-25 Message)

Elizabeth's mother prepared a favorite dinner for her family: leg of lamb with mint jelly and all the savory trimmings. She and the family celebrated the homecoming of her "big girl" after a few nights away with her grandparents.

During the meal, Elizabeth suddenly stopped eating and stared at her plate. When questioned, Elizabeth replied tearfully, "I keep thinking about that poor little lamb, hopping around the meadow with only three legs."

We smile at Elizabeth's innocence. But sometimes the whole truth becomes more painful than an imagined scenario. Did her parents further ruin the meal by telling her the truth—that not only was a lamb *not* hopping around on three legs, but the whole lamb had been sacrificed (another euphemism) so that many people could enjoy many meals?

Jesus was the only person who knew his future with certainty. I choose to believe I can trust him with my questions. He sees the "big picture."

Can we trust God with our biggest fears, doubts, and questions?

Caring heavenly Father, when I worry about unanswerable questions—about health, my children and grandchildren, the future—may I stop and remember to turn over all my worries and cares to you, "for [you are] always thinking about [me]" (1 Peter 5:7 TLB). Amen.

Hymns of Faith

MARTHA CHAMBERLAIN

APRIL 1 O LORD, WHAT A MORNING!

I'm ready, God, so ready, ready from head to toe. Ready to sing, ready to raise a God-song: "Wake, soul! Wake, lute! Wake up, you sleepyhead sun!" I'm thanking you, GOD . . . The deeper your love, the higher it goes; every cloud's a flag to your faithfulness.
(Psalm 108:1-4 Message)

This month we'll focus on hymns of faith, from ancient to modern. Though many of the hymns we explore may be familiar, others may be new to you. Even so, may their messages deepen our faith-roots and, in turn, inspire us to help deepen the faith-roots of our grandchildren.

Closing my eyes, I imagine hundreds of boarding school boys shuffling their bare feet on the concrete ochre in a mission church. Deep voices resound with, "O Lord, what a morning!" It's not in my church hymnbook, but I hear the call to worship in the early morning heat, already wrapping around them like a warm cotton blanket.

The girls' voices drift closer; we watch a steady stream of pink-uniformed schoolgirls marching into the church, their rich contralto voices blending with boys' bass voices. Missionary Reynolds's pet monkey seats himself at an open window.

I can see it, hear it, feel it again as my memory picks up the refrain, and my feet shuffle with the rhythm, "O Lord, what a morning!"

Praise God for this day! Praise God for life and family and health—however fragile. Praise God for memory and music and the great hymns of faith. Amen.

APRIL 2   THOU HIDDEN LOVE OF GOD

It is no longer important that I appear righteous before you or have your good opinion, and I am no longer driven to impress God.... The life you see me living is not "mine," but it is lived by faith in the Son of God, who loved me and gave himself for me.   *(Galatians 2:20 Message)*

God's "hidden love" hardly coincided with my understanding of bountiful, obvious, extravagant divine love. In fact, I really didn't like the hymn until I noticed that John Wesley translated it!

So, studying it more closely, I understood. It's not that God's love is *hidden*, as though to hinder our faith. Rather, this hymn illustrates that God's love is so deep, so high, so beyond our comprehension that we can't begin to fathom it. Even though we sense divine love, most of it, like an iceberg, is still "hidden" far beyond our understanding.

How do we quantify our love for precious grandchildren? How do we describe "being in love" to young people who ask its meaning? When Ray and I "fell in love" nearly half a century ago, I thought I could define being in love; now, in comparison, it's as though I hadn't a clue then about its meaning.

Love for our Creator God, our Savior God, increases each day. Yet we cannot fathom God's love that's still "hidden" in eternity.

Beloved One, may we receive and give generously of your abundant love. Amen.

APRIL 3   JESUS CALLS US O'ER THE TUMULT

A mighty windstorm hit the mountain ... but the Lord was not in the wind ... there was an earthquake, but the Lord was not in the earthquake ... there was a fire, but the Lord was not in the fire. And after the fire, there was the sound of a gentle whisper. **(1 Kings 19:11-13 TLB)**

At fifteen months old, Pearl is beautiful, loving, and bright. She even loads her dish and spoon into the dishwasher after a meal.

But her mother reported a disturbing incident. While playing in the children's play paradise, Pearl momentarily got "lost" in the maze of tunnels and rooms. Her mother called frantically, but Pearl played on.

"Well, does she know *how* to answer when she's called, even out of 'the tumult' of playtime with dozens of other children?" I asked.

"Oh no," her mother said.

"But at home, when you call her," I insisted, "doesn't she *answer* in some way?" I had learned that "answering" a call is beyond a young toddler's ability.

How do our youth—or any of us—hear God's call with the sounds of the world gushing through headphones, Internet, and busyness during every waking hour? Perhaps we've lost some of our hearing; perhaps "answering" is beyond our ability.

William Wordsworth cried out against the world's cacophony, "The world is too much with us; late and soon, / Getting and spending, we lay waste our powers."

"Jesus calls us! By thy mercies, Savior, may we hear thy call."*
May our little ones grow to "hear" your call. Amen.

*Cecil Frances Alexander, "Jesus Calls Us," 1852.

APRIL 4   WHAT A FRIEND WE HAVE IN JESUS

"The greatest love is shown when a person lays down his life for his friends; and you are my friends if you obey me. I no longer call you slaves, for a master doesn't confide in his slaves; now you are my friends. . . . You didn't choose me! I chose you!"
(John 15:13-16 TLB)

One night our foster daughter Sandy sat in her bedroom with her friend with the door closed. Sandy had run away before; her friend had an unbearable home life. Sandy had been abused in every way. So, we wondered what they might be planning and considered eavesdropping on their whispered conversation.

Deciding against that and praying for wisdom, we suddenly heard, as my husband tells it, the sweetest sound on earth: "What a friend we have in Jesus, all our sins and griefs to bear! What a privilege to carry everything to God in prayer." These young teens sang their hearts out. They were learning, in spite of extraordinary odds, the source of lasting, trustworthy friendship that would never fail them.

On some Indian roads, small shelves called "soma tonga" are mounted on stands inviting travelers to stop, lay down their burdens, and rest awhile. Jesus' invitation comes as friend to friend. He becomes "soma tonga" for us. Then we, in turn, become "soma tonga" for others on the Way.

Heavenly Friend, how incredibly fortunate we are to be called "friend." May our grandchildren accept you as a lifetime companion. Amen.

APRIL 5   HOW GREAT THOU ART

Then you send your Spirit, and new life is born to replenish all the living of the earth. Praise God forever! How he must rejoice in all his work! The earth trembles at his glance; the mountains burst into flame at his touch. I will sing to the Lord as long as I live. I will praise God to my last breath!

(Psalm 104:30-33 TLB)

Superfluous exclamation marks? The scripture translators could not help themselves, nor could this hymn writer, or the secular writer who penned a piece that shook the musical world with exclamation.

Igor Stravinsky saw beyond the visible signs of spring that we typically see. His biographer wrote of "The Rite of Spring" as "brutal, savage, aggressive, chaotic," for Stravinsky saw spring "from within, from the very bowels of the pregnant earth."*

As spring approaches, the earth gradually pushes up and out

until all around us new life bursts forth. But we see only the birth, not the miraculous gestation.

Consider the life *under* the ground, *in* the depths of the sea, and *beyond* our universe! When I consider all that God has made, "then sings my soul, my Savior God to thee; How great thou art, how great thou art!"†

Creator God, we want to see beyond the surface, as wondrous as that is! Help us to be more childlike in recognizing the splendor and mystery of your creation. Amen.

*Roman Vlad, *Stagebill* (April 1988), vol. XVI, no. 8, 20B.
†Carl Boberg, "How Great Thou Art," trans. Stuart K. Hine. © Copyright 1953 by Manna Music, Inc.

APRIL 6   ON EAGLE'S WINGS

But they that wait upon the Lord shall renew their strength. They shall mount up with wings like eagles; they shall run and not be weary; they shall walk and not faint. (Isaiah 40:31 TLB)

The Bethune-Cookman College choir packs houses to overflowing. Their history energizes their final number as a testimony to what God can do. Surround sound enveloped us as scores of youth circled our congregation, filling us with their rich rendition of "Lord, Lift Us Up Where We Belong"—especially meaningful when one knows the story of their college's humble beginnings.

As she guided the horse-drawn plow through the cotton fields, Mary Bethune told herself that one day she would get an education. Later, chosen as the one child in her family who could attend school, she excelled and began to teach other girls.

After her schoolchildren were invited to a local hotel to sing, Mary approached one of the men in attendance, Mr. James Gamble (of Procter and Gamble), about serving as a trustee for her school. Leading him to the site of her future school—the city dump, which was all she could afford—she requested him to be a trustee of the dream in her heart. Mr. Gamble agreed.

Today, Bethune-Cookman College is an outstanding college

whose students know whereof they sing: Lift us up where we *belong*!

God, we can be trustees of our grandchildren's dreams, helping them to realize their potential, but only you can "raise [them] up on eagle's wings ... and hold [them] in the palm of [your] hand."* Amen.

*"Up Where We Belong" is by BeBe and CeCe Winans in *Greatest Hits*, published by Hal Leonard, p. 78.

APRIL 7   I WAS THERE TO HEAR YOUR BORNING CRY

People brought babies to Jesus, hoping he might touch them. When the disciples saw it, they shooed them off. Jesus called them back. "Let these children alone. Don't get between them and me. These children are the kingdom's pride and joy. Mark this: Unless you accept God's kingdom in the simplicity of a child, you'll never get in."   (Luke 18:15-17 Message)

We don't picture Jesus crawling around with babies, climbing trees with neighborhood kids, or playing tag. But as sure as I am about any facet of my faith, Jesus was there, playing with the children.

Kahlil Gibran wrote: "And if you would know God, be not therefore a solver of riddles. Rather look about you and you shall see Him playing with your children."* While we search for God in many places, we need look no farther than into our children's world.

Not that our children are perfect—you've noticed pushing, shoving, putting other kids down, grabbing toys from others. Although they're *not* perfect, they're teachable.

The hymn "I Was There to Hear Your Borning Cry," sometimes used at children's baptisms, moves me to tears. God's presence from birth continues to death: "When the evening gently closes in, and you shut your weary eyes, I'll be there as I have always been with just one more surprise."†

God, may we look in the right places to see your image, and may our grandchildren continue in their God-given role to help us in our journey. Amen.

*Kahlil Gibran, *The Prophet* (New York: Knopf, 1951), 70.
†John Ylvisaker, "I Was There to Hear Your Borning Cry," 1985.

APRIL 8   GUIDE ME, O THOU GREAT JEHOVAH

I am but a pilgrim here on earth: how I need a map—and your commands are my chart and guide. I long for your instructions more than I can tell.... These laws of yours have been my source of joy and singing through all these years of my earthly pilgrimage.   **(Psalm 119:19-20, 54 TLB)**

Phil Cousineau says that "it is possible to transform even the most ordinary trip into a sacred journey, a pilgrimage."* Cousineau readily understands the revelation of the wandering pilgrim-poet Basho, who named the journey a "glimpse of the under-glimmer, an experience of the deeply real that lurks everywhere beneath centuries of stereotypes and false images that prevent us from truly seeing other people, other places, other times."†

A group of twelve women who meet twice a year stay connected though they are simultaneously "together" and "in every direction." How can this be?

In two ways we connect by recording our journeys and sharing as desired when we gather. We also "meet" weekly in the wayside room of prayer, instantly connecting—in some ways in a more real sense than during our physical gathering. Here we offer gratitude for friendship, thanksgiving for our journeys (regardless of the terrain), and intercession for our companions on the way.

O Guide, keep us tethered to you and to one another. We fear getting lost, but we know we'll not lose our way with you as guide. We pray for our little ones, our middle-sized children and teens, our grandchildren who already have children of their own in this pilgrimage with you. Amen.

*Phil Cousineau, The Art of Pilgrimage (Berkeley, Calif.: Conari, 1998).
†Ibid., ix.

APRIL 9   HOSANNA, LOUD HOSANNA

The next day, the news that Jesus was on the way to Jerusalem swept through the city, and a huge crowd of Passover visitors took palm branches and went down the road to meet him, shouting, "The Savior! God bless the King of Israel! Hail to God's Ambassador!" **(John 12:12-13 TLB)**

Palm Sunday. Good Friday. Easter. All were wrapped in disguises. How ironic that the real meaning in each depth of human experience is often shrouded from our vision.

Hindsight makes Palm Sunday less exciting than it first appeared. The celebrating crowd illustrates our tendency to see only the present moment. From our historical vantage point, we view the events of holy week as the triumph God intended. But how often present circumstances mask what is really happening.

Do you wonder about the purpose as you watch God work in yourself, in the church, in world events? Even Jesus' closest friends often saw only the wrappings. They often examined situations, but totally missed the point.

Consider Palm Sunday: those who lined the streets wanted to make Jesus an earthly king rather than recognize the lordship of life he intended. Think about the garden of Gethsemane: first Jesus' friends slept; then when things got really bad, they deserted him. On resurrection morning, the disciples huddled in fear behind locked doors.

O God, open our eyes to see and to trust. May we be slow to judge, quick to admit our limited view, and ready to praise you "with heart and life and voice."* Amen.

*Jeannette Threlfall, "Hosanna, Loud Hosanna," 1873.

APRIL 10   WOMAN IN THE NIGHT

Martha welcomed [Jesus] and made him feel quite at home.... The Master said, "Martha, dear Martha, you're fussing far too much and getting yourself worked up over nothing. One thing only is essential, and Mary has chosen it—it's the main course." **(Luke 10:38, 41-42 Message)**

The hymn "Woman in the Night" by Brian Wren (1983) refers to biblical women, bound in the darkness of that era's social mores, nurtured in subservience. Some broke with tradition to follow Jesus.

On his way to Jerusalem and his death, Jesus stops for nourishment of body and soul with friends in Bethany. They know him well. He's welcome there.

Preparing to feed Jesus and the disciples, Martha is "distracted," suggests Martha Montgomery. "Distracted from what?" Montgomery writes that this woman with her "efficient hospitality and her knowledge of Christ" is rightly frustrated—distracted from the one with whom she wants to spend every moment.*

Maybe, says Montgomery, Jesus is telling Martha that he recognizes that both sisters have household tasks; both are his friends. Mary has "chosen the better" part, meaning, perhaps, that she is sufficiently free of social customs to sit at the Teacher's feet—reserved for men only. Patricia Halverson suggests Mary may be "better at listening ... than speaking."†

While "Martha [already] knows Jesus is the Christ," suggests Montgomery, "Mary [sits] at his feet learning the same thing."‡

God, our grandchildren display personality traits unique to them. May we not criticize the very essence of their being but help them live out the work you have for them to do. Amen.

*Martha Montgomery, *Priscilla Papers* (Summer 1996), vol. 10, no. 3, 11-12.
†Patricia Halverson, ibid., 12.
‡Martha Montgomery, ibid., 10.

APRIL 11   BY GRACIOUS POWERS

Jesus then said, "I came into the world to bring everything into the clear light of day, making all the distinctions clear, so that those who have never seen will see, and those who have made a great pretense of seeing will be exposed as blind."
                                        (John 9:39 Message)

The fact that we celebrate the tradition of "Fat Tuesday"—with Mardi Gras thrown in—to prepare for Lent is surely an oxymoron. To use up all that fat—and, I might add, sugar—in preparation for the arduous journey to the cross seems incongruous.

I'd purchased Easter cards for our grandchildren; the two older ones are teenagers. "What shall we send them?" I asked my husband, considering a dollar amount to enclose. We agreed they'd outgrown Easter baskets, but *any* monetary or secular gift could obscure Easter's real significance.

It's not the diet or basket or gifts that distorts the meaning. Neither is it the pain from torture that Dietrich Bonhoeffer experienced as he penned this hymn, nor that of disease or loss of a loved one. As long as we acknowledge Jesus as the One, first high and lifted up on a center cross, then turning his back on an empty tomb, we journey as intentional pilgrims, denying *and* feasting, giving *and* receiving, remembering *and* repenting.

"When this cup you give is filled to brimming with bitter suf-f'ring, ... [may] we take it thankfully and without trembling,"* for we know that you are always good and loving. Amen.

*Dietrich Bonhoeffer, "By Gracious Powers," 1944; trans. Fred Pratt Green, 1972. ©1974 Hope Publishing Company.

APRIL 12   HOW FIRM A FOUNDATION

Don't be afraid.... When you go through deep waters and great trouble, I will be with you. When you go through rivers of diffi-culty, you will not drown! When you walk through the fire of oppression, you will not be burned up.... For I am the Lord your God.   (Isaiah 43:1-3 TLB)

An elderly woman called a morning talk show. She'd slept for a number of hours and felt disoriented. "It's semidark outside," she said, "but could you tell me whether it's sunrise or sunset?" Since she lived alone, she had no one to ask, and her clock didn't dispel her confusion. The talk show host was amused.

Following a car accident, my son was taken to the hospital in an ambulance. The attendant asked questions, both for information and to determine his mental state. "What day were you born?" she asked. "Well," he began slowly, "that will take some calculating." Of course, she assumed he didn't remember his birthday. He assumed she wanted to know the day of the week on which he was born.

During Holy Week and the days following the resurrection, all that Jesus had taught and predicted only served to confuse his followers. In the dark night of the soul, even while the Easter sunshine exploded around them, they asked in confusion, "Could someone tell me whether it's sunrise or sunset?"

Almighty God, "When through the deep waters [you] call [us] to go, the rivers of woe shall not ... overflow; for [you] will be with [us], [our] troubles to bless, and sanctify to [us our] deepest distress."* Amen.

*"How Firm a Foundation," "K" in Rippon's *A Selection of Hymns*, 1787.

APRIL 13   I STAND AMAZED IN THE PRESENCE

"Father, remove this cup from me. But please, not what I want. What do you want?"...An angel from heaven was at his side, strengthening him. He prayed on all the harder. Sweat, wrung from him like drops of blood, poured off his face.

(Luke 22:42-44 Message)

The disciples had been on the road with Jesus, and now they were gathering in some upstairs room without family. Some artists have depicted the gathering with women and children participating, because the Seder meal traditionally included the family. Even the children helped tell the ancient story of deliverance from the angel of death who stalked the land that night in Egypt, passing over those homes marked with the blood of a slain lamb.

Whether that Last Supper Seder included only Jesus and the twelve or some of their families who had followed them, they not only weren't "home"; they were implicated in events that were anything but normal or traditional: a meal, a hymn, a walk to the garden, sleepy friends, a Savior praying alone, sweat that flowed like blood, a sudden rush of soldiers, a tussle and a severed ear and, most preposterous of all, a disciple greeting Jesus with a kiss to signal soldiers to capture the innocent God-man.

I stand amazed in your presence, O Christ of Nazareth. "And my song shall ever be: How marvelous! How wonderful is my Savior's love for me!"* May the reality of this love story likewise "amaze" my grandchildren. Amen.

*Charles H. Gabriel, "I Stand Amazed in the Presence," 1905.

APRIL 14   'TIS FINISHED! THE MESSIAH DIES

Jesus knew that everything was now finished, and to fulfill the Scriptures said, "I'm thirsty." A jar of sour wine was sitting there, so a sponge was soaked in it and put on a hyssop branch and held up to his lips. When Jesus had tasted it, he said, "It is finished," and bowed his head and dismissed his spirit.
                                    (John 19:28-30 TLB)

The man who controlled the drawbridge over which the train crossed took his young son to work. He sat before the controls looking toward the tracks. Right on time, the locomotive drew closer. The man placed his hands on the lever and set the controls to lower the bridge.

Suddenly his eyes saw a child. Aghast, he realized his son had left the room. If the father closed the bridge, his little son would be crushed. If he did not close the bridge, scores of passengers would plunge to their deaths.

Seconds remained, and the father pulled the lever to close the bridge with an inner scream that will last to eternity. Gripped in unreality, he stared at the faces of passengers whizzing by—in the dining car, in the lounge, in their compartments, oblivious to the cost of their safety.

It is right for us to recall the old, old story of God's sacrificing his son in order to save humankind from a tragic fate.

O loving Savior, may we remind our grandchildren that God loves them this much, even sacrificing you, God's son, to save us. Amen.

APRIL 15   HYMN OF PROMISE

"Listen carefully: Unless a grain of wheat is buried in the ground, dead to the world, it is never any more than a grain of wheat. But if it is buried, it sprouts and reproduces itself many times over. In the same way, anyone who holds on to life just as it is destroys that life. But if you let it go, reckless in your love, you'll have it forever, real and eternal."

(John 12:24-25 Message)

We can surmise that between the crucifixion and resurrection, Jesus' followers experienced the most gut-wrenching pain they'd ever known. They undoubtedly felt partly to blame and were pressed into despair with their guilt over their desertion and failure to halt the crime, for allowing one among them to have betrayed their master, and for Peter's private grief in his denial of the one he loved.

If it weren't for God's grace and mercy, more than one suicide might have resulted. There seemed to be no hope or comfort anywhere.

But "The Hymn of Promise," written by Natalie Sleeth (1986), speaks of a "hidden promise," demanding faith. Anyone can count the seeds in an apple, but only God can count the apples in a seed. Jesus had revealed the sequence of that week, but not one of the disciples had caught on. And then, he was dead forever—or so they thought.

Merciful God, may we more fully believe through faith in all you try to tell us. And when we don't "get it," please hold on to us until we slow learners can catch up. Amen.

APRIL 16   LOVE DIVINE, ALL LOVES EXCELLING

God is so rich in mercy; he loved us so much that even though we were spiritually dead and doomed by our sins, he gave us back our lives again. *(Ephesians 2:4-5 TLB)*

One evening our grandsons walked with us around Lake Junaluska, in North Carolina. Caden raced ahead while Connor settled into a stroll; so finally we separated, Papa racing ahead with Caden and I sauntering with Connor. We entered the stone chapel as evening sunrays cascaded through stained glass windows. Even young Connor seemed to recognize this as "holy ground." Noticing the wood carving of the Last Supper, he said, "Tell me the story, Nana."

Kneeling at the altar rail, I began with Maundy Thursday, reviewing the Holy Week saga. He'd heard the individual stories before, but he continually prompted me, "Then what?" I continued retelling the story through Easter.

Caught up in a moment of epiphany, he whispered, "You mean, Nana, there's a *connection?*"

Yes, Connor, there *is* a connection! Likewise, tracing our lifetime "stories" that appear unconnected, we may discover that they reveal God's unfathomable, caring love for us.

"Love divine, all loves excelling, Joy of heaven, to earth come down;... Pure, unbounded love thou art."*

May we as grandparents walk reverently into those revelatory moments with our grandchildren. Help us, O God, to connect Christ's Passion with everyday living. Amen.

*Charles Wesley, "Love Divine, All Loves Excelling," 1747.

APRIL 17   O THOU WHO THIS MYSTERIOUS BREAD

That same day two ... were walking to the village Emmaus ... deep in conversation.... Jesus came up and walked along with them. But they were not able to recognize who he was.... [Arriving at the village, Jesus] went in with them [for supper].... Taking the bread, he blessed and broke and gave it to them. At that moment, open-eyed, wide-eyed, they recognized him." **(Luke 24:13-16, 29-31 Message)**

Is faith a gift or a choice?

For some, "believing" is as natural as breathing. From her youth, Mother Teresa seemed drawn irresistibly toward a life of devotion and service to God and humankind.

For others, believing seems beyond their ability. C. S. Lewis structured his atheistic view on the unjust universe until he ultimately embraced the notion that, were it not for the plumb line of ultimate justice, injustice would not exist.

Still others turn from God intentionally, like the rich young ruler who turned his back on Jesus and walked away.

On that first Easter afternoon, Jesus answered his followers' questions, yet they nearly missed connecting the dots. After all, Jesus was "dead" and not expected to show up for an afternoon walk.

We, too, sometimes fail to sense God's presence. But as Alfred Lord Tennyson said, "Closer is He than breathing, and nearer than hands and feet." Jesus himself promised: "I am with you always, even unto the end of the world" (Matthew 28:20 KJV).

This *is* the gift. We choose by believing the unimaginable.

Risen Lord, "Open our eyes to see thy face,"* and lead our grandchildren to make choices that open the door to believing. Amen.

*Charles Wesley, "O Thou Who This Mysterious Bread," 1745.

APRIL 18   WHEN I SURVEY THIS WONDROUS CROSS

"So what do I do with this man you call King of the Jews?"... "Nail him to a cross!"... They nailed him up at nine o'clock in the morning.... "If you're really God's Son, come down from that cross!"... But Jesus, with a loud cry, gave his last breath.   (Mark 15:12-13, 25, 30, 37 Message)

Father Jenko's testimony moved me deeply. Having experienced the paralyzing fear of a political kidnapping in Beirut in the 1980s, he'd been wrapped like a mummy and fastened beneath a truck chassis. Bumping along the road, his nose bled; caked with blood, he could scarcely breathe.

He suffered the ultimate humiliation when they took from around his neck the cross, symbolic of his life and allegiance.

One day a tiny button fell from his garment—so small and

insignificant, yet it became a link to the "normal" world. Increasingly, he realized how much his only possession meant to him. In an act of utter abandonment to God, he flung that last vestige of human hope aside.

"My richest gain I count but loss, and pour contempt on all my pride," Isaac Watts wrote. "All the vain things that charm me most, I sacrifice them to His blood."*

Sacrifice all the vain things—even a button. Father Jenko's deliberate relinquishment of even the smallest idol illustrates the power of losing to gain.

God, we sacrifice bits and pieces and then pride ourselves in the very acts that alienate us from the One who knows the meaning of sacrifice. Forgive us. Amen.

*Isaac Watts, "When I Survey the Wondrous Cross," 1707.

APRIL 19   OPEN MY EYES THAT I MAY SEE

So now the Lord called the third time, and once more Samuel jumped up and ran to Eli.... Then Eli realized it was the Lord who had spoken to the child.... "If he calls again, say, 'Yes, Lord, I'm listening.' "... "My son," [Eli] said, "what did the Lord say to you?"   (1 Samuel 3:8-9, 17 TLB)

It's interesting that God communicated the sad news about Eli's sons to a child. But the little boy listened and reported to Eli. He received a message that no adult would likely accept or relay to one whose connection to God appears to be far beyond his or her own. Even though it was too drastic and too frightening, the message still had to be delivered. And God chose a child.

If only we adults were so humble, admitting our interdependence and need for children's wisdom and connection with God. We pray that communication with the divine does not become so unusual that we regard any such person as foolish indeed—or childish at best.

We want our grandchildren to "hear" God's voice. When our son was five years old, he ran indoors to announce, "I heard God talking to me out there!" Accustomed to playing alone, he used his imagination; but this was different.

God surely speaks to those who listen, regardless of age or circumstance.

Lord, I know you speak through little ones, and I pray that my ears, too, are open. "Silently now I wait for thee, ready, my God, thy will to see. Open my ears, illumine me, Spirit divine!"* Amen.

*Clara H. Scott, "Open My Eyes, That I May See," 1895.

APRIL 20   O LOVE THAT WILT NOT LET ME GO

*I can **never** get away from my God! If I go up to heaven, you are there; if I go down to the place of the dead, you are there. If I ride the morning winds to the farthest oceans, even there your hand will guide me, your strength will support me. If I try to hide in the darkness, the night becomes light around me.*
(Psalm 139:7-11 TLB)

Remember *The Runaway Bunny*? Because he is angry with his mother, he threatens to run away. He'll climb a tree and hide where she can't see him. But his mother says she'll be the leaves on the tree. He'll sail away on a boat. But she'll be the waves surrounding the boat. Little bunny tries to devise an escape, but his mother loves him too much to let him leave her presence.

We all know people who have run away—from God, from families, from responsibilities, even from themselves. I cannot fathom the pain of the one who feels deserted or unloved or simply unable to cope with another day. Nor can I imagine as a mother, grandmother, and foster mother the agony of a child's perception that might cause him or her to run away, either literally or figuratively.

Our precious grandchildren will struggle with issues and decisions, but we remind them that we will always be there—no matter what. Although not everyone is so blessed, for every human being, the heavenly parent is always present.

"O Cross that liftest up my head, I dare not ask to fly from thee."* I know that wherever I go—there you are. You have promised to be with me to the end of the age. Amen.

*George Matheson, "O Love That Wilt Not Let Me Go," 1882.

APRIL 21   WHERE CROSS THE CROWDED
                                        WAYS OF LIFE

"Listen to me, you . . . who hate justice and love unfairness, and fill [our cities] with murder and sin of every kind—you leaders who take bribes; you priests and prophets who won't preach and prophesy until you're paid. (And yet you fawn upon the Lord and say, 'All is well—the Lord is here among us. No harm can come to us.')" **(Micah 3:9-11 TLB)**

A young woman featured in a documentary told of her being kidnapped at age twelve to be trained as a child soldier. I listened tearfully to her story of mind and body control, forced sexual encounters, and instruction in how to shoot and kill. She described the horror of having to kill another child her age who was caught running away.

More slaves exist in the world today than at any other time in world history. Even in the United States, children and young adults work as sex and domestic slaves—even within blocks of the White House—after having been promised work and education. They do work—for nothing. They do learn—sexual exploitation.

"My enemies chased and caught me. . . . They force me to live in the darkness like those in the grave. I am losing all hope; I am paralyzed with fear" (Psalm 143:3-4 TLB).

We protect our grandchildren as long as possible, but consciousness-raising is a necessary part of growing up.

O God, "We catch the vision of Your tears"* as we see your children hurting. Help us to become aware and then to act on behalf of these, our brothers and sisters and children, even in our neighborhoods. Amen.

*Frank Mason North, "Where Cross the Crowded Ways of Life," 1903.

APRIL 22   HAPPY THE HOME WHEN GOD IS THERE

Anna ... began thanking God and telling everyone ... that the Messiah had finally arrived. When Jesus' parents had fulfilled ... the Law of God they returned home....There the child became a strong, robust lad, and was known for wisdom beyond his years; and God poured out his blessings on him.

(Luke 2:36, 38-40 TLB)

A boy waiting for his mother sat beside me at the doctor's office. Conversation flowed. Looking around furtively, he showed me how to hold the fingers of both hands to convey "I hate the devil." He raised his eyebrows dramatically and showed me another hand sign, whispering its meaning: "I love the devil."

"Oh my, I wouldn't want to do that, would you?"

He went on to describe that his dad had surgery because the knee was so huge it looked "pregnant." We explored possible remedies for hiccups, but he went on hiccuping, saying they'd disappear when he ate a big lunch at Denny's. All this and more in a few minutes from a little second grader.

Why did he impress me? Not only was he cute as a button with a sprinkling of freckles and expressive eyes, he seemed, well, hungry—not for food, but for someone to listen.

Was I present for my children? Did I—do I—practice "active listening"?

Heavenly Father, we did our best and prayed a lot in rearing our family, depending on you to fill in the blanks. Now we pray for our grandchildren, and all those children who come into our lives. Lord, "Unite our hearts in love to thee."* Amen.

*Henry Ware Jr., "Happy the Home When God Is There," 1846.

APRIL 23   JUST AS I AM

"And as Moses in the wilderness lifted up the bronze image of a serpent on a pole, even so I must be lifted up upon a pole, so that anyone who believes in me will have eternal life. For God loved the world so much that he gave his only Son."

(John 3:14-16 TLB)

Flannery O'Connor's novels reveal folks from the inside out. In *Revelation*, Mrs. Turpin continually reconstructs the human pyramid with herself at the top, and with "white trash" and "poor blacks" below.

Attempting to engage a young woman sitting in the doctor's office, Mrs. Turpin remarks that it never hurt anyone to smile. When the girl's book connects abruptly with Mrs. Turpin's head, she hears the girl whisper, "Go back to hell where you came from, you old warthog."

Mrs. Turpin later envisions hordes of clean "white trash," blacks in white robes, freaks and lunatics crossing a bridge into heaven—with Mrs. Turpin herself following. Stripped of pretense, she, with others of her ilk, realizes "even their virtues are burned away."

Bishop Will Willimon says the story of grace shows one "whipped, scorned, lynched by a proud, dishonest world . . . a crucified God who, in horrible deformity, nailed to a cross, stared down upon us in our bloody, lying, freakishness and still . . . [said], even to freaks like us . . . 'I love you still'."*

"Just as I am, poor, wretched, blind; Sight, riches, healing of the mind, Yea, all I need, in thee to find, O Lamb of God, I come."†
Draw to yourself our little ones, Lord. Amen.

*William H. Willimon, *Reading with Deeper Eyes* (Nashville: Upper Room Books, 1998), 71.
†Charlotte Elliott, "Just As I Am, Without One Plea," 1835.

APRIL 24   ALL THINGS BRIGHT AND BEAUTIFUL

Sing your praise. . . . Make a joyful symphony. . . . Let the sea in all its vastness roar with praise! Let the earth and all those living on it shout. . . . Let the waves clap their hands in glee, and the hills sing out their songs of joy before the Lord.
(Psalm 98:5-9 TLB)

Every morning, a white butterfly plays in my garden, reminding me of "the ultimate flying machine." However, a *National Geographic* report says that the exquisite, fragile, delicate monarch butterflies are anything but that.

Millions of monarchs fly annually two thousand miles south from the Rocky Mountains to central Mexico. They ascend to seven thousand feet, average a speed of eleven miles per hour, and can accelerate to twenty-five miles per hour, oblivious to wind shear that could down a plane.

Although hurricane season coincides with their flight plans, high wind currents actually provide lift to their four-inch wingspan. How can this be? How can the oriole fly hundreds of miles to build its hanging basket-nest, following an innate blueprint? How can the salmon navigate the sea by sensing earth's magnetic field, ocean currents, and the sun's position? How?

We know how. "I believe in God the father almighty, [Creator] of heaven and earth..."

God of the universe, your creation awes us. As our grandchildren learn of these wonders, may they be mindful of their creator and awake to this gift of nature that nurtures us. Amen.

APRIL 25 CHILDREN OF THE HEAVENLY FATHER

You made all the delicate, inner parts of my body, and knit them together in my mother's womb. Thank you for making me so wonderfully complex! It is amazing to think about. Your workmanship is marvelous.... You were there while I was being formed. **(Psalm 139:13-15 TLB)**

Tomorrow my daughter may learn the gender of the child she carries. O the wonder, the mystery of God's ongoing creation! We treasure these moments of realization from gestation to birth that confirm the miracle of new life.

Before my granddaughter, Pearl, was born, I wrote in a journal to her: "I want you to know how deeply, how unconditionally you are loved.... Little one, a little larger than a lemon, we already love you! How is that possible? Everything about you is mystery and miracle; that much we know."

I wrote to our other granddaughter, Maya Rae, before her birth: "Do you know that many children in our world don't know the meaning of love? But you're already loved and adored by parents, by grandparents, and by God who created you—and who gave Jesus to be sure you know it!"

Just as God's greatest gift to us is love, so is love our greatest gift to our grandchildren.

God, may we show our love for one another so that our little ones—and big ones—will experience the meaning of love that will change their lives. We thank you by loving as you have taught us to love. Amen.

APRIL 26   O ZION, HASTE

"You are to go into all the world and preach the Good News to everyone, everywhere. Those who believe and are baptized will be saved. But those who refuse to believe will be condemned." . . . And the disciples went everywhere preaching, and the Lord was with them.   **(Mark 16:15, 20 TLB)**

After we arrived in India after midnight, I noticed heaps of blankets against the buildings as we made our way to the hotel. I learned that the "blankets" housed street children and others as they slept. We were instructed to "ignore" the beggars, or we would be mobbed.

In Mumbai, Community Outreach Program (CORP) identifies but refuses to surrender to illiteracy, joblessness, homelessness, malnutrition, discouragement, disease, abuse, low self-esteem, hopelessness, crime, and diminished voice.

Instead, street children come home; prostitutes find meaningful employment; teens discover hope; seniors find acceptance; the deaf and lame become whole inside; the abused create new lives; and women learn life skills.

I noticed a toddler watching us through a barred window that is really just an opening in the rough wall. Chubby brown hands gripped black metal bars. On the inside of poverty, he is already a prisoner. He cannot extricate himself. He depends on people like the dedicated staff at CORP. They do *not ignore;* they *act.* Through the bars of poverty, CORP shines the light and love of Jesus.

Our grandchildren live in luxury when compared with precious little ones worldwide who lack even the basics. Help us not to forget or ignore their circumstances. Amen.

APRIL 27   JESUS, JOY OF OUR DESIRING

A person who is pure of heart sees goodness and purity in everything; but a person whose own heart is evil and untrusting finds evil in everything, for his dirty mind and rebellious heart color all he sees and hears. **(Titus 1:15 TLB)**

Kathleen Norris retells a remarkable story in her book *Dakota*.* The monk Nonnus scandalizes the other monks in the order. A notorious courtesan rides through the city, naked except for jewelry. While other monks avert their eyes, Nonnus watches her and praises God for her beauty.

He asks his fellow monks when they chastise him, "Did not her great beauty delight you? Truly it delighted me."

The courtesan, in time, hears of his remarks and goes to Nonnus in disguise, seeking to change her way of life. In time she becomes a nun, and the church acquires a new saint, Pelagia the Harlot.

Of course, this story may have taken a different ending, and we would not have heard of Pelagia—or the monk Nonnus. But I like to believe that whatever the world throws at us can be redeemed, sanctified through God's grace.

We can choose. Our children and grandchildren can choose. God can open our eyes to see holiness in harlots.

"Jesus, joy of our desiring, holy wisdom, love most bright,"† *thank you for your glorious works. Help us to recognize increasingly the imprint of your self on us and all of creation. Amen.*

*Kathleen Norris, *Dakota* (Boston: Houghton Mifflin, 1992), 196-97.
†Martin Janus, "Jesus, Joy of Our Desiring," 1661.

APRIL 28   GREAT IS THY FAITHFULNESS

Thank GOD! He deserves your thanks. His love never quits. . . .
Thank the miracle-working God, His love never quits. . . . God
remembered us when we were down, His love never quits. . . .
Takes care of everyone in time of need. His love never quits.
Thank God, who did it all! His love never quits!
                    (Psalms 136:1, 4, 23, 25, 26 Message)

We kids walked to school, sometimes taking shortcuts through a swampy area. I loved the walk, partly because I listened intently, hoping to hear a baby cry—like baby Moses in the bulrushes. I prayed often to find a "baby" that I could take home to our family.

It was more than imagination. After Grandpa died, my loving parents housed Grandma, an aunt, and an uncle, all in addition to us four children. I knew they would take in an orphaned baby. Fortunately, I never found one.

Finally as an adult, my opportunity to care for abandoned children came through foster child services. One little boy came to us after having been hospitalized with pneumonia, asthma, and scabies. Another told stories of being left in the car while her mother went with a "boyfriend" into the woods.

God answers prayer. Sometimes the answer is *no*; sometimes *wait*. God finally gave me abandoned children—at the right time.

Faithful Friend, you teach us patience and trust in your plan.
Yet sometimes we forget that the omniscient God who created
the universe also has a stake in our little lives. Thank you, God,
for we know your love never quits! Amen.

APRIL 29   O YOUNG AND FEARLESS PROPHET

King Darius signed the law [that demanded allegiance only to
him]. But though Daniel knew about it, he went home and knelt
down as usual in his upstairs bedroom, with its windows open
toward Jerusalem, and prayed three times a day, just as he
always had, giving thanks to his God.   (Daniel 6:9-10 TLB)

It has been said that a mouse will not appreciate your neutrality when it is up against an elephant! Although I'm concerned with world woes, and laud work on social issues, write to officials, and give money and pray, "I am nothing." That's what the letter-writer to the Corinthians said.

Or, did he say I am nothing *without love*? We continually struggle with *how* to "love" our big world. Do we have courage to respond as we should, when we should?

I cringe at the reports of slain soldiers, hungry children, and social stigma against gays or ethnic groups unlike myself. What can I do? Goethe said, "Let everyone sweep in front of his or her own door, and the whole world will be clean." That will do for starters. I can do *that* much today.

Jesus, "thy life is still a summons to serve humanity."* Continue to reveal our place of support for the small creatures in their fight with the looming elephant. Within a radius of ten miles from our doorsteps, grant us courage to seek—and to sweep. Amen.

*S. Ralph Harlow, "O Young and Fearless Prophet," 1931.

APRIL 30   WHEN JESUS CAME TO JORDAN

"I'm baptizing you here in the river, turning your old life in for a kingdom life. The real action comes next: The main character in this drama—compared to him I'm a mere stagehand—will ignite the kingdom life within you, a fire within you, the Holy Spirit within you, changing you from the inside out."...Jesus then appeared.   **(Matthew 3:11, 13 Message)**

Our grandsons were having so much fun in the gigantic pool at the motel that they didn't want to leave for Disney World!

It reminds me of the father who gave his two young sons money to see the circus. They arrived home much earlier than expected. Not only that, they returned all the money. Surprised, he questioned them, "Did you see the circus?"

"Sure, Dad, the circus was free!" With animation and excitement they described the huge elephants lumbering down the street, the lions roaring from their cages, monkeys entertaining the crowds with their antics, and clowns prancing everywhere.

Then the boys returned home. They'd watched the parade on its way to the circus, but they missed the main event.

This similarly happened when the whole countryside turned out to see John the Baptist in the wilderness. John preached. People repented. What a parade!

But John recognized that his parade was only the introduction. In Cotton Patch vernacular, John would have shouted: "You ain't seen nothin' yet!"

Holy Spirit, "Come, give our lives direction, the gift we covet most: to share the resurrection that leads to Pentecost."* Amen.

*Fred Pratt Green, "When Jesus Came to Jordan," 1973.

May

A Legacy of Faith

GEORGIA B. HILL

MAY 1   THE GREATEST LEGACY

Like arrows in the hand of a warrior,
So are the children of one's youth.
Happy is the man who has
his quiver full of them.

(Psalm 127:4-5a NKJV)

I have sixteen grandchildren: Laurie and Lainey (twenty-seven), Kellie (twenty-six), Lindsey (twenty-five), Kimmie (twenty-four), Sarah and Terry II (twenty-two), Lorey (twenty), Daniel (eighteen), Lyle and Robbie II (sixteen), Rachel (eleven), Alexandra (nine), Russ and Ryan (seven), and Catherine (six). My husband, Bob, liked to say that our children took seriously God's command to "be fruitful and multiply." Then he'd add, "But I don't think God meant for them to multiply the whole earth!"

On our fiftieth wedding anniversary, a local newspaper editor asked Bob and me, "What would you consider your greatest accomplishment in fifty years?" Bob could have mentioned the churches he had served, the many books he had written, or the missionary trips we had taken. Instead, we agreed on the answer: When we leave for church, we know all of our children and grandchildren are on their way to church, too.

A legacy of faith is the greatest legacy we can give to our children and grandchildren. Join me this month and next as I reflect on my own experiences as a grandmother—experiences that I hope will create a lasting legacy of faith.

Thank you, Father, for your faithfulness. Grant all I need to "grandmother" the ones you have entrusted to me, so I may leave a lasting legacy of faith. Amen.

MAY 2   PASSING ON FRUIT

I have been reminded of your sincere faith, which first lived in your grandmother Lois and in your mother Eunice.
                                              (2 Timothy 1:5 NIV)

Grandmothering is a wonderful opportunity to be an influence for good and a model of God's grace and mercy. I want my grandchildren to see me "living out" the fruit of the Spirit: love, joy, peace, patience, kindness, goodness, faithfulness, gentleness, and self-control (see Galatians 5:22-23). God is the only One who can produce this fruit in us, and this fruit will remain after we're gone—producing the fruit we desire in the next generation and the next. It's encouraging to know that whatever I missed in rearing their parents (and I missed plenty), I now have a new opportunity to live out in the lives of my grandchildren.

A wise man once said, "The righteousness of a man or woman may be determined by how it shows up in his or her grandchildren." God's Word encourages us as we read Proverbs 22:6 (NKJV): "Train up a child in the way he should go, And when he is old he will not depart from it." That's God's promise!

Dear God, thank you for taking the best we can do and then filling in the gaps where we come up short. Amen.

MAY 3   TIME TO PRAY

It is good to give thanks to the LORD ... O Most High;
To declare Your lovingkindness in the morning,
And Your faithfulness every night.   (Psalm 92:1-2 NKJV)

In her book *It's My Turn*, Ruth Bell Graham recalls a summer day when her young son joined her on the front porch where she was enjoying some quiet moments. Ruth says, "He settled noisily into the rocker next to mine and whispered, 'Shhh. Be quiet, Mom. Don't make any noise ... and you will hear plenty of nuffin.'"

Ruth Graham liked to hear plenty of "nuffin." Her son didn't, so he soon slid out of his chair and ran inside, taking care to create some noise by slamming the screen door.

There are times when I, too, enjoy hearing a whole lot of "nuffin." These are times to worship the Lord and to pray for my family, my sixteen "grands," and their parents. I pray for each one by name, including my granddaughter Kellie, a nurse working a twelve-hour shift; my grandson Terry II, serving in Iraq; and my daughter-in-law Pamela, also a nurse, working the night shift. There's nothing quite like hearing a whole lot of "nuffin"!

Thank you, Lord, for accepting my praise and hearing my prayers. Thank you for special times and places to be with you. Amen.

MAY 4   MY FAVORITE PRAYER TIME

"But we will give ourselves continually to prayer and to the ministry of the word."   *(Acts 6:4 NKJV)*

My favorite prayer time is the dark of night. I turn out the lights and gaze out the window at the night sky. In the dark, I'm not distracted by undone tasks. The darkness, illumined by faraway stars, an outside light, or even a sudden flash of lightning provides solemnity and wonder to my prayerful worship. God seems very close.

I think of these verses: "My mouth shall praise You with joyful lips. When I remember you...I meditate on You in the night watches" (Psalm 63:5b-6 NKJV). I count my blessings and praise God for them—including Jesus, the One who is praying for me (Romans 8:34). I pray for my "grandmother friends"—some who are in nursing homes, some who are very sick, and some who don't have grandchildren or anyone else who really cares about them. I pray for Trula, my retired missionary friend whose only child lives in Southeast Asia.

Prayer is a privilege. It's a way to "bear one another's burdens."

Father, teach me to pray. I pray right now for those grandmothers who need your comfort and guidance. Amen.

MAY 5   SHINING MOMENTS

Children's children are a crown to the aged, and parents are the pride of their children.   *(Proverbs 17:6 NIV)*

In his poem "The Donkey," G. K. Chesterton allows the animal to describe itself. The donkey complains about his sorry appearance, his huge head, and the sickening sound of his screech-like cries. He's the most starved, most beaten of "all four-footed things." But in the end, the donkey declares, "I also had my hour; one far fierce hour and sweet: There was a shout about my ears, and palms before my feet."

One shining moment—yet we grandmothers have lots of shining moments: a car turning into the driveway, carrying those grandchildren for a visit; new school pictures that arrive in the mail; sports events, graduations, weddings, and all the in-between special times. On any such occasion, our hearts swell with love and gratitude. We experience a shining moment!

We want to give God thanks for these shining moments, and we can do this best by *"thanks-living"*—always being aware that we are the "image of Christ" as we live and work as "saltshakers" in our families and our world.

Heavenly Father, thank you for the shining moments in my life. Show me how to "live out" my true thanks. Amen.

MAY 6   A SERVANT SPIRIT

Your attitude should be the same as that of Christ Jesus: Who ... made himself nothing, taking the very nature of a servant.
                                    (Philippians 2:5-7 NIV)

A servant spirit is more *caught* than *taught*. It's an attitude that communicates "I'll take time for you." As I look back, I confess that with my fast-growing family, my servant attitude was a long time "kicking in."

My grandchildren are the light of my life. My grandson Terry, now twenty-two, loves to tell this favorite grandmother story. This is my version.

One day I heard a knock at the back door. I opened it to see little Terry standing there, dripping water from his swimming trunks. He asked, "May I come in and use the bathroom?" I answered, "Terry, you are supposed to use the restroom in the gazebo." He said something was wrong with the door and he couldn't get in. Since I was "up" on his tricks on getting into the house—and into the candy jar—I told him to run on home, which was two houses up the street. The story is that he had an "accident" before he got home, and it was Grandmother's fault.

I guess my servant spirit was out of tune that day!

Lord, thank you for forgiving my shortcomings daily; I desire to be your servant, always tuned in to your spirit for directions. Amen.

MAY 7   A SWEET-SMELLING FRAGRANCE

Now thanks be to God who . . . through us diffuses the fragrance of His knowledge in every place. For we are to God the fragrance of Christ.   **(2 Corinthians 2:14-15 NKJV)**

I met Tammy in a bookstore. She hugged me and sweetly said, "You smell just like my grandmother!" The smell was a link with someone she loved. We became good friends.

One evening I was leading a group of women in a celebration of the life of Frances, a dear church friend who is now in heaven. She was, and remains, a source of strength to us all. I reminded them of the fragrance Frances had left in our church—in classrooms, in various committees, in her creativity with flowers and decorations, in dinners she prepared for our seniors. Through Frances, the fragrance of Christ was throughout our church, and it wafted out into the community, as well.

We Christians are "containers" of God's fragrance. The Holy

Spirit diffuses this sweet-smelling aroma "among those who are being saved and those who are perishing" (2 Corinthians 2:15*b* NIV). We may never know where or to whom that aroma is drifting, but we can pray that our grandchildren, as well as "those who are perishing," will be influenced through our lives.

Heavenly Father, I am humbled at the thought of being a container of your Holy Spirit. Thank you for reaching out to the world through me. Amen.

MAY 8   COLLEGE GRAD

A wise [person] will hear and increase learning.
(Proverbs 1:5 NKJV)

One day when I was fifty-nine years old, my son Rob announced, "Mother, I'm taking some courses at Belmont University, and I want you to go with me. I'll pick you up and bring you home."

I was stunned! I had had two years of Bible College, was an author and a leader of women's groups, and had a record of many accomplishments. I wasn't interested in college.

My other children insisted that I do this, so I conceded and enrolled in the university's thirty-plus program. The local newspaper ran a story about Rob and me attending college together; the story, complete with photos, made a state publication as well.

At graduation, I received my bachelor of science degree in political science and was able to wear the special honor society cords, as well. Most of my children and "grands" were present. They couldn't have been prouder. Tears slid down Rob's cheeks as he held tightly to my degree. We all went to lunch afterward, and my husband, Bob, was pleased to provide the treat!

Thank you, Father, for so many blessings in my life; truly, you are so good! Amen.

MAY 9   MY DARKEST DAY

*"The LORD gave and the LORD has taken away; may the name of
the LORD be praised."*   *(Job 1:21 NIV)*

On Sunday, December 3, my husband, Bob, drove us to St. Louis,
Missouri, to attend the funeral of his ninety-four-year-old mother.
On Wednesday, December 6, my children drove me home, alone.
The events of those four days are forever etched in my mind.

Mom's three sons, Bill, Bob, and Don—her "preacher boys"—
had planned the service. At 10:00 a.m. on Tuesday, December 5,
Bob and his brother Don stepped onto the platform. Bill sat down
next to his sister. Bob walked over to the lectern, directly above his
mother's casket, and welcomed the congregation. He then began
the eulogy he had prepared for his mother.

After only a few words, he slumped toward his right side. Our
three sons jumped to the platform and laid him on the floor. I hur-
ried down the aisle and up the steps and knelt by his side; our
daughter knelt on his other side. I held his hand and prayed our
favorite Scriptures in his ear. There was no response. In just a few
moments, my Bob had slipped into glory.

At the hospital, we were told Bob had suffered a "life-ending
event" due to a major brain hemorrhage. Only two grandchildren
had witnessed this event. The rest of our large family were gathered in the driveway when we returned home—a sad and very different family gathering.

*Our Father, we don't always understand your ways, yet our
hope and our trust are in you. Thank you for the hope of heav-
en and of being with our loved ones again. Amen.*

MAY 10   FAMILY COMFORT

*Blessed be the God and Father of our Lord Jesus Christ, the
Father of mercies and God of all comfort, who comforts us in
all our tribulation.*   *(2 Corinthians 1:3-4a NKJV)*

I had lost my husband of fifty-three years. The memorial service
and burial were over. *What now?* I wondered.

My granddaughter Kellie, a college senior, requested permission to take exams after Christmas so that she could stay with me. I often lay on the sofa as she read from the psalms. Christmas was coming, so I "zombie-ed" around as she took me shopping. I am so thankful for the sacrifice she made and the care she gave me.

Everyone came home for Christmas. We were blessed to have the video from the previous year—to see and hear Grandfather leading us in singing "Joy to the World" and praying before dinner.

My daughter, Sherry, and grandson Lyle remained with me almost two weeks. Then my sister Marilyn came after work every day for several weeks to spend the night with me. My sister Doris and her John, along with my brother Ron, were mainstays for me. I was just beginning to trust what God says in Isaiah 54:5 (NKJV): "Your maker is your husband, The Lord . . . is His name." It was a strange concept at first. Now I know it's true.

Thank you, Lord, for your precious gift of family and for your Word. You are the God of all comfort. Amen.

MAY 11   CRYING OUT

The eyes of the Lord are on the righteous, And His ears are open to their cry.   (Psalm 34:15 NKJV)

I was visiting my daughter, Sherry, and her family just months after Bob's homegoing. Several other family members had joined us for dinner, and I felt very loved. As I ascended the stairs to retire in my granddaughter Lorey's room, however, the dreaded feelings of lost-ness, loneliness, and unreality began to creep over me again. Even with loved ones, my life was very "strange."

Sherry came in to say goodnight, and I tried to explain my feelings. She said, "Mother, you just have to cry out to God; he wants you to."

I began to understand that no one could "fix" my problem or say just the right words. Only God, who created me, understood, and he had a plan. Elizabeth Elliott writes, "In circumstances for which there is no final answer in the world, we have two choices: accept them as God's wise and loving choice for our blessing (this is called faith), or resent them as proof of His indifference, His carelessness, even His non-existence (this is unbelief)."*

Indeed, it is true! Jesus patiently leads us through our pain, and as he does, we learn more of Who he is.

Thank you, Lord, for hearing and responding when I cry out to you. Thank you for being "near to those who have a broken heart" (Psalm 34:18 NKJV). Amen.

*Elizabeth Elliott, *The Path of Loneliness* (Nashville: Thomas Nelson, 1998).

MAY 12   PEACE AND JOY

For the kingdom of God is ... righteousness and peace and joy in the Holy Spirit.   ***(Romans 14:17 NKJV)***

I knew peace through the months and years of loneliness after my husband's homegoing. As Paul tells us in Philippians 4:7, "The peace of God, which surpasses all understanding, will guard your hearts and minds through Christ Jesus" (NKJV). I knew Bob was at peace, so I was at peace. However, I was lonely. I didn't like my new life, and I didn't feel any joy since I associated joy with feelings of happiness and laughter.

Once again my daughter came to my rescue. I mentioned the loss of my joy, and she responded, "Mother, joy is not a feeling; it's a *knowing*." I was comforted because I realized that, as Sherry suggested, joy comes when we acknowledge Who is in control and rest in that knowledge.

A study note in my Bible says this: "Joy transcends the rolling waves of circumstance.... When our lives are intertwined with [God's] ... [we can] walk through adversity without sinking into debilitating lows and manage prosperity without moving into deceptive highs."* The joy of living with Jesus Christ daily enables us to maintain a joyful spirit at all times.

This grandmother is still learning—from my family and from the Word.

Father, forgive me when I trust my feelings more than your Word. Feelings come and go; thank you that your Word is our firm foundation. Amen.

*NKJV (Carol Stream, Ill.: Tyndale House, 1993), p. 1940.

MAY 13 LITTLE SANCTUARIES

"Yet I shall be a little sanctuary for them in the countries where they have gone." *(Ezekiel 11:16 NKJV)*

God had had it with the disobedience of Israel. Soon they would be taken as captives to Babylon. Yet God promised that he would be a "little sanctuary" for them there and, eventually, would return them to Israel.

God has not abandoned us, either. I have learned through my own grief that trials and tribulations are processes wherein God allows us to further discover who he is—if we choose to believe that he has a plan for our good. He's absolutely pure in his motives and deeds, for he is holy. His own promise to us is that he will *never* leave us or forsake us (Hebrews 13:5).

God does not punish us with death, disease, divorce, or other tragedies. These evils are the result of humanity's decision in the very beginning to disobey. Rather, in his mercy, God provides "little sanctuaries" for us when troubles come—precious times alone with him and his Word; times of worship and fellowship with our church family; and wonderful, blessed times with our families and grandchildren. These and other "little sanctuaries" prove that God is faithful.

Dear Father, you say that "even in old age, [we] will still produce fruit and be vital and green" (Psalm 92:14 TLB). This, Lord, is my desire. Amen.

MAY 14 VISITING GRANDCHILDREN

But for right now . . . : Trust steadily in God, hope unswervingly, love extravagantly. And the best of the three is love. *(1 Corinthians 13:13 Message)*

Visiting my grandchildren is exciting, exhilarating, and exhausting! The younger ones, Alexandra, Russ, and Catherine, wear me out—but in a *good* way. We wade through tall grass to reach the creek. We look for minnows and have lots of fun. We trek back to the house, clean up, and maybe watch a video—Catherine on my lap and the other two on each side. What could be cozier?

My older grandchildren fit me into their schedules and take me to the mall, to the gym, to business luncheons, and to ball games and tennis matches. My granddaughter Lainey and her husband, Tom, who is a professional chef, have me over for a scrumptious meal, and I am reacquainted with my great-grandchildren, Joseph and Ellie. What could be more fun?

Visiting grandchildren is one of the best ways to love—and be loved—*extravagantly.*

Father, thank you for the pleasures of grandchildren and for opportunities to give and receive extravagant love. Amen.

MAY 15   THE SAME EVERYWHERE

For there is no distinction ... for the same Lord over all is rich to all who call upon Him.   ***(Romans 10:12 NKJV)***

In 1992, Bob and I joined a team whose objective was to distribute Bibles and present the gospel in the former Soviet Union. We stood in Red Square on Easter Sunday when the church bells rang for the first time in seventy years. During those years, churches had been closed and Bibles and Christian literature had been read in secret.

One day in Evanovo, Russia, we set up our tables near a marketplace where we started distributing copies of a colorful book of children's Bible stories. At once, we were almost crushed! Older people—grandparents, to be sure—were desperate to have one of those books for their grandchildren. They jostled one another around and held up their arms, begging for a copy of the book. Bob noticed a certain older woman who was crying out with tears. Sadly, all at once, she seemed to be gone. Then she appeared right in front of his face. She had crawled between the legs of hundreds of people right to the man with the book!

Dear Lord, thank you for your Word. In 1 Samuel 3:1 we read that "the Word of the Lord was rare and precious in those days" (AMP). It still is. Amen.

MAY 16   I CAN ONLY IMAGINE

I saw the Lord sitting on a throne, high and lifted up, and the train of His robe filled the temple.   *(Isaiah 6:1 NKJV)*

One evening as I was praying in the dark, I looked up at the sky and visualized my Bob, my parents, my grandmothers and grandfathers, and other dear ones who, I believe, are in heaven. I pondered what they might be doing, and I felt a sense of expectancy at the thought of joining them. Then I recalled today's scripture and began to wonder, "How high is God's throne?"

In Revelation 5:11 (NKJV), we read that the angels number "ten thousand times ten thousand, and thousands of thousands." There's a great multitude of saints in heaven, and there are elders. The list goes on. I concluded that God's throne must be very high for so many to see and worship him at the same time. Is the throne a mile high or higher? It's an awesome thought, as songwriter Bart Millard pens in his song "I Can Only Imagine."

Someone said, "If you listen when you're in the dark (hard times), you'll have something to share in the light." For me, the dark of nighttime works also.

Father, thank you for the prospect of heaven and for the reality of seeing you and the glories of heaven. What a glorious thought! Amen.

MAY 17   A SPECIAL BIRTHDAY

I will bless the LORD at all times; His praise shall continually be in my mouth.   *(Psalm 34:1 NKJV)*

My birthday arrived on a cold, dreary January day. I was feeling a little down. My husband of fifty-three years had been in heaven for four years, but I still missed him and the special something we would always do on my birthday.

Hearing the doorbell ring, I peeked through the glass and saw a lovely bouquet of red roses. They had come from my son Rusty's family. I felt blessed and thankful.

A short time later the doorbell rang again. I peeked through the glass to see a second vase of lovely roses! "This is just too much," I thought, "for just a regular birthday." I read the card: "To my sweet and beautiful grandmother, Love Terry II." As the tears ran down my face, I wondered how he had done this since he had been in Iraq for several months. I dialed the florist, and they told me the roses had been ordered online from Iraq.

Gifts and calls arrived the entire day—from children, grandchildren, brothers, and sisters. I was overwhelmed. God is so good.

Father, I'm grateful for my family. Thank you for their thoughtfulness, and for your love and care. Amen.

MAY 18 — A BLESSED "INCONVENIENCE"

For who is God, but the LORD? And who is a rock, except our God?—the God who girded me with strength, and made my way safe. ***(Psalm 18:31-32 RSV)***

My oldest son, Terry, and his wife, Diane, frequently invite me on their ministry trips. We were in Dallas, where I shared a hotel room with my granddaughter Kimmie. One morning as I stood to answer a "bathroom call," my hip decided to take a "break." Flashes of sharp pain enveloped my body as I crumpled to the floor. Kimmie was beside me in an instant, phoning her mother, weeping with me, and crying out to God. We were dismayed as nature, aided by the fall, took its course. She helped me to the wall where I hopped to the bathroom while she got some towels for the floor and some fresh pajamas for me.

I had pulled the top over my head and the bottoms up to my knees when Diane admitted the EMTs. Someone covered me with my robe, and I went "bumping off" down the hall, into the elevator, into the ambulance, and, finally, inside the hospital door.

A huge interruption to our plans? Yes, but surprises lay in store. *To be continued tomorrow...*

Thank you, Lord, for being my source of strength in every situation. Amen.

MAY 19   TREASURES OF THE HEART

For out of the abundance of the heart the mouth speaks.
(Matthew 12:34 NKJV)

I awoke the next morning to see a woman standing by my bed. She introduced herself as the assistant to the doctor who had performed my two surgeries during the night. She chatted a little and then asked, "Did you know you were quoting scripture in surgery?"

I didn't recall saying anything, though I remembered a man saying, "Mrs. Hill, you are going to be all right; the Lord is going to get us through this." Fear never entered my mind. My only explanation is that my system alerted my brain to danger, and I quoted scripture as I would normally do in a time of need.

I stayed in the hospital sixteen days. It was a painful yet wonderful experience, for I received excellent care and made new friends. My dear siblings "chipped in" to provide a luxury SUV for my trip back to Tennessee. My daughter, Sherry, my granddaughter Lindsey, and her husband, Jon, drove to Dallas to take me home. It was a perfect two-day spring vacation! God is good!

"The LORD is my rock, my fortress and my deliverer; my God is my rock, in whom I take refuge" (Psalm 18:2 NIV). Thank you, Father. Amen.

MAY 20   GRANDDAUGHTERS

I will mention the lovingkindness of the LORD and the praises of the LORD, according to all that the LORD has bestowed on us.
(Isaiah 63:7 NKJV)

I have sewed frilly dresses for all ten granddaughters—though the time came when the older ones outgrew my grandmotherly styles. Now I have two great-grands, as well. I have enjoyed helping to make little ladies out of all these granddaughters; I have taught various ones to cross-stitch, sew, quilt, and paint.

One summer when our family went to Disney World, I took the girls (there were seven of them at the time) to do a little shopping, have lunch, and play miniature golf. On the way we composed a "silly song" about playing putt-putt. They were fascinated about that silly song—at least for a couple of days.

On the occasion of the fiftieth wedding anniversary celebration for Bob and me, imagine my surprise when those seven girls, now all grown up, told the story about that special day and sang that "silly song" we had made up! I'm so glad they remembered having that fun day with their grandmother.

Dear Father, thank you for little girls and big girls, and for being so faithful to your Word: "Train up a child in the way [she] should go, And when [she] is old [she] will not depart from it" (Proverbs 22:6 NKJV). Amen.

MAY 21   GRANDSONS

Yet, O LORD, you are our Father. We are the clay, you are the potter; we are all the work of your hand.   (Isaiah 64:8 NIV)

Boys are always on the move. They run, wrestle, carry frogs in their pockets, knock things over, and get into trouble. You can dress them up like little gentlemen, and in minutes shirttails are hanging out, knees are skinned, and hands are dirty. Yet I love my boys—all six grandsons and two great-grandsons.

Six-year-old Lyle once interrupted his mom's phone call by saying, very adultlike, "Hi, Grandmother. How's your day?" Robbie takes out my trash and asks for my help when writing high school papers. Terry II will be a college senior when he returns from Iraq. Daniel writes songs and sends me stories. Russ has trophies in wrestling, and Ryan has trophies in basketball and baseball.

I never really liked "boy" games, so when they were little I made them things to eat and let their grandfather play with them. My hope is that they will value the memories of a loving, caring grandmother from whom they caught values that will hold them steady in the best and worst of times.

Dear Father, thank you for the little and big guys in our family. Help me be faithful in prayer for their obedience to the plans you have for them. Amen.

MAY 22   GRANDMOTHER PORTRAITS

Because of the LORD's great love we are not consumed, for his compassions never fail. They are new every morning; great is your faithfulness.   *(Lamentations 3:22-23 NIV)*

Grandmothers come in all shapes and sizes—and with different challenges. Typical portraits of "grandmothering" involve serving Thanksgiving dinner, having fun with grandchildren at the beach, or doing some other fun thing. Today's grandmother, however, often has a nontraditional role. She faces challenges she didn't choose: grandchildren in trouble, some with special needs; blended families; even the responsibility of rearing grandchildren. Many real-life pictures of grandmothering are far different from the "ideal portraits" we often imagined. My great-grandson, who is three, has very special needs. For a time, we may ask, "Why, Lord?"

Tom L. Eisenman, renowned pastor, author, and speaker, has said that our hard places present new ground for us to plow, and this new ground is a rich place where all we have is all we ever really need: God's faithfulness.

Lord, life is often very different from what we expected. Help me remember you are in control and the best is yet to come. Amen.

MAY 23   WHAT'S IN A NAME?

The name of the LORD is a strong tower; The righteous run to it and are safe.   *(Proverbs 18:10 NKJV)*

Sometimes we are amused as we hear our children struggling over possible names for a new baby. Names often are chosen from relatives, famous people, biblical characters, or whatever name is popular at the time. There are books that give the biblical meanings of names. John, for example, means "gift of God." Some parents and grandparents buy plaques and hang them in children's rooms to challenge them to "live up to" their names.

In the Bible, names are very important because they embody

character. The names ascribed to God also reveal his character: Jehovah Jireh, my provider; Jehovah Rohi, my shepherd; Jehovah Rophe, my healer; Jehovah Adonai, my strength; Immanuel, God with us; and Abba, *my* Father. There are more, but these are the names of God on which I daily depend.

I trust in God's character and pray that all my grandchildren will learn to *run* to the Lord who is their safe, strong tower.

"O Lord, our Lord, how majestic is your name in all the earth!" (Psalm 8:1 NIV). Thank you that your name is a strong tower, the safest place in the world. Amen.

MAY 24   SUBSTITUTE TEACHER

"Show me Your ways, O Lord; Teach me Your paths. Lead me in Your truth and teach me.... On You I wait all the day."
(Psalm 25:4-5 NKJV)

Sometimes I do substitute teaching. One morning I was assigned to a classroom where a young lady named April was doing her student teaching. She was well trained, organized, capable, and prepared. The energy she expended for those seven hours was remarkable. All I did that day was observe and learn! The children loved her, and I'm quite sure they loved me, too, a grandmother of sixteen "grands"—almost as many grandchildren as there were students in that room. (Students are always awed whenever I tell them that.)

Today's classroom can be challenging—difficult family situations, blended families, displaced children. A kindergartner came up to me one day and said, "Mrs. Hill, my mother ran away." I could have wept for him. I pray for wisdom, and that I will be God's fragrance in the classroom—and wherever I may be.

Thank you, Lord, for dedicated teachers—and grandmothers. Help us to pray the words of today's scripture verse and to wait on you "all the day." Amen.

MAY 25   KEEP STANDING

Therefore put on the full armor of God, so that when the day of
evil comes, you may be able to stand your ground, and after you
have done everything, to stand.   *(Ephesians 6:13 NIV)*

The voice of Joni Eareckson Tada, a quadriplegic who has a ministry called "Joni and Friends," caught my attention as she shared
on a radio broadcast the unexpected events of a recent day in her
life.

On the day Joni was describing, she awoke to find that her elec-
tric bed wouldn't work. Her husband, Ken, had to physically lift
and maneuver her body to place her in her wheelchair—an
exhausting exercise. He then went into the kitchen where he found
that the refrigerator had been leaking all night. After mopping up
the floor, other things began to go wrong. By the time they arrived
at Joni's office, both Joni and Ken were tired, discouraged, and
perplexed. They concluded that they were having an "evil day," just
an ordinary day when they felt attacked, harassed, and tempted to
lose faith.

Bad news, illness, temptations—many things cause us to experience "evil days." We must be prepared to "stand," and, after
everything, to still be standing! Our grandchildren are watching
and may learn from our example.

Father, help me remember to stay clothed in your armor so that
I can stand. Amen.

MAY 26   A BIG DECISION

He called a little child and had him stand among them. And he
said: "I tell you the truth, unless you change and become like
little children, you will never enter the kingdom of heaven."
                                          (Matthew 18:2-3 NIV)

I was riding home from church one Sunday with my son Rob, his
wife, Tammy, and their children Robbie, Rachel, and Ryan.
Eleven-year-old Rachel and six-year-old Ryan were in the back seat

of the van. Our conversation up front abruptly stopped when we heard Rachel and Ryan discussing heaven and hell. We were all ears, wondering what had brought up this subject.

Later that afternoon, Ryan had something to tell me. He said, "When I went out to play, I looked up at the sky, and I asked Jesus to come into my heart." We talked about God's response to his "asking." I took out a sheet of paper and made a sketch, showing the earth, the clouds up above, and a large space in between. I told him how we are separated from God because we disobey. Then I drew a cross in the blank space, showing that only through Jesus can we reach God.

I think Ryan understood according to his age level, and we will be watching and praying as he grows along.

Thank you, Lord, for my grandchildren's sensitivity to your Word and the Holy Spirit. May they know you—the way, truth, and life—more and more. Amen.

MAY 27   THE VALUE OF CHILDREN

"Take heed that you do not despise one of these little ones, for I say to you that in heaven their angels always see the face of My Father who is in heaven."   *(Matthew 18:10 NKJV)*

What an amazing truth! Children are watched over by assigned angels who have constant access to the Father! With six younger grandchildren and four young great-grands, that's very comforting to me.

This verse comforts me when I think of the children swept away in the tsunami, the children who perished in the terrorist attack in Beslan, Russia, and the many little children who have been so brutally killed in our own nation. I wonder if, as these children were transported to heaven, our loving heavenly Father directed their angels to hover over them, perhaps shielding them from pain. We know what a loving Father we have.

We have no promise that children will grow up, as we often take for granted. May we value all children!

Father, your Word is very plain: "Whoever receives one little child like this in My name receives Me" (Matthew 18:5 NKJV). Amen.

MAY 28   THE SACRIFICE OF PRAISE

He reached down from heaven and took me and drew me out of my great trials. He rescued me from deep waters.... The Lord held me steady.   (Psalm 18:16, 18a TLB)

In her book *Something More*, the late Catherine Marshall told of her pain in losing her six-week-old granddaughter. Then came the hard work of praising God as he directs us (see Hebrews 13:15; Psalm 34:1; and 1 Thessalonians 5:18). She said we must ask ourselves if we *believe God*, or if we merely believe our beliefs about God.

I first learned about the sacrifice of praise when faced with a situation I couldn't handle. I vowed to stay in my room until I had a word from God. I began reading *Power in Praise* by Merlin R. Carothers, weeping my way through the pages. I remember saying, "OK, God, you're right." I couldn't praise God from my heart, but I said the words with my mouth. It was a start—a true sacrifice.

Since then I've had a lot of practice. Though I can say with the late Catherine Marshall, "The matter of praise is still one of my growing points," I know that thanking God frees him to use any situation for my good.

Thank you, Lord, for loving me enough to keep stretching me; it's part of your "pruning" process to make me more like you. Amen.

MAY 29   TIME FOR A NAP?

**There remains therefore a rest for the people of God.
                                             (Hebrews 4:9 NKJV)**

I read of an invention designed for New York City's downtown workers—and perhaps shoppers. It's a specially designed place called MetroNaps where you can take a "midday power nap." In about twenty minutes you are supposed to be completely recharged and ready to go.

Imagine, you're all "wired" from the morning's fast-paced work track. Then you race down to MetroNaps and get a twenty-minute recharge!

My husband got up early in the morning, and since he mostly worked out of our home, he usually got an afternoon nap. I don't like naps; I wake up irritable. So I find other ways to rest.

God himself rested and invites us to come to him and rest. We grandmothers need to rest. A twenty-minute nap may be fine for some—perhaps rocking a grandchild or lying down beside one. Have you done that lately? It's good for both the body and the soul!

Lord, thank you for your promise to provide rest for our souls, as we physically rest and focus on You. Amen.

MAY 30   THE WORD IS PRECIOUS

And the word of the LORD was precious in those days.
(1 Samuel 3:1 KJV)

Professor Charles Thigpen often reminded us that we should respect and revere the Bible, God's Holy Word. He mentioned that his mother was quite alarmed when their family Bible accidentally fell to the floor one day. With so many copies and various versions readily available today, I wonder if our grandchildren have the same respect for the Scriptures.

In the early years of *glasnost* and *perestroika,* after the fall of the Iron Curtain and the reopening of churches, I was part of a missionary team visiting a house church. The church building had been confiscated by the government many years before. The pastor told us that during those years, there had been only one copy of the Scriptures for his entire church. It was secretly passed around to members, who hand-copied portions of it. It was continually exchanged until each family had a copy of the entire Bible in their own handwriting.

When I stood that morning to share favorite portions from

Psalm 18, the congregation stood, too, and tears rolled down the cheeks of many grandmothers' wrinkled faces. The Word of God is precious, indeed.

Father, thank you for your precious Word that "shall stand forever" (Isaiah 40:8 TLB).

MAY 31   CHANGE

To everything there is a season, a time for every purpose under heaven.   (Ecclesiastes 3:1 NKJV)

In "Song for a Fifth Child," Ruth Hulbert Hamilton poignantly writes about the brevity of childhood. The last lines are as follows:

> So quiet down, cobwebs; dust, go to sleep.
> I'm rocking my baby, and babies don't keep.*

All grandmothers will agree that this mother had her priorities in order. Children grow up; grandchildren grace our years, get married, and have their own families. And the cycles continue.

God provides cycles, or seasons, in our lives. Each season is characterized by new opportunities, challenges, and blessings. Each gives us pause to contemplate the future and prepare for that final "change" that will take us into God's presence.

Penelope J. Stokes writes about the inevitability of change: "Honeymoon weeks give way to the commitments of marriage; children grow up ... things change." She wisely concludes, "If we want to continue to grow in wisdom and intimacy with God, we need to embrace the changes.... We need to learn to view the ends as new beginnings."†

Lord, you know the "season" in which I am now living. With the psalmist I say, "My times are in your hands." Amen.

*Ruth Hulbert Hamilton, "Song for a Fifth Child," *Ladies' Home Journal* (October 1958).
†Penelope J. Stokes, *Faith: The Substance of Things Not Seen* (Wheaton, Ill.: Tyndale), 1995.

June

A Legacy of Faith (Continued)

GEORGIA B. HILL

JUNE 1 FROM GENERATION TO GENERATION

Great is Jehovah! Greatly praise him!...Let each generation tell its children what glorious things he does.
(Psalm 145:3-4 TLB)

My grandpa Barr was a country doctor who delivered many babies, including me, in the Missouri Ozarks. For transportation he rode a horse or drove a horse-pulled buggy; in his later years he acquired a car. He had a reputation as an outstanding, generous man.

My grandmother also had a reputation. She was known as a woman of faith. The story is told of a time when there was a severe drought and the women in the community met at the church to pray for rain. My grandmother arrived carrying her umbrella. When asked why she had her umbrella, her answer was, "Well, we came to pray for rain, and I believe it's going to rain!"

Whether or not it rained on that particular day, we don't know; but the rains surely did come. What a legacy she left to her grandchildren, acting on faith as Hebrews 11:1 defines it: "Faith is being sure of what we hope for and certain of what we do not see" (NIV).

May we pass on such a legacy of faith! This month we will continue to explore how we might do just that.

Thank you, Lord, for your truth passed down from generation to generation. Your truth is still the firm anchor for our souls. Amen.

JUNE 2   EXAMPLES OF FAITHFULNESS

Moreover it is required in stewards that one be found faithful.
                                        (1 Corinthians 4:2 NKJV)

Bob was teaching at the Southeastern Writer's Conference at
Epworth by the Sea on St. Simon's Island, Georgia. The John
Wesley Museum is located on the grounds, so we made sure we
paid a visit one day. The statement was made that when John
Wesley died, he left just four things: a few books, a few coins, two
silver spoons, and the Methodist Church!

What a legacy! Poor in this world's goods, John Wesley was rich
in faith, trust, obedience, and faithfulness to God. Wesley could
not have envisioned the extent of his earthly ministry or how his
hymns and evangelistic outreach would become world-wide in
their scope. As grandparents, we have the same opportunity to be
examples of faithfulness to God. Perhaps there are more "John
Wesleys" among our grandchildren!

Susanna Wesley, John's mother, prayed regularly with all of her
children. What a legacy we leave to our grandchildren by praying
with them when we can and by letting them know that we are
praying for them "without ceasing."

*My Father, teach me to how to pray for my grandchildren,
believing you will hear and answer my prayers. Amen.*

JUNE 3   SHADES OF LEGACY

*A good name is to be chosen rather than great riches, Loving
favor rather than silver and gold.*   *(Proverbs 22:1 NKJV)*

Kay Cole James, a university law professor, told a story I have
never forgotten. Every year she and her husband looked forward
to attending a formal event in Washington, D.C. They were ready
to leave when the telephone rang. It was the principal of their son's
school, requesting that Mr. James come to his office to discuss a
serious situation.

Upon returning home, Mr. James said, "Kay, we can't take our trip." After relating the details, she suggested they could take care of the matter when they returned. He said, "No, Kay, if our son had broken his leg, we would stay home to take care of him. Our son doesn't have a broken leg, but he has suffered a 'break' in his character; and we have to stay home to fix it."

Character breaks are serious business. Do grandmothers suffer "character breaks"? Surely, we do—a slight untruth, a bit of gossip. Matthew 6:33 (NKJV) tells us to "seek first...His righteousness," that is, God's character.

Someone said that reputation is what people think we are, but character is what we really are. Our grandchildren are watching and listening—and imitating!

Dear Father, I want your character to be developed in me. Amen.

JUNE 4   AN OUTBURST OF PRAISE

The LORD lives! Blessed be my Rock! Let the God of my salvation be exalted.   *(Psalm 18:46 NKJV)*

My grandmother on my mother's side was a listener. She was never demonstrative or talkative. However, one day she surprised us all.

Grandma's children, grandchildren, great-grands, and all their families represented a mini-multitude of people; and all were gathered at the old homeplace. We covered the porch and the wide expanse of front and side yards; some even drifted beyond the old rail fence.

Suddenly, Grandma rose from her chair on the porch, stepped onto the yard, raised her cane, and started praising God. Back and forth, with her cane raised, she loudly praised God for this family—and for blessing after blessing. When she was finished, she simply stepped back onto the porch and sat down.

I think as our quiet grandma looked around at her huge family, she was simply overwhelmed with thanksgiving. How many prayers had crossed her lips for all of us? My love and reverence for my grandma spiraled that day. I was grateful and blessed. What a legacy she left us in that outburst of praise!

Father, thank you for grandparents who pray for their families. Only you know the measure of their influence in our lives. Amen.

JUNE 5   A GRANDMOTHER'S DESIRE

All your children shall be taught by the LORD, and great shall be the peace of your children.

(Isaiah 54:13 NKJV)

An old gospel hymn presented worshipers a challenge: "'Must I go, and empty-handed?' Must I meet my Savior so? Not one soul with which to greet Him, Must I empty-handed go?"*

My friend Reba, who has battled multiple sclerosis for twenty-six years, will not go to heaven "empty-handed"! Her one, over-arching desire is to help lead all of her grandchildren into the kingdom of God. Only one remains to accept God's gift of grace.

Surely she has been a witness to her grandchildren—and to the many MS patients she has encouraged through the years. They can't ignore her love for them or her love for the God who keeps her going. As for now, she's out of her wheelchair and walking with a cane. What a legacy Reba leaves!

Dear God, thank you for enabling us to model your mercy and grace, and for helping us to be faithful in prayer and in example. Amen.

*Charles C. Luther, "Must I Go, and Empty-Handed?" 1877.

JUNE 6   A TIRED GRANDMOTHER

Jesus therefore, being wearied from His journey, sat ... by the well.   *(John 4:6 NKJV)*

Julia Ward Howe (1819–1910) was an American patriot known for her work promoting women's rights and helping to get the United States Congress to write the law making Mother's Day an official holiday. She was a wife, mother, grandmother, lecturer, and columnist. During the Civil War, she also cared for the wounded. It was on a night surrounded by battle sounds that she sat down and penned the words to America's most-loved patriotic hymn, "The Battle Hymn of the Republic."

One day she was asked by a friend, "Julia, how are you feeling?" She answered, "I'm tired—way down into next year!" Wow, that's tired! Yet she left a legacy not only to her family but also to her nation.

We grandmothers today are tired, as well—though our days are far different from those of Julia Ward Howe. We are not only involved with our grandchildren but also have many other responsibilities. Whatever our days involve, Jesus gives us an example to follow. He was weary, but he sat down and rested.

Jesus, may I daily heed your invitation: "Come to Me, all you who labor and are heavy laden, and I will give you rest" (Matthew 11:28 NKJV).

JUNE 7   LUNCH TIME

One of His disciples, Andrew, ... said to Him, "There is a lad here who has five barley loaves and two small fish, but what are they among so many?"   *(John 6:8-9 NKJV)*

A young Jewish boy wakes up early. It's a special day—he's going to see and hear this man called Jesus tell more wonderful stories. He dresses hurriedly, eats a bite, and takes the lunch his mother has prepared for him: five barley loaves and two small fish— enough to share with his pal who joins him down the road. To be among a crowd with Jesus is a huge event, and Jesus doesn't disappoint them on this day.

Eventually, the crowd gets hungry. Jesus tells his disciples to look for food among the crowd. Andrew comes upon our young lad and collects the only food to be found. Then Jesus prays over the food, and suddenly there's more than enough to feed everyone—with twelve baskets full left over!

Imagine the faces of two wide-eyed boys as they watched what happened to their lunch! No doubt they became believers that day. They had a story to tell their children and grandchildren—and generations yet to be born. May we tell it too.

Dear Father, what a compassionate God you are, taking care of our needs and providing even more than enough. Amen.

JUNE 8 THE REWARDS KEEP COMING

Being confident of this, that he who began a good work in you will carry it on to completion until the day of Christ Jesus.
(Philippians 1:6 NIV)

My granddaughter Lorey was recently married. The time I spent with the older granddaughters and their families was so special: Laurie and Lainey are stay-at-home moms; Lindsey assists her husband in a restaurant business; Kellie is a nurse; and Kimmie is a staff member with the Fellowship of Christian Athletes in Philadelphia.

Though my older granddaughters are grown, I still play an important role in their lives. A few years ago I had the opportunity to mentor Kellie in preparation for a summer missions trip. It was a blessing to me, and she calls it her special time with Grandmother.

Kimmie's job with FCA provides spiritual outreach opportunities with many high school, college, and professional athletes, including the Philadelphia 76ers basketball team. On my last visit, she invited me to attend her weekly Bible study with the 76ers wives and staff women, and to share some grandmotherly wisdom with them.

The Lord will carry on his work in and through us as long as we live, which means the rewards of grandmothering will just keep on coming!

Lord, thank you for the rewards of grandmothering. I'm thankful that your work in and through me will continue as long as I live. Amen.

JUNE 9   A MOTHER'S SONGS

Sing praises to God, sing praises! Sing praises to our King, sing
praises!   *(Psalm 47:6 NKJV)*

Bob and I celebrated our fifty-third anniversary just twelve days
before he went to heaven. He had given me a wonderful little book
called *Abundance from God's Heart in Autumn*. It is lovingly
inscribed, and I treasure it. The collection of stories was so perfect
for me after he was gone.

    I love one story especially, a nostalgic memory written by pastor
and author Leonard Sweet. He says that his mother followed the
Susanna Wesley "child-rearing manual" to the letter. In their
nightly ritual, after devotions, Sweet's mother took her three boys
upstairs and tucked them into bed. She then returned downstairs
to the living room where she would sit down at their old upright
piano. The boys would then "shout" downstairs the names of their
favorite hymns, which their mother would sing while she played
the piano. "Mother lulled us to sleep singing the hymns of the
faith,"* Sweet writes.

    What a legacy for this mother's children, grandchildren, and
great-grandchildren! And the piano survives as well, a reminder of
childhood memories and a music-loving mother.

Thank you, Lord, for the gift of music—and for grandmothers
who leave whatever gifts you have given them as loving legacies
to their grandchildren. Amen.

*"A Tool in the Hands of God," *Abundance from God's Heart* (Nashville: J. Countryman, 1998).

JUNE 10   SOUNDS OF MUSIC

Praise the LORD! For it is good to sing praises to our God; For
it is pleasant, and praise is beautiful.   *(Psalm 147:1 NKJV)*

Martin Luther said, "Next to the Word of God, music deserves
the highest praise." I cross-stitched and hung these words near my
piano. They echo the essence of family times through generations.

My dad played the guitar and piano. The organ in my grandma Barr's living room was the gathering place for the young people on Sunday afternoons in that Ozark Mountain community more than a century ago. The foot-pedaled organ of my grandma Turnbough became my mother's, and I learned to play it from the instruction book still intact in the stool.

My husband, Bob, had a preacher-grandfather who played the violin. Bob and his brothers played instruments, as did their father; their mother was the church pianist. Today the sounds of music live on in our family.

Paul and Silas prayed and sang hymns to God in prison, and the jailer and his household were saved. No wonder Martin Luther gave such credence to music. May we teach our grandchildren the beauty and power of musical praise.

Father, thank you for the gift of music; it rejoices our hearts and bonds us together as we praise and worship you. Amen.

JUNE 11   FAMILY REUNIONS

But concerning brotherly love you have no need that I should write to you, for you yourselves are taught by God to love one another. *(1 Thessalonians 4:9 NKJV)*

"It's time to sing!" My children have fond memories of hearing this announcement at family reunions where their honored grand-mother was the center of attention. The "family sing" was my mother's favorite time at any family gathering. My brother Finis, or my nephew, Ron, would go to the piano, and we would sing our favorite gospel songs and hymns; we still do this even though Mother now lives in heaven. This legacy seems destined to continue as the younger ones have come to enjoy music, as well.

Family reunions are a great time to show our love for one another as we mend relationships, share, learn from one another, and praise God, the Creator of families. All of my children have some version of this challenge to families displayed in their homes: "Lord, keep us close together and help us to be good, and always love each other the way a family should. And when our lives are over, please let us meet again, where we can be a family, up in heaven, Lord, Amen."

Father, your Word says that you "[set] the solitary in families" (Psalm 68:6 NKJV). Please help us not to neglect this privilege to "love one another" and to remember that love is an action word. Amen.

JUNE 12   REDEEMING THE TIME

Walk in wisdom toward those who are outside, redeeming the time.   (Colossians 4:5 NKJV)

Redeeming the time we have been given, using our time well, making the most of every opportunity—these are sobering words to consider.

When my husband was an assistant editor of *Moody Monthly* magazine in downtown Chicago, we, along with most Moody employees, lived in the suburbs. The guys took the commuter train every morning into the city, and back home in the evening. During these one-hour trips, they enjoyed reading the daily newspaper or engaging in some interesting conversation.

One man chose to sit on the upper deck alone. He was not anti-social; he just had important work to do. He had ten children, and he used this time to paraphrase the portion of scripture he would use for family devotions that evening. That man was Ken Taylor. In time, his paraphrased portions of the Scriptures were published as *The Living Bible*. By 1997, sales of *The Living Bible* had exceeded forty million copies.

Ken chose to "redeem the time," first to benefit his own family, and then to spread the gospel around the world.

Dear God, teach me to redeem the time you have allotted to me, knowing that only what's done for Christ will last. Amen.

JUNE 13   GOD'S HEALING MERCIES

But to you who fear My name the Sun of Righteousness shall arise with healing in His wings.   *(Malachi 4:2 NKJV)*

Some years ago a magazine said that Grandmother's homemade chicken soup was the penicillin of her generation. When grandmothers of the past made chicken soup, it was quite a job. They had to catch a chicken, end its life, pluck it, boil and "feather" it, and cook homemade noodles for the broth. I have made chicken soup for my children and grandchildren, and I agree that it seems to have healing qualities for some ailments. I, however, have always bought my chickens at the store!

Healing is something we all desire—for ourselves, spouses, children, grandchildren, and many others. It's an area where questions abound. Sometimes we are disappointed when a loved one is not "healed" in the way we want or expect.

Actually, healing may occur in one of four ways. First, there may be instant healing, which we call a miracle; second, there's progressive healing through doctors and medicines; third, God may choose to give us the grace to bear our situation (which is a miracle in itself); and fourth, God may choose the ultimate healing for us by taking us to heaven. In any case, we may be sure that God always acts in perfect love.

Lord, thanks for grandmothers who sacrificed their time for us; thanks, too, for all the ways you bring healing to us and loved ones. Amen.

JUNE 14   GOD IS FAITHFUL

So far you have faced no trial beyond what man can bear. God keeps faith, and he will not allow you to be tested above your powers, but when the test comes he will at the same time provide a way out, by enabling you to sustain it.
                                        (1 Corinthians 10:13 NEB)

Recently I came across this statement in Oswald Chambers's *My Utmost for His Highest*: "There are spots [in our lives] that faith has not worked in us as yet." In essence, God has more for us to learn about trusting him, and this requires a continual stretching of our faith.

My immediate thought was to get into the Word, work at changing some spiritual weakness myself, and thereby save myself from difficult faith-building experiences—an exercise in futility, to be sure! Only God knows how I fall short of his mark, and how to correct and perfect me according to his plan. The tests of life are designed by the Great Teacher himself, and, as I once read, during a test the teacher is usually silent. Yet, God faithfully shows us the way to not only endure but also "pass" every test.

We grandmothers have the challenge of getting through difficult experiences while still praising God and remaining on the path—a model to our grandchildren of God's sufficiency.

Thank you, Father, for your faithfulness and sufficiency—especially through the tests of life. Amen.

JUNE 15   HIS LIGHT FOR MY STEPS

Your word is a lamp to my feet And a light to my path.
(Psalm 119:105 NKJV)

A friend gave me Stormie Omartian's book *Just Enough Light for the Step I'm On*. The book title characterizes my journey through grief after losing my husband, Bob.

When Bob was with me, I could count on some plans for the future (I thought); and if things didn't work out, Bob would "fix it." I had to learn the truth of James 4:14: "You do not know what will happen tomorrow. For what is your life? It is even a vapor that appears for a little time and then vanishes away" (NKJV). It is true what they say, that life is what happens when we plan something else.

In his final letter to Timothy, the apostle Paul was approaching the end of his thirty-year ministry; yet he was not afraid because he knew his departure had a destination: heaven. I want my grandchildren to know that I, like Paul, am not afraid of death because I am sure of my destination! In the meanwhile, when God gives me "just enough light for the step I'm on," I'll be thankful—and expectant of the blessing that awaits me on the next step!

Thank you, Father, for the life you have given me, for life eternal, and for so many blessings along the way. Amen.

JUNE 16 NIGHTTIME SPECIALS

I will lie down in peace and sleep, for you alone, O LORD, will keep me safe. *(Psalm 4:8 NLT)*

Author Beth Moore says that in her childhood she slept in a feather bed with her grandmother. She asks, "What could make a child feel more secure than that?"

I, too, have slept with my grandchildren. Once when I was in the hospital, Kimmie came to sleep in my room. I've slept with eleven-year-old Rachel in her bed, and with my grown Lorey in her big bed. When I visit Catherine, age six, and Alexandra, age nine, I sleep on their day bed with the trundle. I've even slept in eight-year-old Russ's room on one of his bunks.

For years, it was just Alexandra and me. We formed the nightly habit of reading from a book, saying four special Bible verses, and praying. In no time she had memorized the Scriptures. When Catherine turned four, she decided she had to sleep with grandmother, too. Now Catherine knows the verses. I believe these nights will one day be special memories for them, and that God's Word, sown in their hearts, will find a deep lodging place.

Lord Jesus, I pray that the seeds sown in "together times" will find deep resting places and bring forth fruit in the future. Amen.

JUNE 17 NEW THINGS

Trust in ... the living God, who gives us richly all things to enjoy. *(1 Timothy 6:17 NKJV)*

I like "new" things—a new outfit, new shoes, new furniture, even a new car— though I've become more selective through the years, making purchases as my budget allows.

God knows the appeal of the word *new*. We see this word throughout the Bible: "Sing to Him a new song" (Psalm 33:3 NKJV); "We, according to His promise, look for new heavens and a new earth" (2 Peter 3:13 NKJV); "If anyone is in Christ, he is a new creation" (2 Corinthians 5:17 NKJV); "To him who overcomes I will give ... a white stone, and on the stone a new name written " (Revelation 2:17 NKJV); "Behold, I make all things new" (Revelation 21:5 NKJV).

Yes, God has lots of new things in store for us. In 1 Corinthians we read, "Eye has not seen, nor ear heard...the things which God has prepared for those who love Him" (2:9 NKJV). Our new things here will perish with use, or they will belong to our grandchildren or someone else in a few years. God's new things, however, will last forever!

Thank you, Lord, for new things, and for all the new things that will be ours throughout the ages. Amen.

JUNE 18   POSITIVES VS. NEGATIVES

Finally, brothers, whatever is true, whatever is noble, whatever is right, whatever is pure, whatever is lovely, whatever is admirable ... think about such things.   (Philippians 4:8 NIV)

I remember these words from a song of many years ago: "Accentuate the positive...eliminate the negative." I doubt that anyone paid much attention to what those lyrics said; it was the rhythm that was appealing.

Bob was a very positive person. My nature is not bent that way. I look out the window on a cloudy day and say, "It's so gloomy, and it's going to be that way all day!" He would look out the same window and respond, "Oh, the sun's up somewhere, and we'll see it later on." He liked to frame his words in positive statements.

Bob's favorite saying was "The best is yet to come," and these words are printed on his gravestone. I wrote them down after he died, and they've been on my refrigerator for four years.

It's my prayer that we grandmothers will believe that the best of life—and a future in heaven—is yet to come; and that the message of Philippians 4:8 is more than just a suggestion!

Father, please replace my pattern of thinking with your pattern of thinking. Amen.

JUNE 19   A SILENT LEGACY

Be an example ... in word, in conduct, in love, in spirit, in faith, in purity.   ***(1 Timothy 4:12 NKJV)***

I met Jennifer as I was substitute teaching one day. She's a beautiful, vivacious young woman who is poised, positive, and skilled in her profession. And she loves her kids.

It was near the end of the school year, and we were at recess—the last class of the day. I noticed Jennifer talking to three students who had been in trouble several times already that day. She was frustrated and about to lose it. I walked over to Jennifer, who was close to tears, and she said to me, "Prayer is the only thing that keeps me going; I pray for my students every morning." I was so impressed to hear this.

Teachers, like grandmothers, often leave a silent legacy. I still remember principles and truths taught and modeled by my own teachers and grandmothers. God is always watching, and he gives the final awards!

Heavenly Father, teach me how to pray for my grandchildren— and for their teachers, who have so much influence on their values and character. Amen.

JUNE 20   CAREGIVING

I tell you the truth, anyone who gives you a cup of water in my name because you belong to Christ will certainly not lose his reward.   ***(Mark 9:41 NIV)***

At the age of ninety-two, my mother was living in an assisted-living facility. My oldest brother, Finis, and his wife, Dianne, lived two miles away and took care of her transportation needs and much more. My older sister, Erm, and her husband, Jesse, also lived nearby.

However, my mother's primary caregiver was her granddaughter Christi. Each week Christi drove two hundred miles round trip to visit her grandmother. She brought Mother's favorite things to eat, gave her feet and legs a good rub with lotion, trimmed her toenails and fingernails, and took care of any other personal needs. Sometimes she made the trip more than once during the week.

Christi was a natural caregiver. While other granddaughters loved and cared about their grandmother, Christi was the one to minister "love in action" on a regular basis. She considered her gift of time a blessing, not a chore.

Our family presented Christi with a framed piece of Mother's hand embroidery at Mother's funeral service. We were all so grateful for Mother to have had this special care.

Father, thank you for your special gifts you give to each of us. Help us use them faithfully to help others and honor you. Amen.

JUNE 21   NEVER GIVE UP

"I know the plans I have for you," declares the LORD, "plans to prosper you and not to harm you, plans to give you hope and a future."   *(Jeremiah 29:11 NIV)*

A boy was sitting on his grandmother's lap. He lovingly patted her face, feeling the soft lines. Then he asked, "Grandmother, how old are you?" Grandmother thought for a while and then said that she couldn't remember. Her grandson replied, "If you don't know, I can tell you how to find out; you can look in your underwear. Mine says four."

Bob earned a doctorate in gerontology when he was sixty-three and then taught seminars for seniors. He learned of a reclassification in which Americans who were once considered "old" are now divided into three groups. From the age of seventy-two to eighty-one years, we are young old; from eighty-two to eighty-nine years, we are mid-old; and from age ninety and older, we are truly old. Maybe that is encouraging news for some of us!

A valuable tool for grandmothers of all ages is mental exercise. Physical exercise is good for the body; mental exercise keeps the brain healthy and happy. Reading new books, working all kinds of problems, and learning to use a computer are marvelous and rewarding challenges. "Never give up"—that's a legacy we can leave our grandchildren.

God, you have plans for good for all the days of my life. Help me be ever learning, a source of inspiration to my family. Amen.

JUNE 22   PRAYING FOR ONE ANOTHER

Pray for one another.   *(James 5:16 NKJV)*

When my mother went to heaven, we wondered, "How are we going to continue to keep this large family together?" It was a timely question, for the number of her children, grandchildren, great-grandchildren, and all the "in-laws" equaled ninety-two. Mother had always been the focus of our family gatherings, and she had been the reason so many still attended them.

Bob came up with a plan that would help keep us together through prayer. On his computer, he designed an annual prayer calendar that included everyone's name—with several family members being listed on each day of the month. Since Bob's death, my sister-in-law, Joan, has assumed responsibility for the prayer calendar.

We still honor our mother and grandmother. My youngest brother, Tom, and his wife, Patty, host the annual reunion, and quite a number manage to spend Christmas Day together. We still sing one of mother's favorite songs, "That Glad Reunion Day." Truly, one day in the future, there will be a great reunion day!

Father, thank you for the tie that binds families together, and for the privilege of praying for one another. Amen.

JUNE 23   THIS IS MY STORY

"My words which I have put in your mouth, shall not depart
from your mouth, nor from the mouth of your descendants, nor
from the mouth of your descendants' descendants," says the
LORD.   *(Isaiah 59:21 NKJV)*

For Christmas one year, I gave my family copies of stories I've
written about my life and our family. A local office supply store
reduced the pages for me, and I placed them in loose-leaf binders
so that I may continue to add more stories. Photographs accom-
pany some of the stories.

The story of our collie, Cassie, was included. When she died, she
had been part of our family for sixteen years. I called the story
"Ode to Cassie." Just about everyone read it on the spot, and not
many of us were dry eyed.

I gave a notebook to each of the four couples, and to the grand-
children who were twelve and older. My title, "This Is My Story,
This Is My Song," was taken from a favorite hymn, "Blessed
Assurance."

Although some of the stories may not be read for a while, I'm
trusting that the words I'm passing on "shall not depart ... from
the mouth of [my] descendants" down through generations.

Father, thank you for all the events of our lives through which
family history is recorded. Amen.

JUNE 24   FAR ABOVE RUBIES

Who can find a virtuous wife? For her worth is far above
rubies.   *(Proverbs 31:10 NKJV)*

Did you know that rubies are valuable because they are red all the
way through? The author of Proverbs seems to place great value
on something that is beautiful all the way through. He asserts that
a virtuous (righteous) woman is worth far more than a perfect
ruby. She's an extra special gem!

This proverb speaks to me about character. Jesus says in

Matthew 6:33, "Seek first the kingdom of God [his rule and reign in our hearts] and His righteousness [character], and all these things [material needs] shall be added to you" (NKJV).

As a grandmother, I need to be the "real thing" all the way through. The tests of life are my opportunities for God's character to be developed in me. I become more righteous each time I respond to God in faith and obedience. One day, in God's timing, I will be perfect—like the ruby—and then I will be in heaven!

Lord, you know that I am imperfect, yet you don't give up on me. Thank you for loving me and perfecting "that which concerns me" (Psalm 138:8 NKJV).

JUNE 25   ADVENTURE IN BELIZE

"Go therefore and make disciples of all the nations.... And lo, I am with you always, even to the end of the age."
(Matthew 28:19-20 NKJV)

I flew with my son Terry and my granddaughter Kellie to Belize to assist in vacation Bible schools and a preaching ministry. Mothers, grandmothers, and other family members accompanied the children in each village or community where we set up shop.

On our last day, I didn't think I could participate. The previous ten days we had experienced exhausting temperatures. But I knew I couldn't stay in our quarters all day alone, so I decided to go along and just sit on the bus.

When we arrived at the community, "duty" urged me inside to greet the ladies. I sat next to a mother named Eva. Entirely unplanned, the opportunity arose for me to give my Christian witness. She was ready to respond to Jesus—and she did! Then she introduced me to her friend, Yvonne, and said, "Tell her what you told me!" I did, and she also received Jesus. I walked to another area and encountered two more women, Lena and Shirleen, who also received the Lord.

Though I was too tired to comprehend what God was doing, I surely was happy I had gotten off that bus!

*Father, thank you that your ways are not our ways; and that
you get your work done even when we least expect to participate. Amen.*

JUNE 26 "DOERS" OF GOD'S WORD

*How beautiful upon the mountains are the feet of him who
brings good news.* **(Isaiah 52:7 NKJV)**

In the Nilgiri Mountains of India, Miss Laura Belle Barnard
brought the good news to a caste of people called the
Untouchables, which is also the title of a book I was honored to
cowrite with her.

She tells the story of a very old grandmother of the Kota tribe
whom she had heard was ill. Taking her medical bag and other
supplies, Miss Barnard walked several miles to visit the old
woman and give the grandmother her first bath.

The patient vigorously resisted the removing of her clothes and
being washed, but Miss Barnard was determined. After the bath,
she sprinkled talcum powder all over the grandmother's wrinkled,
sick body, and helped her put on soft pajamas; and a miracle was
accomplished! A look of complete satisfaction adorned that smiling grandmother's face.

Sometimes we share the good news with words, and other times
with deeds of love. As grandmothers, we have many opportunities
to share the good news of God's love with our grandchildren
through our actions. May they remember us as "doers" of God's
Word.

*Lord, thank you for all those who share your good news all over
the world. Help me to be a "doer" of your Word. Amen.*

JUNE 27 ON PILGRIMAGE

*Blessed is the man whose strength is in You, whose heart is set
on pilgrimage.* **(Psalm 84:5 NKJV)**

A gospel song we sing at family gatherings sweetens our spirits and confirms what we believe: "This world is not my home, I'm just passing through." As we get older, we know more about what we're singing. We have more loved ones in heaven, and this makes heaven more real.

Hebrews 11 gives us the "roll call of faith," those who believed God and confessed that they were strangers and pilgrims on the earth. Pilgrimage was the theme of our pastor's message at Bob's celebration service. Expounding on Psalm 84:5, he spoke these words: "Dr. Hill, while he was living, was on pilgrimage; he understood that, and he lived his life on that premise. He was a pilgrim; his heart was set on making the most of the journey, making it count for Christ."

My heart is also set on pilgrimage—making the most of the journey, making it count for Christ, trusting God to bring along my grandchildren and those who follow me.

Lord, I confess I'm a needy pilgrim; grant me strength for the journey and light for the way. Amen.

JUNE 28   HEAVEN

Now I saw a new heaven and a new earth, for the first heaven and the first earth had passed away.... Then I, John, saw the holy city, New Jerusalem.   ***(Revelation 21:1-2 NKJV)***

Bob's brother Bill battled cancer for five years and died months after Bob's own death. Bill's homegoing was a joyful experience for him personally, and a revealing and reassuring time for the family. In his last hours, surrounded by his wife, Julia, his children, and his grandchildren, Bill—who was entirely coherent—began to talk about heaven. He said, "They're all here!" Someone asked, "Who, Dad?" He answered, "Bob, Mom, and Dad," and he went on to name other family members. His daughter, Debbie, took out a pen and tablet and began to record what he was saying.

Someone asked, "Is heaven real, Dad?" He answered, "Yes, it's real, and it's beautiful." Bill expected to go any moment and was disappointed that life was lingering. Eventually, he drifted off to sleep and into the arms of God.

The story of Bill's homegoing was shared at the funeral service, and the impact of that story will spread as it is passed on as a witness to God's faithfulness and the heaven prepared for all who believe.

Father, thank you that heaven is a real place where we will be reunited with our loved ones. I'm grateful for your eternal plan for our lives. Amen.

JUNE 29   MORE CONTEMPLATIONS ON HEAVEN

After these things I heard a loud voice of a great multitude in heaven, saying, "Alleluia! Salvation and glory and honor and power belong to the Lord our God!"   *(Revelation 19:1 NKJV)*

My friend Trula and I were delighted to have time for a visit. Trula and Dan had been missionaries in India for many years, and Dan had recently gone to heaven. Our conversation soon turned to heavenly things. Trula wondered, "What is Dan doing in heaven?" I had done the same kind of wondering about my Bob. She also wondered, "Why does God give us so many talents and abilities and then not let us live long enough to use them all?"

I shared with her from an article written by Dr. Irwin Lutzer, whose words had comforted me. Writing to widows, he had said that he believes our husbands continue to love us in heaven as they did on earth, but with a sweeter, purer love—a love purified by God. He also believes that artists and musicians will still create in heaven, but that their creations will be on magnificent levels.

Two grandmothers had a wonderful talk about heaven that day, and we were encouraged to consider that everything about us will be perfected and purified in heaven.

Father, thank you for the hope of heaven and of worshiping you in true perfection. Amen.

JUNE 30   BEULAH LAND

You shall no longer be termed Forsaken,...but you shall be called Hephzibah [my delight], and your land Beulah.
(Isaiah 62:4 NKJV)

In Isaiah's prophecy, Beulah was a symbolic name for the land of Israel, the promised land. We may be more familiar with the term as it's used in Squire Parsons's song "Beulah Land"—a reference to our eternal home in heaven.

Ecclesiastes 3:11 says, "[God] has put eternity in their hearts" (NKJV). Author Max Lucado describes this as a computer chip that God installed in us when we were being created; we are programmed to hunger for God. This hunger witnesses to a Creator God. We're all looking for Beulah Land.

A retired missionary couple had returned to the United States. As they disembarked their plane, they found a celebrity had been on board. He received loud cheers from a large crowd. The wife said to her husband, "There's no one to welcome us home." He replied, "But, my dear, we're not home yet!"

As grandmothers, we have the awesome privilege of leaving a legacy of faith—a legacy that will help our grandchildren to satisfy the hunger of their hearts and find their true home.

Lord, some day I will be at home in Beulah Land. In the meantime, help me to teach my grandchildren that their true home is with you. Amen.

July

Living Freely and Lightly

ELLEN GROSECLOSE

JULY 1   THE UNFORCED RHYTHMS OF GRACE

"Learn the unforced rhythms of grace. I won't lay anything heavy or ill-fitting on you. Keep company with me and you'll learn to live freely and lightly."   *(Matthew 11:29-30 Message)*

July days in the northern hemisphere are filled with light and warmth. School's out and people are on vacation. This time provides wonderful opportunities to spend quality time with grandchildren and to learn with them the unforced rhythms of life. In today's hectic world where schedules would make my grandmother's brain spin, summer months are perfect for a relaxed lifestyle. I go barefoot every chance I get and encourage my grandchildren to do the same. July is perfect for snuggling on our porch in the evening; playing card games like "Go Fish" and "Crazy Eights"; swinging the grandchildren high into the leaves of our old maple; or going to the soda fountain for banana splits.

July offers possibilities for focusing on life's spiritual dimensions—for gently drawing others, including grandchildren, into God's circle of love. When our family is relaxed; when wristwatches remain on dressers; when meals are served only because everyone's hungry—these unforced rhythms become precious gifts. I look forward to July, to sharing God's and my family's company, and to living "freely and lightly."

Come on. Let's "keep company" this month—with God and with each other.

Dear God, grant me unhurried moments and sweet times with you and with my grandchildren. Slow me down and let me bask in your grace. Amen.

JULY 2   A NATURAL GRANDMOTHER

How natural it is that I should feel as I do about you, for you have a very special place in my heart.   *(Philippians 1:7 TLB)*

Becoming a parent involved considerable work. I remember being very tired from frequent feedings, long nights, and time spent worrying about being a good mother. My husband and I were successful with our six children, but both of us have gray hair now. Being a grandmother, however, has seemed to come naturally. Perhaps the reason comes from my not having the same level of responsibility and getting my full eight hours of sleep every night. It could also be that my being separated by another generation—their parents—helps to create an intuitive and deep bond with my grandchildren.

All I know is that grandmothering feels very comfortable, and that all eleven of my grandchildren have a very special place in my heart. In a world where there are powerful forces trying to pull us apart, how very wonderful to have the most powerful force ever, God's gift of love, holding us tight and secure.

Thank you, God, for making love an essential, beautiful, and natural part of life, and for the strong bonds between grandmothers and grandchildren. Amen.

JULY 3   THEY ALSO SERVE WHO SIT AND SNUGGLE

[God] will feed his flock like a shepherd; he will gather the lambs in his arms, and carry them in his bosom, and gently lead the mother sheep.   *(Isaiah 40:11 NRSV)*

I take pride in my ability to snuggle with grandchildren. I've spent years perfecting that art, one I learned from my mother, who had a world-class lap. The other day while I was crammed in the back seat of our small car with two granddaughters, one of them laughed and said, "Grandma, you're not a bag of bones like my mother; you're a pillow." I plead guilty because it's really a gift of mine.

Some grandparents may take their families to fancy places and lavish them with expensive gifts. That's fine. I occasionally do special things for mine. More important, however, is that I'm available for them. For those of my grandchildren who live a distance away, I talk with them on the phone, e-mail them, send pictures, and visit as often as possible. But nothing can take the place of gathering them—even my tall, gangly teenage grandkids—into my arms and holding them close. If that's good enough for God, then it is good enough for me, too.

O gentle and kind God, you hold me in your loving arms. Help me snuggle my family with both my lap and my heart. Amen.

JULY 4   CELEBRATE LIFE!

Celebrate God all day, every day. I mean, revel in him!
(Philippians 4:4 Message)

On this birthday of our nation, celebrate with your grandchildren whether they're close and you can get your hands on them, or whether they're far away. If they're at a distance, send them loving thoughts. Lift them up in sincere, genuine prayer. But wherever they are, celebrate God and your family. And do so not just on special occasions. Take delight in your clan everyday.

Like this nation, our families have a long history, complete with glorious successes and a number of imperfections. But we're family, and that's something worth celebrating! We don't need fireworks to express our joy in one another. We have hugs and kisses and a sparkle in our eyes. The pride we grandmothers have in our hearts is enough to tell the whole world how we feel about our grandchildren. With such blessings, you and I will also revel in God. So let the celebration begin!

Gracious God, I know you love celebrations. You love it when we dance, sing, and rejoice in being your people. Help me celebrate being a grandmother all day, every day! Amen.

JULY 5   SHAPE YOUR WORRIES INTO PRAYERS

Don't fret or worry. Instead of worrying, pray. Let petitions and praises shape your worries into prayers, letting God know your concerns. **(Philippians 4:6 Message)**

There are a multitude of things in this world that cause me to worry, from personal and family issues all the way to major global concerns. It's important for me as a grandmother, though, to look at life from a historical perspective. I can draw from the deep wells of experience. I've seen fashions and trends come and go. I've learned that by sharing my anxieties with God, the two of us can reshape all my worries into prayers.

I do get worn out physically and emotionally when I hold tightly to my fears about this world, the one in which my grandchildren are growing up. But if I gather my fretting and stewing and explain them to God, a sense of peace comes over me. As Paul writes in Philippians 4:7, "Before you know it, a sense of God's wholeness, everything coming together for good, will come and settle you down. It's wonderful what happens when Christ displaces worry at the center of your life" (*Message*).

Dear Jesus, shape my worries into prayers. When I read the headlines or watch the evening news, calm my anxious spirit and help me entrust my grandchildren into your loving care. Amen.

JULY 6   THE "HAPPIMESS" OF SUMMER VISITS

"[Your life] shall be bound in the bundle of the living under the care of the Lord your God." **(1 Samuel 25:29b NRSV)**

When grandchildren come to visit, especially for an extended period of time, the result is what I lovingly call a "happimess."

There's joyful noise from dawn to dusk. The refrigerator door is opened more than shut. I spend considerable time cleaning up soap bubble spills, glitter on the floor, and glue everywhere. The washing machine goes constantly. But I don't mind at all, because it's wonderful to be "bound in the bundle of the living," even when the bundle is active and constantly moving grandchildren.

The bundle in which we're bound obviously extends beyond our own family circle. And that big world comes complete with stress and strain. Yet that's how God planned our human lives to be, a mixture of peace and turmoil. Regardless of whether my house is controlled chaos from visiting family, or our nation is struggling to cope with global tensions, I will rejoice in my God, the Lord of "happimess."

Wise and patient God, thank you for placing me in an imperfect world that's still in the making. Just give me adequate courage and strength. Amen.

JULY 7   EACH OF US IS AN ORIGINAL

We will not compare ourselves with each other as if one of us were better and another worse. We have far more interesting things to do with our lives. Each of us is an original.
(Galatians 5:26 Message)

Sometimes I compare myself with my grandchildren's other grandmothers, the ones who take them to professional ball games, spend a week with them at an elegant beach house, or buy them rather expensive gifts. After all, I am human. But the apostle Paul says I'm an original. I'm one of a kind! And God simply asks me to be the best grandmother I can be.

It's also true that sometimes we compare our children or grandchildren with one another. But each of them is a unique individual, too. Three of our children are "store bought" (adopted), and three are "homegrown" (biological). In addition, several of our grandchildren are technically of the "step" variety. But that's inconsequential. Family is family regardless of how they join our clan. Each member has special gifts and abilities. Each is equally loved. And praise the Lord, each is God's original work of art!

God of unconditional love, inspire me to love my children and grandchildren in exactly the ways each of them needs. Amen.

JULY 8   A TIME FOR WATERING

It is possible to give away and become richer! It is also possible to hold on too tightly and lose everything. Yes, [generous people] shall be rich! By watering others, [they] water [themselves].
(Proverbs 11:24-25 TLB)

The hot, frequently dry days of our Northwest summers are important times for watering lawns, flowers, and gardens. They're also excellent opportunities for grandmothers to water—that is, to nurture and lovingly tend their family relationships. It's fun to stock my refrigerator and cupboards with good food in order to help my grandchildren's physical growth. I know the favorite dishes of each child, and I try to serve them whenever they visit. But summer months are also the perfect opportunity to nourish their souls.

I like to think of it as getting out my spiritual watering can and sprinkling them with words of encouragement, helping them blossom in their faith, and gently guiding them into producing a bumper crop of the fruit of the Spirit. The marvelous truth is that as I water their lives, I can't help getting splashed with some of it myself. Along with them, I, too, experience inner growth; I, too, am refreshed by the Holy Spirit.

God of watering cans and sprinklers, thank you for spiritually nourishing all of my grandchildren and me. Keep the waters of your Spirit flowing free. Amen.

JULY 9   MY JOB IS TO BLESS

Be agreeable, be sympathetic, be loving, be compassionate, be humble. That goes for all of you, no exceptions. No retaliation. No sharp-tongued sarcasm. Instead, bless—that's your job, to bless. You'll be a blessing and also get a blessing.
(1 Peter 3:8-9 Message)

My job as a grandmother is to bless my grandchildren, although that doesn't give me the right to spoil them. Well, once in a while it's OK. But far more significant than offering our grandchildren candy bars or ice cream is blessing them with the gift of ourselves.

How precious it is to sit with a grandchild and really hear his or her joys and concerns. The apostle Peter said that one's true blessings are to be sympathetic, loving, and humble. Perhaps you'll get down on the floor, if you still can, and play with your grandchildren. For me, it's the getting back up that's a problem! Or it might involve teaching them to sew, crochet, or throw a baseball. I try to bless them, whenever possible, by sharing in their birthdays and attending their special church and school functions.

Of course, praying regularly and faithfully for them may be the best blessing of all. What a joy to work with God in blessing my grandchildren! And what a great feeling to receive countless blessings myself!

You know, Lord, how I occasionally spoil my grandchildren. But you also know I wish deep in my heart to always be a blessing to them. Amen.

JULY 10 GRANDMOTHERS NEED OPEN MINDS

The intelligent [person] is always open to new ideas. In fact, he [or she] looks for them. **(Proverbs 18:15 TLB)**

We grandmothers bring a wealth of experience and a solid foundation of beliefs to our interaction with grandchildren, giving us a perspective younger folks don't have. We can enthrall our grandchildren with stories from our pasts, ones that get better with every telling. We can also be a strong support for them in the swirl of current fads, fashions, and attitudes.

But we need to remain open to the new ideas and fresh ways of youth. I've learned to cope with some amazing technology, though admittedly I have a long way to go. My limitations in the fields of electronics and computers allow my grandchildren to feel superior to me, as well as learn patience as they teach me. I, however, have been quite accepting of some of their new lifestyles—from the clothes they wear to the music they enjoy.

While I shall try to be open to all their new ideas and ways, I shall hold tightly to the basics of my faith. Some things are the same "yesterday and today and forever."

Wise and perceptive God, help me sort through all the changes I've experienced in my lifetime, while accepting the helpful, creative ones that will abide. Amen.

JULY 11   THE FUTURE STARTS NOW

Because Jesus was raised from the dead, we've been given a brand-new life and have everything to live for, including a future in heaven—and the future starts now! God is keeping careful watch over us and the future. (1 Peter 1:3b-5a Message)

This grandmother has been given a brand-new life! Oh, it's still housed in the same mature body, but even so, my heart and mind and soul are fresh and pure. Those who accept Christ, and especially we grandmothers, have everything to live for. We anticipate the joys of eternal life, but here and now we have reason to praise God, to rejoice and laugh and dance a happy jig about our present lives. We love and are loved.

Grandchildren are God's gift to help us stay fully alive and get us out of bed every morning with words of praise to God on our lips and a twinkle in our eyes. The younger generations give us a reason for thinking positively and seeing the promise in every day. There are phone calls, e-mails, and pictures to share; letters to send or receive; birthdays to celebrate; visits to make; hugs and kisses to give and to get. And to think, this foretaste of heaven starts here and now!

God of this very moment, thank you for the joys I have right now! I look forward to each new day, knowing you watch over my whole family and me. Amen.

JULY 12   ELOQUENT GRANDMOTHERS
NEED NOT APPLY

Has not God made foolish the wisdom of the world? For since, in the wisdom of God, the world did not know God through wisdom, God decided, through the foolishness of our proclamation, to save those who believe. (1 Corinthians 1:20d-21 NRSV)

I'm thankful I no longer have to impress this world with how intelligent, brave, and beautiful I am. I'm a grandma with hands that show the signs of age, a few wrinkles on my face, and a head of gray hair I earned from being a parent of six teenagers. I'm old enough to be foolish—to hold hands with my grandchildren as we skip through the park; to draw in chalk on the sidewalk; to blow bubbles into a summer breeze; to play dolls on the floor, and not be embarrassed to ask for help when it's time to stand up.

I no longer need to be anxious about where I am on the ladder of success. I've discovered that having a rocking chair and a grandchild to cuddle is the best of all worlds. I don't need filet mignon when I can have hot dogs or grilled cheese sandwiches with my grandchildren. Of course, God entered into human life as a tiny baby. That wasn't foolishness. That was pure, sweet love!

O God, you who are usually out of step with the ways of us humans, I appreciate your divine foolishness. Let me be foolish for the sake of my grandchildren and you. Amen.

JULY 13   A PRECIOUS TREASURE

This precious treasure—this light and power that now shine within us—is held in a perishable container, that is, in our weak bodies. Everyone can see that the glorious power within must be from God and is not our own. (2 Corinthians 4:7 TLB)

Our house's family room is filled with treasures, but not of the rare or unavailable variety. It's crammed with toys for grandchildren to use. Some are vintage and date from their parents' era—Fisher-Price pull toys, old LEGOs, Matchbox cars, and an ancient riding horse. They absolutely love "Grandma's Room," including the cupboards loaded with arts and crafts material. It's difficult for them to leave when their visits are over because they always have unfinished business. I rather like that because it means they will want to come back soon.

In all humility, however, there's a more valuable and rare treasure in our house, and that's Grandma and Grandpa. We're showing signs of wear and tear and have a few wrinkles here and there, but we really are treasures in perishable containers. For our grandchildren's sakes, it's important for us to let them see that "the glorious power within" isn't our own but is from God.

Gracious God, my grandchildren are precious treasures to me. May I truly be a treasure to each of them. Amen.

JULY 14   FLEXIBLE GRANDMOTHERS

We who have strong faith ought to shoulder the burden of the doubts and qualms of the weak and not just go our own sweet way. We should consider the good of our neighbour and help to build up his character.   (Romans 15:1-2 JBP)

I make considerable effort to learn my grandchildren's tastes, schedules, habits, and likes and dislikes. I believe it makes them feel important, which they are. I don't cater to their every whim, but I do try to enter as fully as possible into their busy and active worlds. I attend as many school programs, piano recitals, soccer and baseball games, and church concerts as humanly possible. I often have to readjust my schedule to accommodate theirs. Ah, but it's worth it! A grandmother's role isn't just to go her own sweet way. Rather, it's to be there for them—to support their activities, listen to their questions and fears, and lift them in prayer. It also includes loving and undergirding their parent or parents.

Whenever I hear myself start to say, "But I always did it this way," I try to stuff these words back in my mouth and replace them with statements of affirmation, compassion, and genuine caring.

Dear God, in Jesus you entered fully into our human world. Lure me into the lives of my grandchildren that I may help build up their characters. Amen.

JULY 15   THIS GRANDMOTHER IS RICH!

Now I have everything I want—in fact I am rich. Yes, I am quite content.   (Philippians 4:18 JBP)

This particular grandmother is rich indeed! No, I'm not wealthy in economic terms. We're on a fixed income, but have adequate resources to meet our basic needs and then some. Our home isn't elegant, but it's comfortable and it's paid for. We have investments and many nice things. But what makes me rich isn't anything I have; it's whom I love, and those who love me. I'm content because I'm privileged to spend quality time with most of my grandchildren. I am rich beyond measure!

I cherish the months of July and August because there's more time for movie matinees, for lunch at our favorite bagel place, and for Sunday mornings snuggled on a church pew. These two months for me have a sacramental quality and a holiness of relationships. I understand the importance of school and actively support their attendance and hard work, but I feel so very rich and content during summer when I'm able to be with my grandchildren for extended periods of time.

I praise and thank you, Lord, for the precious gift of time with my grandchildren; and if you ever see fit to give me more, I'll gladly take it. Amen.

JULY 16   O TASTE AND SEE

O taste and see that the LORD is good; happy are those who take refuge in him.   (Psalm 34:8 NRSV)

Eating with grandchildren is a happy and holy time. A special bonding occurs when we break bread together. Sometimes, of course, the elements of our "family communion" are chocolate chip cookies, warm from the oven. On other occasions it may be pizza and soda, or microwave popcorn and a movie. I try to respect their parents' wishes, so I do monitor their sugar intake. But once in a while I let them sneak a piece of candy from my secret bowl.

God not only relates to us through our minds, hearts, and souls, God also speaks to us through our taste buds and tummies. Why do you think God gave us church potlucks? All of us, and especially grandchildren, can feel God's presence when enjoying the fellowship of a shared meal. When the food is prepared and served by a grandmother who loves them very much, surely the presence of the Lord is at that table. I want my beloved grandchildren to "taste and see that the Lord is good," and to partake frequently!

Dear God, may I do whatever it takes to help my grandchildren know how sweet and good it is to experience your presence. Amen.

JULY 17   WHILE AWAITING PERFECTION, DO SOMETHING

If you wait for perfect conditions, you will never get anything done.   ***(Ecclesiastes 11:4 TLB)***

There's never enough time to be as prepared as you'd like. There's seldom enough money to afford everything you want to buy or do. There's usually a lack of energy for us grandmothers to be all things for all people. That being acknowledged, however, doesn't mean we have to sit and twiddle our thumbs. Perfection is a quality God apparently has reserved for heaven. In the meantime, you and I on this earth need to do our best with the limited resources we have. If we wait for everything to be just right, those grandchildren of ours will be all grown up and gone before we know it, and we'll have missed many chances to celebrate life with them.

Do what you can with them now, when you can, and as often as you can. Trust God to replenish your body, refresh your mind, and restore your soul. God is obviously the One who invented the system of fast recovery.

O God, gently nudge me so I don't postpone fun times and expressions of love with my family and friends, and hold my hand if that's what it takes. Amen.

JULY 18   GRANDMOTHERS DO GREAT WORK!

"I am doing a great work and I cannot come down."
(Nehemiah 6:3a NRSV)

Nehemiah had returned from the Babylonian captivity to lead in the rebuilding of Jerusalem and its walls. His detractors didn't appreciate his work ethic and wanted to slow down the project. But Nehemiah's response was steadfast and firm. He probably said something like, "I'm busy following God's instructions and can't go to coffee with you." He had his priorities in good shape. Well, I consider what we do as grandmothers to be a great work. The nurturing we provide, the lessons we teach, the stability we offer, and the faith that we share are vital gifts our grandchildren—and this whole world—need.

We may not be paid much monetarily for our services, but what we give is priceless. We're anchors in the storms of life, the storytellers of family history, the sharers of continuity, the safety nets and support systems for the generations behind us. Oh, we're doing a great work! And don't you forget it. I know God certainly won't.

Remind us grandmothers, O God, that we're doing a great work for our families, for you, and for your kingdom on earth; and inspire us to keep going. Amen.

JULY 19   REJOICE EVERY DAY!

It is a wonderful thing to be alive! If a person lives to be very old, let [her] rejoice in every day of life, but let [her] also remember that eternity is far longer. (Ecclesiastes 11:7-8 TLB)

Perspective can be a very helpful by-product of living many years. The older you become, the more experience you gain. Much of it for me, however, seems to have come the hard way. But whether you learn quickly or have to repeat the course multiple times, we mature Christians do learn along the way. One of the lessons I've learned is that it really is wonderful to be alive, and that no matter how gray the day or difficult the circumstances, I have every reason to rejoice. Sometimes life is so good I'd turn cartwheels if I still could. At other moments I struggle to make sense of problems within my own family circle.

I want to stay truly alive every day I'm on this earth. I don't want to shuffle through each day, merely surviving. I'd like to live and love to the fullest. And whether my days are calm and serene, or hectic and stressful, may I remember that "eternity is far longer."

God, I really do try to rejoice every day. Some days I do well; some days I don't. Please be patient with me, your faithful student. Amen.

JULY 20   THE WEAKER I GET, THE STRONGER
I BECOME

For whenever I am weak, then I am strong.
                   (2 Corinthians 12:10b NRSV)

As my physical strength and stamina diminish, my spiritual power seems to increase. Perhaps it's because I've learned that true strength comes from within. I've experienced a great deal through my decades of life. I've seen my share both of successes and sorrows. I've laughed until it hurts, and I've shed many tears because of that pain. But through it all, I've grown in my trust and faith in God. My love for family has come to fill every fiber of my being. It matters little that I can no longer successfully use a hula hoop. Well, actually, I never could. I don't need to keep pace with my active grandchildren. My strength these days is more inward than outward. It's not my physical prowess now but my availability; not my endless supply of energy but my inner peace; not my wealth but my wisdom.

Yes, I'm not as strong as I once was. But in this weakness, I am stronger and more vital than ever! Thanks be to God!

O God, who for our sakes became weak upon the cross, walk with me as my outward strength declines, and give me an extra measure of your inner power. Amen.

JULY 21   MAKE HAY WHILE THE SUN'S SHINING

Lord, help me to realize how brief my time on earth will be. Help me to know that I am here for but a moment more.
(Psalm 39:4 TLB)

At every age, life is precious. But for grandmothers, even the youngest of us, each moment of each day takes on new meaning. We have new, fresh, young lives to help nurture. We find excitement in watching them grow and mature. What joy every time a grandchild comes to visit, to have this child take off his or her shoes and stand against the "measuring wall" in our kitchen. With eleven grandchildren, that wall makes quite a cluttered sight. It also reminds me how quickly they grow up, and how quickly I'm growing older.

I feel as though this is harvest time in my life. I've planted seeds, and now the fruit of the Spirit is being produced. I have no idea how much longer I shall be in the land of the living. But while I'm here, I intend to make use of every minute. So do not postpone writing that letter, sending that e-mail, making that phone call, or giving that hug. Quite literally, you and I are here "but a moment more."

I know well, dear God, that each day is precious. But sometimes I have trouble remembering this truth. Please remind me; then remind me again. Amen.

JULY 22   GOD'S EXQUISITE PLEASURES

You have let me experience the joys of life and the exquisite pleasures of your own eternal presence.   *(Psalm 16:11 TLB)*

What a wonderful verse of scripture! What a gifted poet the psalmist was. We mere mortals can actually experience the delight of God's presence. As a grandmother, I would have to say that being with grandchildren is one of God's most exquisite pleasures. Perhaps it's God's special way of making this verse from the psalms come to life, demonstrating how God's Word is wonderfully embodied in our world.

Grandchildren have a way of making concrete and real the love of God. They often do so in simple, common ways. I experience these exquisite pleasures when sharing a meal of macaroni and cheese with them; when helping them with their homework—although I confess I'm over my head with today's fifth grade math; and when they stay overnight and I tenderly tuck them into bed. I'm not naive. Being a grandmother isn't all fun and games. But even then, it's an exquisite experience.

What can I say, Lord? You've outdone yourself by giving me the chance to be a grandmother. How I do appreciate it! Amen.

JULY 23   HANDING DOWN THE FAITH

Every time I say your name in prayer—which is practically all the time—I thank God for you. . . . That precious memory triggers another: your honest faith—and what a rich faith it is, handed down from your grandmother Lois to your mother Eunice, and now to you! **(2 Timothy 1:3a, 5 Message)**

Lois, the mother of Eunice and grandmother of Timothy, is commended by the author of 2 Timothy, probably the apostle Paul, for her honest faith and the nurture she's provided succeeding generations. It is both pure joy and a little intimidating to know that my words, touch, and homespun wisdom can be such powerful influences within my family circle. I do wish to affirm their growth in faith every chance I get.

I am fortunate to have several grandchildren living close by. We're part of the same congregation, so I'm able to snuggle with our teenage autistic grandson on the back pew in the balcony, beam with pride as a granddaughter serves as acolyte, and listen to several of them sing in the children's choir. But whether they're near or far, we grandmothers can have spiritual authority in our grandchildren's lives. They notice how we live and love. I choose to quietly and consistently model my faith for them, and I never cease praying for them.

God of Lois and Eunice, and of me, too, may I be a worthy influence in helping shape my grandchildren's faith and nurturing their love for you. Amen.

JULY 24   A LONG DISTANCE LOVE AFFAIR

Let love be your greatest aim.   (1 Corinthians 14:1a TLB)

I know the word *aim* in 1 Corinthians 14 refers to our focus or purpose in life. Perhaps we might also define it like the shooting of an arrow; that is, our love needs to be right on target. We grandmothers like to keep our eyes on the objects of our affection. Sometimes, however, they live too far away, and we're not able to be with them frequently enough. We then have to find and use all the opportunities for communication at our disposal. I suggest sending greeting cards at times other than birthdays; or e-mail them their own special messages; occasionally telephone them—and only them; try sending a small gift for no reason other than that you love them. Be creative, be constant, and always be positive.

Of course, you can do these same things for grandchildren who live close by. But the farther away they live, and the more infrequently you're with them, the better your loving aim needs to be. So practice, practice, practice.

Teach me your secrets, O God, of how to be close to my grandchildren no matter where they are or what they're doing. Amen.

JULY 25   O SING A NEW SONG

O sing to the LORD a new song; sing to the LORD, all the earth.
(Psalm 96:1 NRSV)

My late mother-in-law, Great Granny, as we affectionately called her, lived in our home for several years toward the end of her days.

She had a cozy apartment in the house's lower level, so sounds drifted up into our living space. She rose at 5:30 every morning to have her devotions. She usually prayed out loud and sang a rousing selection of old gospel hymns. Her voice often served as my alarm clock, whether or not I was ready to face the new day.

But over the years she learned, and joyfully offered to God, a number of new songs and choruses of praise. In spite of myself, I also learned them. She kept her faith alive and remained up to date with current world affairs. She embraced new ideas and could visit with her grandchildren and great-grandchildren and speak on nearly any topic.

Even though I don't like singing solos, I do try to learn what new things God is doing. If you listen closely, that's me *humming* a new song from God.

O God of new life, constant growth, and frequent surprises, keep me awake and alert. I don't want to miss anything you—or my grandchildren—are doing. Amen.

JULY 26   A PLACE OF PEACE AND PROSPERITY

Everyone will live quietly in [her] own home in peace and prosperity, for there will be nothing to fear. The Lord himself has promised this.   *(Micah 4:4 TLB)*

Grandmothers have the time and opportunity to make their homes a sacred space, to create a sense of peacefulness where grandchildren feel safe and secure. In times when young persons need to be alert to potential dangers in the world, they should find total acceptance at Grandma's place. When my grandchildren visit, they immediately kick off their shoes and head for the candy dish in the kitchen. They sprawl out full-length on our family room floor to color, or sit at the computer creating imaginary zoos filled with marvelous animals.

An eleven-year-old granddaughter recently paid me a high compliment. "Grandma," she said, "when you and Grandpa have to go to a nursing home, I'm going to buy your house. I just love it!" In all likelihood, that will never happen. But obviously she feels comfortable here. She and her younger sister frequently leave a few possessions with me, perhaps as a pledge they'll soon be back. No matter what size your dwelling place may be, or how humble it is, may peace and love always abide within its walls.

Gracious One, I pray for that day when all the world's children will be able to "live quietly...in peace and prosperity." Amen.

JULY 27   ACCEPT LIFE AND BE PATIENT

Accept life, and be most patient and tolerant with one another. (Colossians 3:12 JBP)

We grandmothers, who have probably "seen it all" and "been there, done that," seem to be a patient and accepting lot. There's not much grandkids can do that will surprise us. Most of us had our patience tried so often when we were mothers that it's now extremely strong. Grounded in our faith, settled and solid in our values, we're not easily upset. You've got to get up early and work hard to perturb us.

We live in an age of instant everything—instant food, immediate success, and a quick fix for every problem. But some things, the really important ones, take time to develop. You don't learn to play a musical instrument quickly. It requires years of faithful practice. Well, we humans don't seem to learn patience and tolerance quickly, either. We grandmothers of this world can offer a priceless gift to our offspring by modeling acceptance and tolerance. After all, it takes patience to learn patience.

Patient God, remind me that I still have a way to go in that department. But let me use what patience I already have to be a calming, healing presence for others. Amen.

JULY 28   TAKE GOOD CARE OF YOURSELF

Oh, that you would choose life; that you and your children might live! Choose to love the Lord your God and to obey him

and to cling to him, for he is your life and the length of your days. *(Deuteronomy 30:19b-20a TLB)*

It's wonderful in these "golden years of life" to have the time and resources to give to others. In my days of active mothering and working outside the home, I was just too busy or tired to help much in the community. Yes, I taught Sunday school, worked on the PTA, and had a Bluebird group. I did my share. But these days with only Grandpa and me in the house, I can now invest myself more deeply in other good works.

I need to be careful, however, not to overextend myself. Especially for my grandchildren's sake, I want to enjoy many more years of living and loving. I hope to see them grow to maturity and, one day, to hold great-grandchildren on my lap.

God wants to give me length of days and expects me to cooperate by choosing life—by taking care of my health, eating well, exercising, and keeping my mind active. Being a grandmother brings such joy that I want to experience it as long as possible.

God of each day and God of eternity, remind me to care for my physical, mental, emotional, and spiritual health. Help me choose life! Amen.

JULY 29   SOWING SEEDS OF KINDNESS

Keep on sowing your seed, for you never know which will grow—perhaps it all will. *(Ecclesiastes 11:6 TLB)*

Being a grandmother is all about planting seeds in other people's lives. Of course, that also involves watering, weeding, and tending your very special garden. I enjoy planting positive thoughts in grandchildren's fertile brains. It's satisfying to sow seeds of kindness whenever and wherever I can. Then it's pure joy to wait and watch for the harvest.

"You never know which will grow," so you and I ought to be generous in scattering seeds. If there were retail stores where such seeds could be purchased, I'd buy packages of hope, courage, wisdom, laughter, praise, faithfulness, rejoicing—well, I'd probably buy out the whole store. Some seeds I plant in others' lives, especially in my younger grandchildren, may not bear fruit in my lifetime. So be it. That won't stop me from preparing the soil of their hearts and minds, or from tenderly placing seeds of love in the lives of everyone I know. Our task is to scatter; God gives the growth. We'll receive our reward—if not now, then later.

Dear God, what comfort and joy it brings to know that, one day, "we shall come rejoicing, bringing in the sheaves." Amen.

JULY 30   FOREVER VITAL AND GREEN

The godly shall flourish like palm trees, and grow tall as the cedars of Lebanon. For they are transplanted into the Lord's own garden, and are under his personal care. Even in old age they will still produce fruit and be vital and green.
                                                   (Psalm 92:12-14 TLB)

There are a myriad of ways in which to be an effective grandmother. My dear mother in her later years could only sit and smile, keep her cookie jar filled, and watch my children study maps and read *National Geographic* magazines. She'd sit in her rocking chair, and they'd sprawl all over the floor. What a delightful sight! What a gift she was! She quietly imparted to them a love for God's creation and for all his creatures.

Great-grandma Emert often expressed frustration that she couldn't do more, that her failing health limited her activities so much. But I don't know how, had she been in perfect health, she could have been a greater blessing to our six children. Her body may have grown weak and weary, but her mind and her spirit remained ever "vital and green."

My prayer is that I, too, shall keep myself under God's personal care, and by so doing stay active and be an inspiration to those who follow in my footsteps.

Water me some more with your Spirit, O God, whenever I start getting a little wilted. I want to stay vital and green for the rest of my earthly life. Amen.

JULY 31   LIVE AND LOVE DEEPLY

Receive and experience the amazing grace of the Master, Jesus Christ, deep, deep within yourselves.
                                (Philippians 4:23 Message)

When we receive and experience the amazing grace of Jesus Christ, we discover who we are at the depths of our being. There's no other way to be the grandmothers we're called to be than to go deep into the love of God. We simply can't do it by ourselves. We quickly run out of energy and answers when we try it solo.

Everyone around you, including your precious grandchildren, will sense the depth of your caring and the power of your love. You won't have to say a word, give any outward gifts, or spoil your grandchildren in the slightest. They'll feel the strength of your faithfulness and intuitively experience the power of your commitment.

It's helpful to learn from the experts about being a grandparent. It's important to talk to others who share your same role and responsibilities. But it's not just a matter of trying harder. It's a matter of faith and trust in God. It's the courage to go deep within yourself, knowing that the Holy Spirit goes with you every step of the way.

O God of amazing grace, hold my hand and go with me as I explore the depths of your power and love. Amen.

August

A Life of Love

ELLEN GROSECLOSE

AUGUST 1   LET LOVE HAVE THE RUN OF THE HOUSE

God is love. When we take up permanent residence in a life of love, we live in God and God lives in us. This way, love has the run of the house, becomes at home and mature in us, so that we're free of worry.   **(1 John 4:16b-17 Message)**

Though school will be starting sometime this month in many places, it is still summer—a time for outdoor activities and family fun. It's a perfect time to reflect on how our very lives can be expressions of love—especially to our grandchildren.

One of the best ways I can show love to my grandchildren is to spend time with them. In the summer, I enjoy camping with them, although I'm not into roughing it. I prefer the comforts of our small travel trailer. But what I like best is being with them in my home.

I delight in sharing my earthly dwelling place—my home for more than thirty years—with my grandchildren. I want them to have "the run of the house," to feel very much at home and accepted here. Yes, it gets cluttered and messy. But tidy and spotless just have to take a back seat to warm and cozy. I've discovered Grandma's house cleans up easily after they're gone, much more quickly than the ache in my heart does.

God of infinite love, I feel so comfortable with you. You're such a gracious host. May my home be as inviting and welcoming as yours is—well, almost. Amen.

173

AUGUST 2   LOVE GOES THE DISTANCE

Love knows no limit to its endurance, no end to its trust, no fading of its hope; it can outlast anything.
                                        (1 Corinthians 13:8a JBP)

Love is sweet, kind, and gentle; yet it is strong, tough, and enduring. As the apostle Paul writes, "it can outlast anything." In our family life, I've learned to never, ever underestimate the power of love. It has stayed close with us through some serious tensions, a few deep disappointments, a bunch of misunderstandings, and several profound times of grief. God's gift of love isn't a fairweather friend. It's strong and determined, unconditional and abiding.

I remember this saying, the source of which I've long since forgotten: "There is nothing you can do to keep me from loving you." Not even rebellious teenagers or cantankerous old grandpas can cause me to withhold my love. I choose to love; or perhaps more accurately, divine love has chosen me.

God's love starts with us as babies—actually before our birth—and goes with us the whole distance, all the way to death and right on into everlasting life.

O God, when I try to hold on to love, I end up losing it. When I give it away, I get even more. Though I don't understand the math, you're sure a great God. Amen.

AUGUST 3   NEW LIFE—A TUMULT OF JOY

Do not remember the former things, or consider the things of old. I am about to do a new thing; now it springs forth, do you not perceive it?   **(Isaiah 43:18-19a NRSV)**

Whenever a grandbaby is born in our family, I forget everything that lies behind—tasks and responsibilities at home—and I'm off and running to welcome that gift of life. Wild horses can't keep me away. First, however, I've had to go on a number of shopping sprees. There are so many cute baby clothes and clever new toys to buy.

I do feel an overwhelming need to be present when the sacred moment of birth occurs. Once there, I'm able to be a calming presence. I share my wisdom about the birthing experience, but only when asked. Something in my soul mysteriously causes me to forget other duties and demands, and makes me totally embrace that new life. When I eventually get to hold that precious little bundle, nothing can distract me from my labor of love.

The wonder of birth, of course, quickly gives way to the constant demands of new life. No wonder God makes babies so cute, adorable, and cuddly.

Creative One, thank you for new life—for rosebuds, kittens, puppies, and human babies! They affirm my faith and jumpstart my joy. Amen.

AUGUST 4   ADD GENEROSITY TO YOUR VIRTUES

Already you are well to the fore in every good quality—you have faith, you can express that faith in words; you have knowledge, enthusiasm and your love for us. Could you not add generosity to your virtues? **(2 Corinthians 8:7 JBP)**

I enjoy being a grandmother because I consider that one of my significant jobs is to be generous. Sometimes when it comes to candy and cookies, perhaps I do it too well. The *American Heritage Dictionary of the English Language*, fourth edition, defines generosity as "nobility of thought or behavior." I would add that it means to give freely and without the expectation of any return. To be truly generous, you and I must take the initiative, not waiting for someone else to act first.

Generosity includes being a cheerful giver (2 Corinthians 9:7), and not only with material things. One of my most valuable gifts is time. In today's busy world, time is a rare commodity and, therefore, something grandmothers should offer in abundance. I realize that we mature women aren't just sitting around waiting for the phone to ring. We, too, have full schedules. Yet my priority is grandchildren first, everything else second. Okay, I'll put Grandpa up there, as well. What I wish to be is an open, available, flexible, approachable, and, yes, generous person.

Dear God, you've been so generous with your people! Inspire me to be gracious and generous with the people close by and those around the world, too. Amen.

AUGUST 5   A SUPPLY OF "LOOK FORWARD TO'S"

Because of [God's] great kindness... now we can share in the wealth of the eternal life he gives us, and we are eagerly looking forward to receiving it.   *(Titus 3:7b TLB)*

I try to keep an ample supply of "look forward to's." I have a few tucked in my bedroom dresser, a couple stashed with the pots and pans, and several more in my desk. I need things to look forward to—like a camping trip two weeks from now; a trip to Ohio to see our son, daughter-in-law, and their family in late autumn; and an Almond Joy candy bar for when I finish sewing on this button. It's important to my emotional and spiritual health to have joyful experiences planned in the future—some soon and some perhaps years away. They help me make it through stressful times and live a life of love even on the toughest of days.

Because of God's kindness, I can look forward to life forevermore with him and all the saints in glory—though I hope that's quite some distance away. In the meantime, I'll watch for the first buttercup to bloom in spring, the first ripe tomato to peek out from the leaves this summer, and everybody in our family to come home next Thanksgiving.

Lord, let me be on my tiptoes to see all the wonderful surprises and beautiful experiences you have in store for me. And could you send another one soon? Amen.

AUGUST 6   PRACTICE PLAYING SECOND FIDDLE

Love from the center of who you are; don't fake it. Run for dear life from evil; hold on for dear life to good. Be good friends who love deeply; practice playing second fiddle.
(Romans 12:9-10 Message)

Most folks probably assume violinists play second fiddle in the orchestra because they aren't quite good enough, or lack the stage presence, to be in the first section. Perhaps there's some truth in that from a human perspective. But that's not how God looks at it. The great God of the universe asks us to choose second violin; that is, to practice being supportive, to willingly play harmony while others get the glory of playing melody.

I wish to be the best grandmother I can be, and often discover it means having a supportive role. I don't always need to be the center of attention; in fact, I probably do better work when I'm not. My family frequently needs me to love them by being supportive and encouraging, flexible and dependable.

So under the direction of the Master Conductor, I've been practicing second fiddle, and getting pretty good at it if I do say so myself—in all humility, of course.

God of the whole human orchestra, I'll play whatever instrument you need me to play, as long as you'll teach me how, and then direct my every note. Amen.

AUGUST 7   EVERY MORNING AND EVERY EVENING

Every morning tell [God], "Thank you for your kindness," and every evening rejoice in all his faithfulness.   (Psalm 92:2 TLB)

The psalmist offers sage advice: Live one day at a time; begin each day with thanksgiving and end it by rejoicing in God's faithfulness. No matter what joys or sorrows, successes or tribulations come your way, give thanks and rejoice. This sounds easy. But when you've had a sleepless night and awaken more tired than when you went to bed, and when anything that can go wrong does go wrong during the day, it may not be quite so simple. Yet the psalmist doesn't list any fine print or exclusions. Those words are right there in the Bible: *every* morning, *every* evening.

Whether I thank God and rejoice for twenty-five grandchildren or I am waiting for my first one to arrive; whether my family lives next door or on the far side of the planet; whether they're doing well or struggling to stay together, it's a great way to begin and end each and *every* twenty-four hours. It's like having two special bookends from God around my life—thanksgiving and praise—that faithfully hold me together.

First thing tomorrow morning, O God, I'm going to thank you. And tonight, my last words before sleep will be to rejoice in you. May I do so every day. Amen.

AUGUST 8   SAFELY UNDER GOD'S WINGS

I am trusting you! I will hide beneath the shadow of your wings until this storm is past.   (Psalm 57:1b TLB)

Summer storms occasionally visit our small valley in north central Washington State. To the west, dark clouds quickly billow up; then a few big raindrops splash on the ground. Distant rumbling of thunder becomes more insistent as it draws ever closer. As the storm cell passes overhead, the sky lights up with flashes of lightning, and the thunder rattles our windows. But it soon passes by, the sky clears, and the air smells so fresh and fragrant. The whole experience is beautiful and a bit frightening, awesome and intimidating. I personally prefer waiting out the storm from the safety of our solidly built home, although I can be coaxed onto the front porch for brief moments.

When grandchildren are visiting during storms, I serve as a loving mother hen, taking them under my wings. I offer my lap and arms to my little ones for comfort. And I'm reminded that in everyday life, too, storms unexpectedly rumble through, but God's wings are always spread over us until the unsettled weather passes.

Dear God, when the storms of life are present, comfort me; but especially protect my grandchildren. They're your precious babies, too. Amen.

AUGUST 9   GOD'S CHILDREN RIGHT NOW!

Here and now, . . . we are God's children. We don't know what we shall become in the future. We only know that when he appears we shall be like him, for we shall see him as he is!
(1 John 3:2 JBP)

This grandmother is one of God's dear children—every bit as much as his tiny, smooth-skinned babies. Granted, I can't crawl on hardwood flooring more than a few minutes without my knees hurting. And if I tumble down the stairs, it will take forever to get back up—after having checked to make sure all my parts are still working. At first glance, you may notice nothing but a pleasant looking, obviously older and slower model of the human race. But don't be fooled. I am a beloved child of God!

What we shall become is not yet revealed (see 1 John 3:2), but right now you may consider me a sweet two-year-old with wrinkles and gray hair. I'll bet from God's vantage point I'm almost as cute. To understand what I'm saying, you need to know that God sees us from the inside, focusing on our hearts and minds and souls.

No matter how tired, lonely, stressed, or troubled you or I may be, *we shall be loved!*

It's thrilling to know I'm your beloved child! So pardon me, Lord, while I turn a cartwheel! Amen.

AUGUST 10   STEADY AS SHE GOES

The LORD is my light and my salvation; whom shall I fear? The LORD is the stronghold of my life; of whom shall I be afraid?
(Psalm 27:1 NRSV)

Contrary to what some of my family may think, Grandma doesn't have all the answers, especially when it comes to computers and anything electronic that has buttons and makes beeping sounds. But when it comes to changing a diaper, emotionally handling a child's first day of school, and arbitrating between arguing teenage siblings, I have a PhD. Let me tell you, I earned that degree raising six children. I'm not bragging, but stability and constancy could be my middle names.

Truth be told, I'm not the strong one here. God is! He's my light and my salvation, the stronghold of my life. Basically, all I'm doing is passing on to others the calmness, wisdom, and strength God has given me. My goal, of course, is to help all my family cut out the middlewoman, namely me, and go directly to the Source: God.

Dear God, so many times you've been my strength between that rock and a hard place. Guide me now as I love others by sharing the inner power I've received from you. Amen.

AUGUST 11   CLINGING TO GOD'S COMMANDS

I cling to your commands and follow them as closely as I can. Lord, don't let me make a mess of things.   (Psalm 119:31 TLB)

I've made my share of mistakes. Over the years I've learned the delicate art of tactfulness, and I'm quite accomplished at staying out of the middle of family issues. I'm happy to share any insights I may have—most of them of the commonsense variety. I have, however, learned to wait to be asked for advice. It's then much more likely to be appreciated and heeded. Even so, there are times when I find myself in tight spots, in one of those ticklish situations.

That's when I cling to God's commands and to wisdom, such as always speaking the truth in love. The book of Proverbs contains a wealth of common sense: "We can always 'prove' that we are right, but is the Lord convinced?" (16:2 TLB); and "It is an honor to receive a frank reply" (24:26 TLB). My role as grandmother is to help family members sort out the issues, encourage them to be honest about their feelings, and invite them to join me in clinging to God's commands.

Eternal God, thank you for giving me your commandments. Some may cause me to squirm a little, but help me to follow them as closely as I can. Amen.

AUGUST 12   HANG IN THERE, GRANDMA!

Be truly glad! There is wonderful joy ahead, even though the going is rough for a while down here.   *(1 Peter 1:6 TLB)*

This text is perfect when times are tough—when you're weary and facing an uncertain future. We all have struggles from time to time. It's part of being human. We can either allow those difficult experiences to drag us down, or we can move forward to those wonderful joys that surely lie ahead.

One of my roles as a grandmother is to pass this bit of wisdom on to my little brood. Each one of them seems to learn at her or his own speed. We teachers of truth just need to be patient and keep gently offering our knowledge. I tend to share advice by using my own experiences—both my successes and failures. I have quite a collection of family anecdotes at my fingertips. I do try to keep them fresh and repeat them only as absolutely necessary. But stories rather than lectures are often better received and longer remembered.

This verse is one truth I want my grandchildren all to retain: "There is wonderful joy ahead" no matter what happens down here.

Gracious God, I admit I sometimes chew my fingernails, but I affirm with all my being that I believe in your promises. I am truly glad! Amen.

AUGUST 13   THE JOY OF FAMILY REUNIONS

Lift up your eyes and see! For your sons and daughters are coming home to you from distant lands. Your eyes will shine with joy, your hearts will thrill.   *(Isaiah 60:4-5a TLB)*

Our family reunions are quite the affairs! If everyone can make it, we have a crowd of twenty-three excited, noisy, happy bodies— from a baby to a sixty-five-year-old grandpa. To use a phrase from the Christmas carol "There's a Song in the Air," it's a "tumult of joy." There's a reason we hold these events somewhat infrequently.

By the time we all return home, everyone's happy but totally exhausted.

Summer is the only time—at least in our family—when these large gatherings are possible. I anticipate them with much excitement. My eyes shine and my heart thrills just in planning and anticipating the occasion. When they all arrive from "distant lands," our house is suddenly bursting with life. The words *bustling, hectic,* and *noisy* don't do justice to the ambiance. *Loving chaos* is closer to the truth. My kitchen's a mess and the refrigerator is opened and closed a hundred times—and that's every ten minutes. Our cats take refuge under beds; that is, until a two-year-old discovers them.

There's nothing quite like your sons and daughters coming home to you.

O God, it was hard letting them leave, so thank you for letting them return to the old nest. Remind them they're welcome anytime, as long as they bring my grandchildren. Amen.

AUGUST 14   ENCOURAGING WORDS DO WONDERS

Anxious hearts are very heavy but a word of encouragement does wonders! ***(Proverbs 12:25 TLB)***

I'm not a wonder worker; although when grandchildren think I am, I laugh and don't correct them. But when I speak affirming and encouraging words, it does wonders. So I tell my flock how special they are. I praise each grandchild whenever he or she does a good deed, creates something special, or gives a thoughtful gift. Frequently I tell them what wonderful people they are for no particular reason—other than that I love them.

I enjoy standing on the sidelines during soccer matches, cheering for my granddaughters. I tell a grandson, who will struggle academically his whole life, what a brilliant young man he is—and that's the truth. I also let their parents know what good children they have. Moms and dads need affirmation, too. I try to encourage in creative ways so I don't sound like a broken record. Oops, I meant to say a scratched CD.

We're all susceptible to heavy hearts, so kind and gracious words are always appropriate and well received.

Your words encourage me so much, O God. How can I do anything else but share kind words with those I love? May encouraging words flow directly from my heart to theirs. Amen.

AUGUST 15   GENEROUS, GRACIOUS, AND FAIR TO ALL

"You're kingdom subjects. Now live like it. Live out your God-created identity. Live generously and graciously toward others, the way God lives toward you."   *(Matthew 5:48 Message)*

I have a strong sense of equality and fairness when it comes to people, and especially when it involves grandchildren. In my book, favoritism doesn't even deserve one sentence. I try hard to be equally available for all my family. I seek to love each as a unique individual, as a one-of-a-kind gift from God.

I must admit this deeply ingrained attitude makes birthdays and Christmases something of a challenge. It puts my list-making talents to the test. I do enjoy shopping for each person. It allows me the opportunity to think about his or her special talents, favorite colors, and passionate interests. What joy there is when I find exactly the right gifts! I do want each grandchild to know she or he is equally loved and appreciated.

In addition, I do not compare grandchildren to one another. Each of them is God's original work of art, and a masterpiece at that!

O God, I know you love us for exactly who we are. Help me to be fair, just, and accepting in my dealings with each and every family member. Amen.

AUGUST 16   THE OLD, OLD STORY

I plan to keep on reminding you of these things even though you already know them and are really getting along quite well!
                    (2 Peter 1:12 TLB)

I want my family—from the youngest to the eldest—to be familiar with the "old, old story of Jesus and his love." They don't have to sing the same spiritual songs I enjoy, belong to the denomination I've been loyal to my entire life, or spend as much time in church as I do. But I want to be able to say with the disciple Peter that they're all "really getting along quite well."

So I shall continue to remind them to be kind and work for peace; to accept the promises of God and use the gifts they've been given; to be patient and genuinely loving to other people. I've learned that sermonizing, admonishing, reproaching, or otherwise browbeating them is counterproductive. If you want them to listen and respond favorably, then share God's message kindly and with a smile. Add a big hug for the really important ideas. Better yet, set them to music!

I've heard somewhere that "the truth bears repeating." Personally, I speak most eloquently when I let my actions do the talking.

O God, hush me when I start to preach or nag. Let me live every day in such a way that my daily life becomes a powerful vehicle for your good news. Amen.

AUGUST 17   FASHION IS FLEETING

"If you decide for God, living a life of God-worship, it follows that you don't fuss about what's on the table at mealtimes or whether the clothes in your closet are in fashion."
(Matthew 6:25 Message)

I don't fuss much about fashion. Of course, rural eastern Washington State isn't exactly the fashion capital of the country. I do like to dress appropriately on Sunday mornings, which for my generation means no jeans, shorts, or sweatshirts. However, I've learned that what we wear outwardly to church can't compare with who we are inwardly. I tend to wear practical clothes—so it won't matter when a grandchild spills a soft drink on my lap or squirts catsup on my blouse. Utilitarian always trumps elegant—except perhaps for a night on the town with Grandpa.

It's okay to be a little out of date fashionwise as long as I'm up to date in terms of my beliefs, my caring, and my compassion. Fashion is fleeting and changes faster than my grandchildren are growing. Faith and hope and love are forever!

Dear God, my priorities seem to be tested every day. Refresh my memory about what's temporary and what's eternal, and help me live accordingly. Amen.

AUGUST 18   LEAVE ROOM FOR GROWTH

As we live with Christ, our love grows more perfect and complete.   (1 John 4:17a TLB)

No matter how old I become, how financially secure I may be, how much I know, or how many grandchildren I have, God expects me to keep growing spiritually. He also asks that I continue expanding the horizons of my love for others. A faith that doesn't grow is one that will soon be shriveled and useless.

My father-in-law was a preacher, and one of his favorite stories was about a small girl who kept falling out of bed every night. When her mother asked her why it was happening, the girl replied, "I guess I go to sleep too close to where I climbed in." Similarly, a number of Christians stop growing in their faith and nod off to sleep in their service to God.

I want my love to continually expand. It seems hard to believe, but if I live by this verse, I'll love my grandchildren even more in the years ahead. And if more of them should join our family fold, I'll have quite enough love for them, too.

God, your love never runs out. I've heard that if you give love away, you end up having more. Thanks to you, I'm proving that truth day by day. Amen.

AUGUST 19   GOD IS GOOD ALL THE TIME

I had fainted, unless I had believed to see the goodness of the LORD in the land of the living.   (Psalm 27:13 KJV)

It's a tough world out there. Life isn't always fair. You can get hurt when you venture into the problems, pressures, and competitive nature of society. Yet in all those tensions and potential struggles, God is present, working to make it better. The Spirit of God is constantly seeking people to help in the shaping and molding of a just world.

I want my entire family, and especially my grandchildren, to know in their hearts that God's goodness isn't just words on paper, a figment of human wishing. God's caring and compassion are genuine. I do believe that the goodness of the Lord is abundantly present in the land of the living. God's love is there in school classrooms, hospitals, and office buildings, as well as in the tenements and ghettos. If we know where to look, and don't let the negativity of our age distract us, we'll see abundant evidence of God's goodness in our midst. And I hope we'll find it within our own hearts, as well.

God of grace and God of glory, remind us that you are with us. I'm not about to faint, because your Spirit hovers over us and dwells within us. Amen.

AUGUST 20   LORD, MAKE IT PLAIN

Tell me what to do, O Lord, and make it plain.
(Psalm 27:11a TLB)

I'm a person of basic, simple faith—no frills. I study and seek to learn more about God's Word and ways. But when push comes to shove, when my back is against the wall, I hope God will give me very clear instructions. Life today is a little confusing, especially when it comes to electronic gadgets. PalmPilots, cell phones, Xboxes, DVDs, and all their electronic "buddies" make my head hurt and my hands tremble. After all, I grew up with calculators and slide rules. It makes my head spin when our son-in-law, who works for a computer software company, tries to explain how our computer works. It's all very logical, he patiently explains. *Sure it is*, I think to myself. I keep his phone number handy at all times.

I don't think I'm being hardheaded or stubborn. But I do appreciate God's clarity and even his bluntness when I need it. And yes, thank God for grandchildren who are at home in this world of the Internet, Google, and SpongeBob SquarePants on CD-ROM.

O God, I'm part of the generation who needs you to be down-to-earth and to the point. I'm glad there's still the Good Book where I can read about your ways. Amen.

AUGUST 21   TEND TO YOUR KNITTING

Eventually, we're all going to end up kneeling side by side in the place of judgment, facing God.... So tend to your knitting. You've got your hands full just taking care of your own life before God.   (Romans 14:10b, 12 Message)

I don't knit. My dear mother tried to teach me, but I wasn't particularly interested. I enjoy doing needlepoint, making quilts, and altering clothes for grandchildren. But I do get the point of this scripture: Don't meddle in other people's lives, especially those of your own family. I actually do have more than enough to keep me busy without poking my nose where it shouldn't be. Of course, I sometimes sneak in little sermonettes when I think family members need them, though I try to avoid intruding into their major decisions. I'm quite accomplished at being quiet, listening intently, and simply nodding my head. Even when they ask for my opinion, I reply cautiously.

When that day comes when I kneel before my Maker, I'm guessing he'll not inquire about what church I attended, what my annual net income was, or what make of car I drove. He'll look into my eyes and ask, "Did you really, really love?"

God of infinite love, I promise to tend to my own knitting. And if I fail, teach me how to undo every one of my stitches. Amen.

AUGUST 22   I WILL TRUST AND NOT BE AFRAID

"See, God has come to save me! I will trust and not be afraid, for the Lord is my strength and song; he is my salvation."
(Isaiah 12:2 TLB)

I vividly recall watching each of my kindergartners head off to their first day of school in their new clothes, clutching their lunch pails, and looking very handsome or pretty with their neatly combed hair. I recall my feelings of pride and my gnawing apprehensions. Will their teachers know how wonderful and clever they are? Will other children include them in games during recess? What in the world am I going to do all day while they're gone?

These days I observe secondhand as my children telephone and share with me these same feelings I once experienced. And I find those feelings from years gone by sweeping over me again. What I do now is pause and say a silent prayer that my grandchildren will have a safe environment, teachers who will appreciate and nurture them, and budding friendships with a wide variety of children. I also think kind thoughts for their parents, and whisper to myself, "I will trust and not be afraid."

God of parents and students, bless them in their excitement and anxiety. Bless us grandmothers as we relive those years gone by. Be the strength and song of us all. Amen.

AUGUST 23   INVENTIVE HOSPITALITY

Don't burn out; keep yourselves fueled and aflame. Be alert servants of the Master, cheerfully expectant. Don't quit in hard times; pray all the harder. Help needy Christians; be inventive in hospitality.   *(Romans 12:11-13 Message)*

I'm not what you'd call a "hostess with the mostest." I enjoy having guests in our home; although, if they come for dinner, they're likely to get my special recipe for "company chicken" or my mother's famous meatloaf. But even if I cooked hot dogs, it would be enough if my guests felt welcomed and at home.

I try not to fuss too much when we have guests. That's Grandpa's department. Especially when children come, it's important *not* to notice everything that goes on. I would burn out if I fussed over every out-of-place toy, every kitchen floor spill, or every soaking wet bathroom towel. I try not to look at the dirty clothes pile in our utility room.

Inventive hospitality is my goal. To me, that means focusing on my guests' needs, listening to their stories, sharing their laughter, and expressing love for their children. I know I've succeeded when, as they leave, other people's kids or my own grandchildren ask excitedly, "When can we come back?"

Gracious and welcoming God, you make me feel so at home with you. Please let other people, young and old and in-between, feel that way with me. Amen.

AUGUST 24　　THE MEASURE OF YOUR GREATNESS

"Your care for others is the measure of your greatness."
(Luke 9:48c TLB)

God's standards of measurement and our human ones don't always seem to agree. Our yardstick of greatness often includes wealth, fame, political clout, and physical prowess. But God's way of measuring greatness is based on "your care for others." My stature as a grandmother isn't calculated by whom I know in high places, how flashy my wardrobe is, or how much I spend on gifts for each grandchild. It's so much more basic than that. Do I care for my grandchildren in my heart? Whenever possible, do I spend quality time with them? Am I patient and attentive, forgiving and loving?

I hope all my family, including my beloved grandchildren, will base their lives upon this premise of God. They will succeed in my mind if they truly care for others. I want them to reach out to less fortunate persons, offer help to victims of disasters, and lend a helping hand to anyone in need. In so doing, they will bless me as well.

Loving God, I'd be pleased if on my tombstone it read, "Her care for all others was the measure of her greatness!" Amen.

AUGUST 25   PERFECT TIMING

There is a right time for everything: A time to be born, a time to die; A time to plant; A time to harvest. . . . A time to cry; A time to laugh. . . . A time to hug; A time not to hug. . . . A time to be quiet; A time to speak up." (Ecclesiastes 3:1-2, 4a, 5b, 7b TLB)

In sports, timing is everything. When my grandchildren play baseball (the plastic variety) in our front yard, I marvel at how hard and far they can hit the ball. Even my four-year-old grandson makes solid contact nearly every pitch. For someone athletically challenged like myself, it's pure joy to watch their coordination and energy.

But don't worry about me. I have perfect timing, too. I often know exactly when to make that phone call to a family member in crisis, and I know when to wait before dialing his or her number. I know when to offer advice, and when to listen to her or his ideas. I know when a bandage is needed, and when a kiss will do. I understand there's a time to hug, and a time to give my children or grandchildren room. I didn't learn all this overnight. And I still don't always get it right. But of this I am absolutely certain: It's always the right time to follow the Spirit's leading.

O God, you always do the right thing at exactly the right moment. Even when I fall far short, may I continue to pattern my human life after your perfect standards. Amen.

AUGUST 26   OUT OF THE DEPTHS

Out of the depths I cry to you, O LORD. Lord, hear my voice!
(Psalms 130:1-2 NRSV)

"Launch out into the deep."   *(Luke 5:4b KJV)*

I often assume that "the depths" refers to troubles and sorrows. I do know that grief takes us deep as we search our own souls, as well as the depths of God's Spirit. Yet doesn't joy also go deep into our lives? This particular grandmother feels joy all the way to the tips of her toes. There are certainly times when I cry to the Lord from the depths of anxiety or pain. But there are surely more occasions when God and I laugh deeply—when he and I rejoice and I feel it with every cell in my body.

People of faith are called to venture out into the spiritual depths, not just wade in the shallows. I want to go deep in my relationships with my husband, children, and grandchildren—and with my God. I want them all, including my Maker, to know me fully and love me unconditionally.

God of the high places and God of the depths, thank you for going with me on this rollercoaster called life. Amen.

AUGUST 27   MATURE CHRISTIANS

Our greatest wish . . . is that you will become mature Christians.
(2 Corinthians 13:9b TLB)

I have many hopes and dreams for my grandchildren. I want them to be whole persons, healthy in body, mind, and soul. I'd like them to grow up in a safe environment and be surrounded by people who care for them. I want them to be disciplined and work hard, but also to laugh, play, and enjoy life. I hope they succeed in their endeavors, maintain a sense of humility, face their failures with courage, and always remember how much their grandparents love them.

I know it takes a village to raise a child. Adding a congregation of God's people to the mix helps even more. My greatest wish is that whatever my grandchildren do and wherever they go, they will become mature Christians. Their favorite songs will not be the same as mine. Their outward forms of worship may be radically different from what's familiar to me. But there is one Lord, one faith, and the same God and Parent of us all (see Ephesians 4:5-6). While I'm thinking about it, I better get busy maturing in my faith.

God of all generations, you've always been my faithful companion. Walk now with my grandchildren and gently shape them into your faithful disciples. Amen.

AUGUST 28   AN EXTENDED FAMILY

The truth is that we neither live nor die as self-contained units. At every turn life links us to the Lord and when we die we come face to face with him. In life or death we are in the hands of the Lord.   *(Romans 14:7-8 JBP)*

It can be a little scary to watch your children and grandchildren leave home and go off into the big world. There are things there that go bump in the night. The good news is that far greater numbers of wonderful, caring people are also there. We tend not to hear or see much of them in our media. Truth be told, we're part of a special extended family that begins in this life and extends all the way to the saints in glory. We still need to educate our young people about the dangers they may encounter, but we should do so without making them overly cautious or perhaps even frightened.

This extended family is the church. It comforts me to know there are people of God present everywhere my family may go; a beloved community of the faithful who truly care, will welcome them, and are willing to serve. In no time, I'm certain a whole host of people will discover how brilliant and clever all my offspring really are.

God, thanks for creating the church, not only for how it nurtures my own family, but also for the way it encircles the entire world with your love. Amen.

AUGUST 29   THE FINAL OUTCOME IS IN GOD'S HANDS

We can make our plans, but the final outcome is in God's hands.   *(Proverbs 16:1 TLB)*

Yes, I have hopes and plans for my grandchildren! I'm wise enough, however, to keep them to myself, with the exception of sharing them with my husband. Grandpa knows how to keep a secret, too—well, most of the time. But I can't help dreaming about their future, about where they'll be and who will love them. I know that worrying is unproductive and never changes anything.

Even so, I'll no doubt continue to make my plans; but I pray I'll remain flexible and open to whatever God has in store for them.

I left home and my small community, where everybody knew me, when I was eighteen. I went off to college, got married the next year, and then trekked all the way across the nation. In my busy life, I seldom considered that my parents and grandparents might be concerned about me. I'm certain, though, they prayed daily for me, and that made all the difference. May my prayers for my grandchildren do the same.

O God of the universe, I'm so grateful you watch over everyone I love and listen to my suggestions, yet hold the final outcome of their lives in your hands. Amen.

AUGUST 30   SHAPING THE FUTURE

[God] has given you all of the present and all of the future. All are yours, and you belong to Christ, and Christ is God's.
                                        (1 Corinthians 3:22c-23 TLB)

In some small way, I hope to shape the future and make it better for those who come after me. I may not be able to change it very much, but that doesn't stop me from trying. I do have some influence with my family, and I wish to use it creatively and wisely. I pray that I'll never be manipulative or coercive, but will listen carefully to their wishes and to God's will. I always seek to speak the truth in love. I'm willing to go the second mile or even beyond if necessary. I know I've been forgiven by God, and I've been faithfully practicing the art of forgiving others.

God has given us grandparents all of the present and a small portion of the future. My grandchildren, I hope, will have a more significant part of it. They obviously have a greater stake in the future than I do. If we belong to Christ, however, our future will be secure no matter what happens.

Dear God, help me to make the most of this present moment, and to trust you to guide my family and this whole world into a future filled with promise. Amen.

AUGUST 31   LIVE FULL LIVES

I ask [Christ] that with both feet planted firmly on love, you'll be able to take in with all followers of Jesus the extravagant dimensions of Christ's love. Reach out and experience the breadth! Test its length! Plumb the depths! Rise to the heights! Live full lives, full in the fullness of God.
(Ephesians 3:16-19 Message)

I've lived a rich, full life. I'm a parent of six children—three "store bought" (adopted) and three "homegrown" (biological). Eleven grandchildren now grace my life. I've lived in a comfortable home for more than three decades. My husband has recently retired, and we're looking forward to a more relaxed lifestyle. I'm not rich in things, but I'm wealthy beyond measure in terms of people and hope and love.

And that's what I want for all my family—to live full lives, full in the fullness of God. I don't care if they earn advanced academic degrees, make billions, have adoring fans in every city, or possess political clout. If those things should happen, so be it. But I yearn for something far deeper: that they'll be filled with the Spirit, speak the truth in love, and grow in faith. I wish for them to plumb the depths and rise to the heights.

I joyfully anticipate the unfolding of God's plan in the lives of my grandchildren. And I shall forever remain their most enthusiastic cheerleader.

God of amazing grace, what a rich, full life you offer all your children! And what extravagant love and blessings you've given me! Amen and amen!

September

Special Blessings

HELEN C. SCOTT-CARTER

SEPTEMBER 1   SPECIAL TIMES, SPECIAL BLESSINGS

[Grandchildren] are a heritage.... Blessed is [she] whose quiver is full of them.   *(Psalm 127:3, 5 NIV)*

I have sixteen grandchildren. Many of them are grown and pursuing careers. Most of them live out of town. So I only see them three times a year: Thanksgiving, Resurrection Sunday, and some time in the summer. What special times these are!

Even though I have many grandchildren, there is room in my heart for many more. So on July 3, 2005, I received some wonderful news. My daughter who has been married for thirteen years has started the process for adopting a child, a six-year-old boy. When my daughter told me about the new venture in her life, I could hear the pride and joy in her voice. She had waited so long to have a child, but that was not to be. Yet God always answers prayer. The answer may not come when we want it or how we expect it, but God is always on time.

I am blessed to have a "quiver full" of grandchildren. Yet even if we have only one grandchild, how blessed we all are to be grandmothers! This month we will consider some of the special blessings of grandmothering—those we receive and those we give.

Thank you, Lord, for the blessing of grandchildren. Amen.

SEPTEMBER 2   A LASTING LEGACY

God is our refuge and strength, an ever-present help in trouble.
(Psalm 46:1 NIV)

A TV commercial for an insurance company shows a grand-mother with two grandchildren. She approaches a parking meter just when the "expired" flag pops up. As she deposits a quarter in the meter, she remarks, "Wouldn't it be wonderful if we could do this and life would go on?"

There is a way for life to go on—by creating memories, leaving a lasting legacy. Memories and legacies are not about things. Things are transient. They can be destroyed. They can lose their meaning.

What kind of legacy can we leave our grandchildren? We can leave them the strength of character that comes with reading God's Word and applying it to our lives. In times of stress when they are being challenged by the storms of life, our grandchildren need to know where to go. In Psalm 46, God is referred to as "our refuge," a place of protection during times of danger and distress. According to Proverbs 14:26, a God-fearing woman is one who leaves a lasting legacy—an awareness that God is their refuge.

Dear Lord, thank you for being my refuge, and for being the legacy I leave my grandchildren. Amen.

SEPTEMBER 3   LIVE LIFE TO THE FULLEST

I urge you to live a life worthy of the calling you have received.
(Ephesians 4:1 NIV)

One of the highlights of my year is Thanksgiving. It is at that time that my grandchildren make one of their three yearly visits to Grandma and Grandpa's house. And it is the time when I pull out all the stops. Preparation for their visit gives me the opportunity to live life to the fullest.

Before the grandchildren leave home, they are given a task to complete. They must put together the menu for the special day. Since there are usually seven of them coming, they must collaborate on what the menu will be. Even though there will be some compromise, each grandchild is allowed to select one special food, just for himself or herself. Over the years, the menu has become fairly standard: honey-baked ham, collard greens, string beans, cranberry sauce, shrimp cocktail, hot rolls and butter, pie, cake, and ice cream. Then I add the special requests from each of the "grands": dill pickles, cucumbers, and strawberries, to name a few.

What a joy it is for me to see my "grands'" faces as they enjoy the special Thanksgiving dinner! The memories linger.

Dear Lord, thank you for the opportunity to live life to the fullest. Amen.

SEPTEMBER 4   A FAMILY TRADITION

She provides food for her family.   *(Proverbs 31:15 NIV)*

Workers look forward to Labor Day, the last holiday of the summer. The purpose of Labor Day is to recognize workers and set aside a day of rest with pay. But Labor Day is usually celebrated with cookouts. When my children were young, we started the tradition of gathering at Grandma's house, so Labor Day became a day of labor for my mother. I remember how diligently she prepared for all of us—children, grandchildren, other relatives, church members, and friends. Labor Day at Grandma's was the stuff memories are made of. Not only did we partake of a sumptuous spread of various foods, but we also had fun preparing a special dessert: homemade ice cream. Momma had prepared the ice cream mix in advance. It was the guests' job to make the mix into real ice cream. Each one participated by turning the crank of the old-fashioned ice-cream maker.

What fond memories my children have of those special times at Grandma's house. As a grandmother, I, too, enjoy providing similar memories for my grandchildren.

Lord, give grandmothers everywhere the heart to make lasting memories for our grandchildren. Amen.

SEPTEMBER 5   WHAT'S IN YOUR HAND?

The LORD said to [Moses], "What is that in your hand?"
(Exodus 4:2 NIV)

Ecclesiastes 9:10 (NIV) says, "Whatever your hand finds to do, do it with all your might." God has given everyone a talent. Often we think that we need extraordinary ability to make a difference. But the Lord says to us what he said to Moses, "What is in your hand?" The Lord uses small tools to perform great tasks.

Imagine the Lord asking Paul while he was in prison, "What is in your hand?"

The answer: a quill! It was enough to write letters to keep in touch with the new churches. Thus, Paul wrote the greatest portion of the New Testament.

In 1994, God asked me, "What is in your hand? I answered, "A pen." God said, "Write a book to help the children understand the Apostles' Creed." Then twelve books followed, as well as various curriculum pieces for the children in my church and denomination.

The Lord wants us to use what he has given us to bless not only our grandchildren but others as well.

Lord, help me to discover what is in my hand that will benefit others. Amen.

SEPTEMBER 6   LITTLE APPRENTICES

Imitate me.   *(1 Corinthians 4:16 NIV)*

The phenomenon of grandparents raising grandchildren is increasing in our country. Because of this, grandparents—particularly grandmothers—have an increasing responsibility to pass on family beliefs and traditions.

Grandchildren become little apprentices when they learn from their grandparents how to live, how to put their beliefs into practice, and how to be like Jesus. They learn from conversations at mealtime, in the car, in the store, at church, and in the neighborhood. They imitate what they see and hear. Even though we may tell our grandchildren what to do or offer advice, they are more likely to follow our example than heed our words.

We can teach our grandchildren to live for Christ by our example. May we always remember that they are watching how we live.

Lord, help me so to live that my grandchildren have a good example to imitate. Amen.

SEPTEMBER 7   WOMAN OF GOD

Look, in this town there is a man of God; he is highly respected.
(1 Samuel 9:6a NIV)

How would your grandchildren describe you?

There is a street in London named Godliman. The story is that a man who once lived on this street led a saintly life. People began to refer to where he lived as "that godly man's street." In time the street was named Godliman. What a tribute to a holy life!

Today's verse refers to a godly man. Kish sent his son Saul to look for some donkeys that had wandered off. Saul and a servant searched long and hard for the donkeys but could not find them. Saul became discouraged because he could not find them. The servant told Saul that "a man of God," Samuel, lived nearby. But Saul did not have any way of paying the man for his services, so he was reluctant to go to the man. Because Samuel was a godly man, he told Saul that the donkeys had been found;, and he did not charge Saul.

Are you a godly woman? Take time to be holy. Let your grandchildren see Jesus in you.

Dear Lord, guide my feet and hold my hands so that I may be like you. Amen.

SEPTEMBER 8   PRAISE THE LORD!

I will bless the LORD at all times; his praise shall continually be in my mouth.
(Psalm 34:1 NRSV)

In the hustle and bustle of daily life, we often take God's blessings for granted. Many of us forget to meditate daily on God's goodness and greatness. In fact, some of us consciously think about God only when things go awry.

Each day we should count our blessings and praise God for bestowing these blessings on us. There are some blessings I don't take for granted—the sunshine, the rain, birds, flowers, blue skies, green grass, and trees. I continually praise God for children's laughter, babies' cries, and family time together.

In addition to praising God for his blessings, I enjoy praising God for his majesty and greatness. The psalms not only describe God but also give reasons for praising God. For example, God is...

a shield
King
Judge
Most High
strength, rock, fortress
Deliverer
Redeemer
Shepherd
God of my salvation
light and salvation
God of glory
Lord God of truth
help in trouble.

For all that God is and all that God does, we can never praise God too much!

Lord, thank you for all your blessings. Amen.

SEPTEMBER 9   SPIRITUAL EXERCISE

Enoch walked with God.   *(Genesis 5:24 NIV)*

"Step with It" was a program sponsored by a soft drink company in public schools. I spearheaded the program at the school where I had been called out of retirement to mentor teachers. The object of the program was to encourage young people to walk. Each student was given a pedometer to keep track of the number of steps he or she made in three days. Every participating student was given a certificate, and the winning class received gifts.

Just as walking for our health keeps us physically fit, walking with God keeps us spiritually fit. Walking with God is developing an intimate, growing relationship with the Lord. To walk with God, we need to "keep in step" with him. This involves talking with him, listening to him, and enjoying his presence.

Our walk with God will be a walk of trust, for God will guide us when we cannot see what lies ahead. We can rest assured that we will be headed in the right direction when we walk with God. Best of all, it's an exciting lifelong journey!

Lord, help me to keep spiritually fit by walking with you. Amen.

SEPTEMBER 10   GOD'S FAITHFULNESS VS.
                                       MY FAITHFULNESS

Because of the LORD's great love we are not consumed, for his compassions never fail. They are new every morning; great is your faithfulness.   (Lamentations 3:22-23 NIV)

We sing, "Great is Thy faithfulness! . . . Morning by morning new mercies I see." Indeed, God is faithful to us. But what about our faithfulness to God?

We make promises to God that we do not keep. For example, we might suffer a devastating illness and promise God that we will do this or that if only we recover. Maybe we keep our promise for a while, but then the pressures of life begin to creep in and take precedence over our promise to God. Not so with God. His compassions never fail. They are new each day.

When I was twelve, I took the "Christian Endeavor" pledge. In part, I promised to "do whatever [God] would like to have me do." Of course, I'm not perfect. There have been many times when I haven't done what God would have me to do. Yet, God has been faithful to me all of my life. Each day I see God's compassionate acts in my life. I can truly say, "Great is Thy faithfulness, Lord, unto me."

Dear Lord, help me to keep my promises to you. Amen.

SEPTEMBER 11   WHAT HAVE YOU DONE FOR
                                              GOD LATELY?

[God] is able to do immeasurably more than all we ask or imagine, according to his power that is at work within us.
(Ephesians 3:20 NIV)

The human mind cannot grasp all that God can do; it is immeasurable. Yet God chooses to work in and through us! We are God's feet and hands. What we do for others, we do for God. As the words of an old gospel hymn remind us, "If I can help somebody as I pass along... Then my living shall not be in vain."*

There are so many ways we can help others. When I lived in Wilmington, Delaware, I spearheaded a program that assisted grandparents who were thrust back into parenthood. I worked with city and private agencies to secure clothes, food, and furniture for grandparents who had to raise their grandchildren on a fixed income.

One of many heartwarming experiences was helping a grandmother who had moved into her little dream home and then, a week later—one week before Christmas—had received three grandchildren to raise. What a joy to see her tears of happiness and the smiles of the grandchildren when my staff and I delivered food, clothes, and toys to their home.

What have you done for God lately?

Dear Lord, show me how I may help someone today. Amen.

*Alma Bazel Androzzo, "If I Can Help Somebody," 1912.

SEPTEMBER 12   RANDOM ACTS OF KINDNESS

As we have opportunity, let us do good to all people, especially to those who belong to the family of believers.
(Galatians 6:10 NIV)

Bumper stickers carry some wonderful messages. One of my favorites is "Please be patient with me. . . . God is not through with me yet." Recently I saw another bumper sticker that caught my eye and appealed to my heart: "Commit random acts of kindness and senseless acts of beauty."

Even though "random acts" and "senseless acts" sound like reckless acts, I realized as I thought about these words that this is how I have tried to teach my adopted "grandchildren"—the children I serve in my church. For example, quite to the surprise of their mothers and grandmothers, the children presented gifts to them on Mother's Day. Also, I have started a ministry with the children called "Adopt a Shut-in." The children make cards to send to the members who are listed on the church's sick and shut-in list. The children have received notes and cards thanking them for their "random acts of kindness."

As grandmothers, may we teach our own grandchildren—by example and encouragement—to commit random acts of kindness.

Lord, show me what "random acts of kindness" you would have me and my grandchildren to do together. Amen.

SEPTEMBER 13   KEEPING SPIRITUALLY FIT

Physical exercise has some value, but spiritual exercise is much more important, for it promises a reward in both this life and the next.   *(1 Timothy 4:8 NLT)*

We know how important it is to stay physically fit—especially as we increase in years. Yet, as Christians, we are called to be not only physically fit but also spiritually fit. Just as we must exercise regularly and eat a nutritious diet to stay healthy, so also we must constantly feed on God's Word and exercise our faith to stay spiritually fit.

Like David, we should praise the Lord daily: "I will bless the LORD at all times; his praise shall continually be in my mouth" (Psalm 34:1 NRSV). Like the Bereans, we must search the Scriptures daily: "These Jews ... welcomed the message very eagerly and examined the scriptures every day" (Acts 17:11 NRSV). Like Daniel, we must set aside time to pray: "[Daniel] continued to go to his house ... and to get down on his knees three times a day to pray" (Daniel 6:10 NRSV).

If we will diligently follow the spiritual disciplines of praising God, reading the Scriptures, and praying "without ceasing," we will be spiritually fit.

Thank you, O Lord, for showing me the ways to stay spiritually fit. Amen.

SEPTEMBER 14   TRAIN UP A CHILD

Train a child in the way he should go, and when he is old he will not turn from it.   (Proverbs 22:6 NIV)

The toy manufacturers are already actively advertising their new toys for the Christmas season. Each year parents and grandparents spend thousands of dollars on all kinds of toys, CDs, video games, and other gifts.

The best gift we can give our grandchildren, however, is our time. It takes time to "train up a child." It takes time and effort to teach God's principles, as he instructed: "Only be careful, and watch yourselves closely so that you do not forget the things your eyes have seen or let them slip from your heart as long as you live. Teach them to your children and to their children after them" (Deuteronomy 4:9 NIV).

Let us take time to give our grandchildren the wisdom to be fair: "Bring them up in the training and instruction of the Lord" (Ephesians 6:4 NIV). May we remember that it takes perseverance to discipline: "The LORD disciplines those he loves" (Proverbs 3:12 NIV). And may we be encouraged that through discipline, our grandchildren will learn self-control. Through discipline they will learn the truths and biblical principles that will keep them on the right path.

Lord, thank you for helping me keep my grandchildren on the right path by teaching them your Word. Amen.

SEPTEMBER 15   CROWN OF GLORY

Gray hair is a crown of splendor; it is attained by a righteous life.   (Proverbs 16:31 NIV)

Autumn is perhaps the most beautiful season of the year. Unlike winter, when nature sleeps, and spring, when nature buds, and summer, when nature blooms, autumn is the season when nature bursts forth in vibrant colors of red, yellow, and orange. These vivid hues the Master Painter uses to adorn the landscape are a glorious sight.

Springtime is usually equated with youth, which is considered the most beautiful time of life. The body is strong and the mind is sharp. But people in their fifties, sixties, seventies, and beyond are even more beautiful if they are "found in the way of righteousness" (Proverbs 16:31 KJV).

Those who know and love the Lord and have allowed him to lead them throughout their lives develop an inward beauty and a loving heart that shine through a beautifully seasoned face. The years that "seniors" walk with God have a way of refining them and imprinting "character" on their faces. Thus, the "crown of glory" reveals what "seniors" really are in Christ.

Thank you, Lord, for lines of character in our faces and silver "crowns of glory." Amen.

SEPTEMBER 16   GOD GIVES US SEEDS

A man reaps what he sows.   (Galatians 6:7 NIV)

When a farmer plants his field, he expects a harvest. If he wants a harvest of wheat, he must plant wheat. The farmer reaps only what he sows.

So it is with us. If we want to reap good fruit in our lives, we must sow good seeds in good soil.

There is a fable about a man who was browsing in a store when he discovered that the salesperson was God. The man asked God what he was selling. God responded, "What does your heart desire?" The man said, "I want happiness, peace of mind, and freedom from fear for me and the whole world." God smiled and said, "I don't sell fruit here. Only seeds."

God has given us the seeds we need for any harvest we desire. It is up to us to sow the seeds God offers so that we can reap good fruit. We must do our part if we want to experience God's blessings. If we want changes in our lives and in our world, we must sow seeds of new actions—a new way of living. In due season, God will give us the fruit we desire.

Lord, may I accept and sow your seeds to make a difference in my life and in the lives of others. Amen.

SEPTEMBER 17   GROWING OLD

They will still bear fruit in old age.   **(Psalm 92:14 NIV)**

Our world is preoccupied with youth. Open any magazine and you will find products to keep us young—makeup, fashions, and hair dye. I bought *Seventeen* magazine when I was a teenager. Although I could buy the magazine with my meager allowance, I could not afford the fashions advertised in it. Now that I am older and can afford both fashion magazines and the fashions, I no longer have the youthful body. What irony!

The Bible speaks about old age in encouraging terms. We need not feel unproductive as we grow older. Growing older is a precursor of becoming stronger in our faith. The autumn of our lives is a time of abundant fruitfulness. We can happily confess, "Even though our outward [woman] is perishing, yet the inward [woman] is being renewed day by day" (2 Corinthians 4:16 NKJV).

We must ask ourselves: Are we growing "in the grace and knowledge of our Lord and Savior Jesus Christ"? (2 Peter 3:18 NIV). The psalmist wrote an answer for us: "Those who are planted in the house of the LORD...shall still bear fruit in old age. They shall be fresh and flourishing" (Psalm 92:13-14 NKJV).

Thank you, Lord, for making the autumn of our lives fruitful. Amen.

SEPTEMBER 18   LET YOUR WALK MATCH YOUR TALK

You, then, who teach others, do you not teach yourself?
(Romans 2:21 NIV)

One of our daughters in the ministry preached a challenging sermon titled "Talking Right and Walking Left." The central thought of the sermon was how we say the right thing but do the opposite. We don't practice what we preach.

We are commanded to "train up a child in the way he should go." But this training involves more than giving instruction. It also means that we should do as we say. Children and grandchildren imitate what they see us do and hear us say. Often we tell them not to do something, but we do the very thing we tell them not to do. God is pleased with us when our walk matches our talk.

So we must live the life Jesus taught—love God and love neighbor—so our grandchildren will obey the commands while imitating us. No matter how much we strive to prepare our grandchildren for life, nothing matters without the "training and admonition of the Lord" (Ephesians 6:4 NKJV).

Lord, may I learn what I teach others. Amen.

SEPTEMBER 19   A GRANDMOTHER IS...

What kind of people ought you to be? You ought to live holy and godly lives. **(2 Peter 3:11 NIV)**

I asked some children to describe a grandmother. Their descriptions were vivid and varied:

"A grandmother is always there for you."

"A grandmother lets you stay up late and eat anything you want."

"A grandmother always has time for you."

"A grandmother likes to fix you goodies."

We grandmothers have an impact on our grandchildren's lives—far greater than we can imagine.

Paul believed that Timothy's faith and goodness were influenced by his grandmother Lois. Not only did she teach Timothy the Scriptures but she also modeled a "sincere faith." Paul wrote: "I have been reminded of your sincere faith, which first lived in your grandmother Lois" (2 Timothy 1:5 NIV).

In his wisdom, God has given children grandmothers to influence their lives as well as guide them.

Thank you, Lord, for grandmothers everywhere. Amen.

SEPTEMBER 20   WHY WORRY?

"Your heavenly Father ... knows all your needs."
(Matthew 6:32 NLT)

Worry can overpower our lives. We can worry so much that we fail to recognize all the good things in our lives.

In all of our worry, we forget that everything is in God's control. Jesus gave an antidote for worry when he told his listeners about the birds of the air and the lilies of the field. Everything that they need is out of their control. But God takes care of them; he "dresses" the lilies so beautifully that "not even Solomon in all his splendor was dressed like one of these" (Matthew 6:29 NIV). God provides for the birds even though they don't sow, reap, or store in barns.

Jesus asked the question, "Who of you by worrying can add a single hour to his life?" (Matthew 6:27 NIV). So, why worry? For every area of our lives, God tells us to trust him.

Worry is the foam atop the dither of our lives.
God feeds the birds and clothes the fields with flowers.
Pay heed to the birds and honor the flowers

And peace will gild your life with calm and power.

Author Unknown

Thank you, Lord, for providing all of my needs. Amen.

SEPTEMBER 21   GETTING BETTER

Though outwardly we are wasting away, yet inwardly we are being renewed day by day.   (2 Corinthians 4:16 NIV)

We often hear people say that they are not getting older, they are getting better. If we are walking with God, this statement is true. Although our bodies are deteriorating daily, we can remain young at heart. Through the constant renewal of our spirit, we grow closer to God.

No amount of exercise, food, or cosmetic products can hold back the aging process. As Paul wrote, "Our outward man is perishing" (2 Corinthians 4:16 NKJV). But we should not allow the disappointment and pain of physical aging to cause us to lose sight of our goal.

Our spiritual age is the opposite of our physical age. We are youthful and vital as we walk with God. Our steps are sprightly. Our spirits are light. The more we fellowship with God, the better we get because we are "being renewed day by day" (2 Corinthians 4:16 NKJV). The more we develop our inner strength, the more Christlike we become—and the more beautiful we grow.

I thank you, O Lord, for helping me to get better as I grow older. Amen.

SEPTEMBER 22   FROM A DISTANCE

Nothing in all creation is hidden from God's sight.

(Hebrews 4:13a NIV)

Bette Midler recorded a song called "From a Distance" that includes these words: "God is watching us from a distance."

Did you ever stop to think that God sees everything we do,

hears everything we say, and knows everything we think? At Christmastime we hear these words: "He sees you when you're sleeping; He knows when you're awake; He knows when you've been bad or good, so be good for goodness sake."* The songwriter was referring to Santa Claus, but these words better refer to the Lord. The rest of Hebrews 4:13 (NIV) says this: "Everything is uncovered and laid bare before the eyes of him to whom we must give account." Yet, even though God sees all we do, hears all we say, and knows all we think, he still loves us!

God is watching us, and so are our children and grandchildren. Let us be careful, then, of what we say and do. Let us imitate Jesus so that our grandchildren may learn to imitate Jesus by watching us.

Lord, may my grandchildren see that I have clean hands and a pure heart. Amen.

*J Fred Coots and Henry Gillespie, "Santa Claus Is Coming to Town," 1932.

SEPTEMBER 23   SURROGATE GRANDMOTHERS

[Barnabas] . . . encouraged them all.   *(Acts 11:23 NIV)*

I never knew my biological grandmothers. Both of them were deceased before I was born. But there were several women in my life who stood in the place of my grandmothers. What I remember most about these women was their encouragement.

Before I went to kindergarten, I was encouraged to learn my ABCs and to count. An older cousin even took time daily to help me learn these things. As a result, I went to school at age four. Several women encouraged me to get a college education, and they periodically paid for books that I needed. Some of the older women at church, particularly Dr. Josephine H. Kyles, encouraged me to participate in national religious activities and organizations.

Whether or not we have any biological grandchildren, we all can "adopt" some grandchildren in our church or our community. As encouragers, we are called to be friendly, to be generous, and to take a genuine interest in our "grandchildren."

Thank you, O Lord, for allowing me to have a relationship with my grandchildren as well as the ones I have "adopted." Amen.

SEPTEMBER 24   PATIENCE

Clothe yourselves with compassion, kindness, humility, gentleness and patience.   *(Colossians 3:12 NIV)*

Patience is a virtue."

Jesus demonstrated patience with Peter on several occasions, yet I love the story of Jesus' reunion with Peter on the Sea of Galilee after Jesus' resurrection. Peter and some of the disciples had given up fishing for men and had returned to fishing for fish. Jesus provided an enormous catch (153 fish) for them. Then he joined them for breakfast. After breakfast, Jesus confronted Peter. Remember, Peter had denied Jesus. With patience, Jesus asked Peter three times if he loved him. Just as Peter had denied Jesus three times, it took three questions to reinstate Peter. How patient Jesus was with Peter.

So must it be with us. We must be patient with our grandchildren. When we speak to them, they may not respond immediately. It may take several times before we get the proper response. We must be both patient and persistent in helping our grandchildren to be like Jesus.

Help me to be patient, gentle, and persistent, Lord. Amen.

SEPTEMBER 25   WHEN YOU THOUGHT I WASN'T
                                                    LOOKING

In everything set them an example.   *(Titus 2:7a NIV)*

We grandmothers greatly influence the lives of our grandchildren. We also touch the lives of other children.

My best friend, a grandmother herself, sent me an e-mail titled "When You Thought I Wasn't Looking." The piece was written by Mary Rita Schilke Korzan and originally appeared in the book *Stories for the Heart.* Here are a couple of my favorite lines:

When you thought I wasn't looking you baked a birthday cake just for me, and I knew that little things were special things.
When you thought I wasn't looking you said a prayer, and I believed there was a God that I could always talk to.

Little eyes are watching, even when we think they're not. We grandmothers touch the lives of our grandchildren—and many other children who come in and out of our lives—even when we are not aware of it.

May my actions, O Lord, be a positive influence in the lives of my grandchildren and others. Amen.

SEPTEMBER 26   WORK AS UNTO THE LORD

In your teaching show integrity, seriousness and soundness of speech.   *(Titus 2:7b-8 NIV)*

Did you know that by age sixty a person who has worked full-time since age twenty-one will have worked about sixty-four thousand hours? That's about thirty-nine years, or two-thirds of a sixty-year-old's life.

How depressing these figures are! Most of our life is spent working. But if we work as unto the Lord, we will have great joy.

I taught school for thirty-seven years. I loved every minute of it. Each day brought a new experience for my students and me. My grandchildren heard me talk about my teaching and my students so much that one of my grandchildren is now in her fourth year of teaching. My son is also changing his career to teaching.

Even though I am now retired, I still have a passion for teaching. I am currently teaching high-school juniors in Sunday school. I enjoy preparing the lessons and am delighted when my students grasp a principle from God's Word.

Teaching is a part of my worship unto the Lord. How we approach our work will greatly affect our grandchildren's work ethic.

Thank you, Lord, for allowing me to worship you through my work. Amen.

SEPTEMBER 27   SHARE THE GOODNESS OF GOD

*We have heard with our ears, O God; our fathers have told us
what you did in their days.*   *(Psalm 44:1 NIV)*

The Scriptures encourage storytelling as a way of witnessing to
the goodness of the Lord. When we tell our story or testify, we may
help others. Our personal stories of God working in our lives allow
us to be firsthand witnesses to what the Lord can do.

A little more than a year ago, I had a total knee replacement.
Within two-and-a-half months of the surgery, I was walking without a cane, pain free. Only God could have healed me in such a
short time. And so I tell my story whenever and wherever I can.
Many people need this surgery, but they fear it. I am a witness that
the Lord and the doctors can bring you through.

The Lord is always blessing us. We must share the goodness of
God, his healing power, his faithfulness, as well as the answers to
our prayers with others.

Our song should be, "I'm gonna tell somebody, just can't keep it
to myself, God's been good to me."

*Thank you, Lord, for your healing power. I pray that those I tell
about my experience will turn to you. Amen.*

SEPTEMBER 28   A JOB FOR EVERYONE

*There are different kinds of gifts, but the same Spirit. There are
different kinds of service, but the same Lord. There are different kinds of working, but the same God works all of them in all
men.*   *(1 Corinthians 12:4-6 NIV)*

The Lord has given special gifts and talents to all of his people.
Everyone's task is important, although many people think that what
they have to offer is not as important as what others have to offer.

We can take a lesson from honeybees, which have a highly
developed social structure. A hive may house as many as eight

thousand bees. At the center of the hive is the queen bee. Each bee has a specific task. The forager bees collect the food. The guard bees protect the hive. The water collectors bring moisture to regulate the humidity of the hive. The plasterers make a kind of cement to repair the hive. There are many more specialized tasks among the worker bees.

The building of God's kingdom depends on us. We must not sit around comparing what we can do with what others can do. Every contribution counts. We must do what God has called us to do.

Lord, may I use my gifts and talents to glorify you. Amen.

SEPTEMBER 29   JESUS, MY VIP

The blessed hope ... our great God and Savior Jesus Christ.
                                      (Titus 2:13 NKJV)

We often hear the expression, "It's not what you know, it's who you know." We like to be on first-name speaking terms with important people. When we are in conversations with our friends, we like to be name-droppers because we think this makes us seem important. If we have met a movie star, a politician, or a singer, we want everyone to know it. We describe in detail our experiences with the VIP. The truth is, none of the "important people" can do much for us.

But there is a VIP we should share with others every chance we get. A popular praise song says that he ...

... came from heaven to earth to show the way
From the earth to the cross, my debt to pay.*

As a result, we need to "lift his name on high." The name we should "drop" everywhere we go is Jesus. To have eternal life, it's who we know and have faith in that counts.

Lord, thank you for being the VIP in my life. Amen.

*Rick Founds, "Lord, I Lift Your Name on High," published by Maranatha! Music, 1989.

SEPTEMBER 30   OUR CHOICES AFFECT OUR FUTURE

Teach us to number our days aright, that we may gain a heart of wisdom.   ***(Psalm 90:12 NIV)***

An old TV program was called "Father Knows Best," but I believe that Mother knew best. You see, when I was young, I liked to crawl around on my knees. I liked to play marbles. I liked to dance. My mother told me I was wearing my knees out. She was really telling me that what I did when I was young would affect my life later. And so it did. I wore my left knee out and had to have a total knee replacement.

Robert Browning wrote: "Grow old along with me! / The best is yet to be / The last of life, for which the first was made."* Browning was saying that each of our days is a foundation for tomorrow. What we become and what happens to us depends on the choices we have made.

It is our responsibility to share this truism with our grandchildren. We have trod the road, and we can share our experiences with them.

Lord, help me to make the choices that will help my grandchildren to lead productive lives. Amen.

*Robert Browning, "Rabbi Ben Ezra."

October

Becoming Like Jesus

HELEN C. SCOTT-CARTER

OCTOBER 1   WHO ARE YOU?

As a Christian, do not be ashamed, but praise God that you bear that name.   *(1 Peter 4:16 NIV)*

Who are you? When people meet you, how do they see you? Do they see a Christian or a "church person"? Do you go to church out of duty or habit, or do you go because you love Jesus and want to become more like him?

The New Testament is our guidebook for becoming like Jesus. The Scriptures list many characteristics of a Christian. For example, we are to bear one another's burdens (Galatians 6:2), forgive one another (Colossians 3:13), comfort one another (2 Corinthians 1:3-4), give others more honor than we want for ourselves (Romans 12:10), and pray for one another (James 5:16).

The most important characteristic of all, however, is love. Jesus taught that the greatest commandments are "Love the Lord your God with all your heart and with all your soul and with all your mind" and "Love your neighbor as yourself" (Matthew 22:37, 39 NIV). Galatians 5:13, one of my favorite verses, admonishes us to "serve one another in love" (NIV). As Christians, love is our calling card. As the song goes, "They will know we are Christians by our love."

This month our focus is on becoming like Jesus, and on leading our grandchildren to do the same—both by our words and by our example.

Lord, may my grandchildren be able to recognize the truth of who I am. May they see you in me. Amen.

OCTOBER 2   BE AN EXAMPLE

You became imitators of us and of the Lord; ... so you became a model to all.   *(1 Thessalonians 1:6-7 NIV)*

Thessalonica was the capital and largest city of the Roman province of Macedonia. When Paul visited Thessalonica on one of his missionary journeys, many of the people heard the gospel message he preached and accepted Jesus as their Savior. In the opening verses of 1 Thessalonians, Paul commended the Thessalonian Christians for following the Lord even though they suffered hardship and persecution because of their faith. Their joy from the Holy Spirit enabled them to become "examples to all in Greece" who believed.

Like the Thessalonian Christians, we must be examples to others regardless of the faith-challenging circumstances we may face. Our unwavering obedience to God will be an encouraging example to others.

Lord, help me to exemplify the Christian life in all I do and say so that my grandchildren will learn to follow and serve you. Amen.

OCTOBER 3   GIVE THANKS

All things come of thee, and of thine own have we given thee.
(1 Chronicles 29:14 KJV)

Each Sunday when the tithes and offerings are dedicated to God at my church, we sing an offertory chant using the words of today's scripture verse.

We should always be mindful of all the Lord has done for us. Instead of coming into God's presence with a laundry list of requests, we should offer the sacrifice of praise.

Paul wrote in 1 Thessalonians 5:18, "In every thing give thanks" (KJV). We need to thank God in good times and in bad times. We can affirm God's goodness and, even in bad times, discover reasons to thank God.

During the seventeenth century, the Reverend Martin Rinkart conducted up to fifty funerals a day as a plague swept through his town. Even though death greeted each new day, Rinkart wrote a hymn of thanksgiving, "Now Thank We All Our God."

Now thank we all our God
With heart and hands and voices,
Who wondrous things hath done,
In whom his world rejoices.

Thank you, Lord, for giving me a heart of thanksgiving and praise. Amen.

OCTOBER 4   HAVE A LITTLE TALK WITH JESUS

Devote yourselves to prayer, being watchful and thankful.
(Colossians 4:2 NIV)

"Pray without ceasing." So we are commanded to do in 1 Thessalonians 5:17 (KJV). One of the great paradoxes of the Christian faith is that God wants us to talk to him about everything in our lives, even though he already knows everything. So why are we commanded to continually be in prayer?

I believe God wants to hear our hearts and our thoughts. God wants to fellowship with us. When we communicate with God through prayer, we strengthen our relationship with him. Talking with God keeps us on the right path. Praying must be as natural as breathing. Just as our lungs need air, so also our hearts need prayer to keep us in tune with God. As we discussed yesterday, our prayers also should offer praise to God.

In addition to praying with our grandchildren and teaching them the Lord's Prayer and other prayers, we should teach them what it means to pray without ceasing.

Thank you, O Lord, for providing a vehicle for me to communicate with you. Amen.

OCTOBER 5   GIVE OF YOUR BEST TO THE MASTER

Whatever you do, work at it with all your heart, as working for the Lord, not for men. **(Colossians 3:23 NIV)**

We all are given one or more talents, or special abilities to do certain things well. Some are teachers. Some are preachers. Some are musicians. Some are chefs. No matter what your task is, you must give your best to the Master. Someone said it this way: "If a man is called to be a street sweeper, he should sweep streets even as Michelangelo painted or Beethoven composed or Shakespeare wrote. He should sweep streets so well that the hosts of heaven will pause and say, 'Here lives a great street sweeper who did his job well.'"

We might be able to do what others do, but whatever we do, we must do it "heartily, as to the Lord." Our grandchildren need to witness us giving our best to the Master in all we do.

Lord, may I continue to give my best to you. Amen.

OCTOBER 6   BE PRODUCTIVE

By their fruit you will recognize them.   **(Matthew 7:16 NIV)**

God expects us to live productive lives. There are several references in the Scriptures that tell us what the results of being unproductive will be. John the Baptizer warned that the "axe of God's judgment is poised to chop down every unproductive tree" (Matthew 3:10 TLB). Likewise, the apostle John wrote that "[God] cuts off every branch in me that bears no fruit" (John 15:2 NIV).

Just as a fruit tree is expected to bear fruit, God expects us to produce a crop of good deeds. If we call ourselves Christians, others must see God's goodness in us. They must see our faith in the way we live. Like Jesus, we must go "around doing good" (Acts 10:38 NIV).

We can lead productive lives by obeying God's teachings, resisting temptation, actively serving and helping others, and sharing our faith. If our lives are productive, our grandchildren will see God in us. Also, our lives will be a message of hope in a sinful world.

Lord, continue to direct me on paths of productivity for you. Amen.

OCTOBER 7   HAVE A MERRY HEART

A cheerful heart is good medicine.   *(Proverbs 17:22 NIV)*

The older we get, the more our physical selves deteriorate. We grandmothers often carry pillboxes in our purses so our medication will be available at the designated time we need it during the day.

Television commercials and magazine ads tell us what various medicines will do for us. According to these messages, we can grow hair, replace cartilage in our knees, lower our cholesterol, and on and on.

Our verse today tells us that our happiness and our healing come from deep within, from our heart. A merry heart is our attitude. Our attitude colors our whole personality. We cannot always choose what happens to us, but we can choose our attitude toward each situation. Our outlook on life has a significant effect on our physical well-being.

In Proverbs 15:13 we read, "A happy heart makes the face cheerful" (NIV). The state of our hearts determines the look on our faces. If we have Jesus in our hearts, our faces will show it.

Lord, thank you for giving me a smile that shows my merry heart. Amen.

OCTOBER 8 BUILD YOUR LIFE ON THINGS ETERNAL

So we fix our eyes not on what is seen, but on what is unseen.
For what is seen is temporary, but what is unseen is eternal.
(2 Corinthians 4:18 NIV)

When we were in history class, our teachers taught us about the "Seven Wonders of the Ancient World." They showed us pictures of what the "wonders" probably looked like. We were charged to learn the names of the "wonders": the Tomb of Maussollos, the Temple of Artemis, the Hanging Gardens of Babylon, the Lighthouse at Alexandria, the Colossus of Rhodes, the forty-foot-tall statue of Zeus at Olympia, and the Pyramids at Giza. Of all of these impressive creations of human genius, only the pyramids remain. The other "wonders" have been destroyed.

How accurate today's scripture verse is! Although we may marvel at the Seven Wonders, we must remember that everything in our world is temporary.

We need to hold tightly to what is eternal. Hebrews 12:28 says, "Since we have a Kingdom nothing can destroy, let us please God by serving him with thankful hearts, and with holy fear and awe" (TLB). Eventually the world, like the Seven Wonders, will crumble, and only God's kingdom will last. The hymnist wrote, "Build your hopes on things eternal." Jesus is the only sure foundation, and his kingdom is unshakable.

Thank you, O Lord, for Jesus, my firm foundation. Amen.

OCTOBER 9   GIVE YOUR GRANDCHILDREN YOUR TIME

There is a time for everything, and a season for every activity
under heaven.   *(Ecclesiastes 3:1 NIV)*

We grandmothers have something that parents have very little of: time.

If children have no significant family member with whom to spend quality time, they will seek outside activities to fill their time. Sometimes these activities may not meet with our approval—such as listening to unwholesome CDs or watching inappropriate videos. The "stars" of such media meet three basic needs of our grandchildren: companionship, acceptance, and identification.

We can do much to meet these three needs by cultivating relationships with our grandchildren, sharing their history, and giving them some unusual experiences.

When four of my granddaughters visited last year, we took them on a tour of the CIA (Central Intelligence Agency). This was special because it is not an open tour; we were able to go because their grandfather is employed there. I also took them to the Great Blacks in Wax Museum in Baltimore so they could experience their heritage. Of course, I also took them to Sunday school and church. And almost every night we played UNO and had a good time together. It was an extremely valuable investment of my time.

How wonderful it is when we spend time with our grandchildren!

Thank you, Lord, for the opportunity to spend time with my grandchildren. Amen.

OCTOBER 10 STRIVE TO BE A GODLY GRANDMOTHER

Add to your faith goodness; and to goodness, knowledge.
(2 Peter 1:5 NIV)

Faith, virtue, and knowledge—these are characteristics of a godly grandmother.

First, there is faith. Faith in Jesus indicates that she is a follower of the Christ, God's only Son. She expresses her faith by how she lives and interacts with others so that she is a "walking sermon" for her grandchildren.

To faith, add virtue. A godly grandmother strives to be a virtuous woman as Proverbs 31 describes: "She is a woman of strength and dignity . . . her words are wise, kindness is the rule for everything she says" (vv. 25-26 TLB). She also "fears and reverences God" (v. 30 TLB), using her talents in ways that honor God. She shows her grandchildren that she honors God by everything she does and says—and hopes they desire to be like her.

To virtue, add knowledge. In addition to having faith and striving to be virtuous, a godly grandmother seeks to know God better. She reads God's Word and discovers God's plan for her life. She also reads God's Word to her grandchildren to help them discover God's plan for their lives.

May we all strive to be godly grandmothers.

Lord, may my grandchildren see faith, virtue, and knowledge in me. Amen.

OCTOBER 11 TEACH THEM RULES FOR LIVING

Train up a child in the way he should go: and when he is old, he will not depart from it. (Proverbs 22:6 KJV)

We grandmothers are special people in the lives of our grandchildren. They look to us for love, guidance, and even correction. When we are not sure what we should do, we must go to our book of instruction: the Bible. God will give us the instruction we need, helping us to give our best to our grandchildren.

The proverbs of Solomon were written for giving "knowledge and discretion to the young." They are rules for living that we should instill in our grandchildren. Here are a few examples:

"Discretion will protect you, and understanding will guard you" (2:11 NIV).

"Fear the LORD and shun evil" (3:7 NIV).

"Honor the LORD with your wealth" (3:9 NIV).

"Preserve sound judgment and discernment" (3:21 NIV).

"Hold on to instruction, do not let it go; guard it well, for it is your life" (4:13 NIV).

"Guard your heart, for it is the wellspring of life" (4:23 NIV).

"Lazy hands make a man poor, but diligent hands bring wealth" (10:4 NIV).

One way we can teach our grandchildren how to live godly lives and become like Jesus is by having them memorize and repeat the wise sayings in Proverbs.

Lord, open my eyes and heart to proverbs that will help me to guide my grandchildren in right living. Amen.

OCTOBER 12   TREASURE GOD'S WORD

All Scripture is God-breathed and is useful for teaching, rebuking, correcting and training in righteousness, so that the man of God may be thoroughly equipped for every good work.
(2 Timothy 3:16-17 NIV)

A group of people was asked, "What is the world's greatest treasure?" Each person offered an answer:

• the Pyramids at Giza
• the ceiling of the Sistine Chapel
• the gold stored at Fort Knox
• Handel's "Messiah"

If all these so-called treasures were suddenly no more, the world would not lose as much as it would if God's Word were blotted out and its influence forgotten, for God's Word is truly the world's greatest treasure.

The psalmist describes the world's greatest treasure, God's Word, in Psalm 119. It is ...

"a lamp to my feet and a light for my path" (v. 105 NIV);
"sweeter than honey" (v. 103 NIV);
"trustworthy" (vv. 86, 138 NIV);
"true" (vv. 142, 151 NIV);
"eternal" (v. 160 NIV).

God's Word leads us to praise God, live pure lives, know God's grace and mercy, pray, give thanks, meditate, sing, know and appreciate God's love, and see God's goodness. Through God's Word, we can lead others to God, experience God's peace, and recognize God's righteousness. What a treasure, indeed!

Lord, "Open my eyes that I may see wonderful things in your law" (Psalm 119:18 NIV). Amen.

OCTOBER 13   PERFORM SIMPLE ACTS OF LOVE

Wherever the gospel is preached throughout the world, what she has done will also be told, in memory of her.
(Mark 14:9 NIV)

One of the most frequently used symbols is the "smiley face." The symbol is used by many, but the creator of the symbol is known by very few. His name is Harvey Ball.

Mary of Bethany probably never guessed that she would be remembered for her act of love toward Jesus. In fact, she was criticized for wasting expensive perfume. She poured a jar of expensive perfume, nard, on Jesus to prepare him for events that would soon occur in his life. Jesus silenced the disciples by saying, "Wherever this gospel is preached throughout the whole world, what this woman did will also be spoken of as a memorial to her" (Mark 14:9 NKJV).

At another time, Jesus also said, "Whatever you did for one of the least of these brothers of mine, you did for me" (Matthew 25:40 NIV). Will we be remembered as those who served, cared, loved, supported, and prayed? Are we teaching these words to our grandchildren by our acts of love? Only simple acts of love for others will be commended by the Lord Jesus Christ.

Lord, help me to practice these verbs every day: love, pray, care, support, and serve. Amen.

OCTOBER 14   GROW OLD GRACEFULLY

The length of our days is seventy years—or eighty, if we have the strength.... Teach us to number our days aright, that we may gain a heart of wisdom.   (Psalm 90:10a, 12 NIV)

Growing old brings its challenges, yet prayer can help us to gain a heart of wisdom and grow old gracefully. A friend of mine sent me this anonymously written prayer that is being widely circulated. I think it speaks to all grandmothers everywhere, regardless of age:

A Prayer as I Grow Older
O Lord, you know I am growing older! Keep me from closing my eyes to the fact. Keep me from becoming a pest, a self-appointed sage with the annoying habit of thinking I must say something on every subject and every occasion. Keep my mind free from the repetition of past experiences and endless details. Seal my lips about my aches and pains. I do not ask for improved memory, but for less cockiness about the memory of others. Teach me to admit that sometimes I am mistaken. Make me sweeter and mellower as my age progresses. Let me never grow old—only older. May it be said of me, "Though our outward man is perishing, yet the inward man is being renewed day by day" (2 Corinthians 4:16 NKJV).

Dear Lord, may I become sweeter and wiser as I grow older. Amen.

OCTOBER 15   COMMUNICATE OUR WORTH

You are a chosen people, a royal priesthood, a holy nation, a people belonging to God.   ***(1 Peter 2:9 NIV)***

While working as a biochemist at Yale University in the 1960s, Harold J. Morowitz began listing the chemicals in the human body and determining how much each chemical would cost. From that information, he determined that the monetary worth of a human being is $6,000,015.44.

Jesus described our worth with a question: "Are you not much more valuable than they [the lilies of the field]?" (Matthew 6:26 NIV). Three years after Jesus taught this lesson, God showed us just how valuable we are. "God ... gave His only begotten Son" to die a criminal's death for the sins of the whole world on an old rugged cross (John 3:16 NKJV). Jesus the Christ's death is the measure of our worth to God. How valuable we are!

Peter was inspired by God to describe our worth in this way: "A royal priesthood, a holy nation." We must teach our grandchildren that they are God's royalty. Their worth is not about clothes or hair or material possessions or popularity or anything else. Their worth is determined by God and God alone. No one else can define them. *Lord, help me communicate to my grandchildren the measure of their worth. Amen.*

OCTOBER 16   DO WHAT IS TRULY IMPORTANT

They will still bear fruit in old age.   *(Psalm 92:14 NIV)*

Many people are preoccupied with how long they will live. The psalmist David addressed our lifespan in several verses, including these:

> An entire lifetime is just a moment to you. (Psalm 39:5 NLT)
> As for man, his days are like grass; As a flower of the field, so he flourishes. For the wind passes over it, and it is gone, And its place remembers it no more. (Psalm 103:15-16 NKJV)

Life is short no matter how long we live. Therefore, we must not put off or neglect doing what is truly important.

We spend too much time securing our lives on earth—collecting things. In the Sermon on the Mount, Jesus commanded: "Don't store up treasures here on earth. . . . Store your treasures in heaven, where they will never become moth-eaten or rusty and where they will be safe from thieves" (Matthew 6:19-20 NLT).

Our greatest priority is whatever dominates our time and thoughts. Money and possessions must not dominate our lives. Instead, we should use our material things to serve God by serving humankind. What is important is not the length of our lives but what we do for God.

Lord, help me to live for you, however long I may live. Amen.

OCTOBER 17   TELL THEM THEY'RE SPECIAL

I praise you because I am fearfully and wonderfully made.
(Psalm 139:14a NIV)

Psalm 139:14 is my favorite scripture verse. I "adopted" this scripture because it not only means much to me but it also helps me to assist children when they question how they look and what they can do.

In my ministry with children, I often hear them compare themselves to their friends and other children they see. They question why they are short or why they are fat or why they don't have long hair. They have an idea of how they should look. I tell them that God makes no mistakes. They are made the way God wants them to be. God gave them their height, chose their hair and eye color, and sculpted their faces. I tell them that how God made them sets them apart; they are unique. There is no one else in the world like them. God made them special. I tell the children that the best way to thank God is to love this special person he has created.

Lord, may I instill in all children how special they are. Amen.

OCTOBER 18   PLANT A SPECIAL GARDEN

By their fruit you will recognize them.   *(Matthew 7:16 NIV)*

Many grandmothers enjoy planting gardens. They take great pride in their gardens, whether they are flower gardens or vegetable gardens. Even I have a flower garden—a heart-shaped flower bed of red flowers—and I don't have a "green thumb"!

But there is a garden that grandmothers who don't have "green thumbs" can plant. This is the garden layout:

Five rows of "peas": prayer, preparedness, promptness, perseverance, politeness.
Three rows of "squash": squash gossip, criticism, and indifference.
Five rows of "lettuce": let us love one another, let us be faithful, let us be loyal, let us be unselfish, let us be truthful.

Three rows of "turnips": turn up for church, turn up with a new idea, turn up with the determination to do a better job today than you did yesterday.

We can share planting this "garden" with our grandchildren. This "garden" will help us to instill values for life in the hearts and minds of our grandchildren.

Lord, help me to plant this special garden with my grandchildren and all children in my life. Amen.

OCTOBER 19　　　　　ENCOURAGE GOOD THOUGHTS

The LORD knows the thoughts of man.　　　*(Psalm 94:11 NIV)*

When I was teaching, I wrote this thought on the board every day: "Thinking is hard work."

Proverbs 23:7 tells us, "As [a man] thinketh in his heart, so is he" (KJV). In Philippians 4:8, Paul listed what we should think about: "Whatever is true, whatever is noble, whatever is right, whatever is pure, whatever is lovely, whatever is admirable" (NIV).

As grandmothers, we need to know what our grandchildren are listening to on CDs and viewing on TV and videos. The language they hear and the images they see are internalized and become a part of their thought patterns. What they put in their minds determines what comes out in their words and actions. We must expose our grandchildren to positive music and images that encourage them to think good thoughts and do good deeds. We must replace harmful thoughts with wholesome material.

Where is the greatest story ever told? The Bible! Let us read God's Word to and with our grandchildren.

Thank you, Lord, for providing your Word to assist us in presenting positive thoughts. Amen.

OCTOBER 20   BE GOD'S MIRROR

So God created man in his own image.   *(Genesis 1:27 NIV)*

Narcissus used the river as a mirror. Then the looking glass was invented. We all like mirrors. Every time we pass a mirror, we pause a moment to see our reflection. Is my hair right? Is my slip showing? Does my makeup need touching up? How do I look to other people? The mirror answers our questions.

But there is another mirror we should look into—God's mirror. Genesis 1:26 says, "Let us make man in our image" (NIV). This means we were made as reflections of God's glory. When we look in God's mirror, do we see ourselves as reflections of God? Are we reflections of the fruit—the characteristics of God—that God wants to develop in our lives? Do others see "love, joy, peace, patience, kindness, goodness, faithfulness, gentleness and self-control" (Galatians 5:22-23 NIV)? When others see us, do they see God?

Our "mirror image" should be a window through which others can look and see God.

Lord, may I reflect your glory to all I see. Amen.

OCTOBER 21   BE A DOER OF THE WORD

Do not merely listen to the word.... Do what it says.
                                          (James 1:22 NIV)

The Bible has been at the top of the bestsellers' list for decades. Many people buy Bibles as coffee-table books. In such homes, the Bible is merely a conversation piece. Other people read their Bibles and even store its truths in their hearts. Yet those of us who possess God's Word have an even greater responsibility.

James reminded us that we must "be doers of the word, and not hearers only" (1:22 NKJV). Understanding the Scriptures makes us responsible for putting their truths into action. God's Word was given to us not only for interesting reading; it is our catalyst for action. Jesus "went around doing good" (Acts 10:38 TLB). We can do no less if we call ourselves Christians.

The Bible is our book of instruction. As grandmothers, we are responsible for assisting our children in putting into action the command "Train up a child in the way he should go, And when he is old he will not depart from it" (Proverbs 22:6 NJKV). Teaching our grandchildren to be doers of the Word will equip them to stay on the right path.

Lord, help me to live up to my responsibility of acting on your Word. Amen.

OCTOBER 22   CHERISH YOUR MEMORIES, PART 1

Even a child is known by his actions, by whether his conduct is pure and right.   *(Proverbs 20:11 NIV)*

Grandchildren are very special, especially when they're young. I recall many special times with mine.

One of my grandsons was prone to high fevers as a baby because of inner-ear infections. As he grew and began to talk, we could not understand him. He was saying what he thought he had heard while he was affected by the ear infections.

The doctor claimed that my grandson would outgrow the problem; but at four years of age, his speech had not improved. The summer before he went to school, I decided I would keep him and work with him one-on-one. The results were astounding. To this day—he is now a freshman in college—he hasn't stopped talking.

During that summer, my grandson was very helpful. One day I was on my knees washing the baseboards in the kitchen. Ryan said, "Grandma, let me do that. I'm short and you won't have to get on your knees." What a wonderful gesture! And, he did a good job, too.

Thank you, Lord, for the wonderful memories my grandchildren have given me through the years. Amen.

OCTOBER 23 CHERISH YOUR MEMORIES, PART 2

Let the wise listen and add to their learning. (Proverbs 1:5 NIV)

I like to reminisce about my grandchildren. One whom I call "Little Bits"—now six feet tall—lived with us for a year. She was a joy because she loved to learn. I was a retired teacher who still loved to teach, so I established "Grandma's School" for her. At four years old, she learned to recognize and spell more than one hundred words, do simple addition and subtraction, print, and even speak some Spanish words. She also learned as we traveled. My husband, a pastor, and I attended several conferences while "Little Bits" was with us. She could name the states we traveled to from Delaware to Mississippi. She even learned to spell Mississippi.

When "Little Bits" went to kindergarten, she was well ahead of her classmates. The teacher challenged her with more advanced activities. Now a ninth grader, she continues her love of learning and is consistently on the honor roll.

"Little Bits," Shantelle, honored me by giving me a license plate that says "#1 Grandma." I'm blessed to add this to my treasure of cherished memories.

Thank you, O Lord, for such special grandchildren. Amen.

OCTOBER 24 DO GOOD WORKS

We are God's workmanship, created in Christ Jesus to do good works. (Ephesians 2:10 NIV)

Throughout the Scriptures are many definitions of who we are as Christians. Unfortunately, some of us who call ourselves Christians are following the ways of the world instead of following and living like the One whose name we bear.

The Bible tells us that we are God's workmanship. In the beginning, God created us in his image. Then, in the fullness of time, God sent Jesus to be our Savior. Nearly two thousand years ago, the followers of Jesus the Christ were first called Christians (Acts 11:26). We have a wonderful name and a glorious heritage because we are identified with God's only begotten Son. As bearers of Christ's name, we also have an obligation to live up to that name.

Ephesians 2:10 says that we were "created in Christ Jesus to do good works." What have you done for God lately? One of the most important works we can perform is teaching our grandchildren to be like Jesus. We also can talk about God and look for opportunities to tell them about God's goodness and love.

Lord, may I gladly do the good works for which you created me, including teaching my grandchildren about you. Amen.

OCTOBER 25   DEVELOP A HUMBLE SPIRIT

A man's pride brings him low, but a man of lowly spirit gains honor.   ***(Proverbs 29:23 NIV)***

I am the director of "children's church" at my church. We try to expose our children to a variety of spiritual experiences outside church. For their summer outing this year, we took them to Lancaster, Pennsylvania, to see "The Psalms of David." As a follow-up, I planned several lessons on David and the psalms. During the first lesson, I reviewed the play. We discussed details about the play—the characters, the scenery, the musical instruments, and the psalms set to music. The children were eager to share.

During the second lesson, I reviewed the first lesson. One of my ministry "granddaughters," Kristina, answered many of the review questions I asked. When she happily reported to her mother, who assists me, that she had answered many of the questions, her mother reminded her not to boast about what she had done. She told her to thank God for giving her the ability to remember and share.

What a timely lesson! My "granddaughter" was reminded that she is not self-sufficient. All that she has comes from God. She must give God the glory. We must do the same!

Thank you, Lord, for lessons in humility. Amen.

OCTOBER 26 LOVE THE LEAST OF THESE

Let us not love with words or tongue but with actions and in truth. *(1 John 3:18 NIV)*

After hurricane Katrina ravaged the Gulf Coast of the United States, the survivors were left to recover from the effects of death and destruction. So many people were left with nothing because of the severity of the storm and its aftermath: flooding.

Even though the continual television images of human need, suffering, and devastation in New Orleans, Biloxi, and Mobile left many people feeling numb, there was an overwhelming response of deeds of love and charity.

In the parable of the Last Judgment, Jesus welcomed into the kingdom those who had fed him when he was hungry, given him something to drink when he was thirsty, taken him in when he was a stranger, and clothed him when he was naked. The righteous asked when they had done all these things. Jesus answered, "Whatever you did for one of the least of these brothers of mine, you did for me" (Matthew 25:40 NIV).

The Sunday following the tragedy, I challenged my church "grandchildren" to do something for the children of the disaster. They immediately began planning—a toy collection, a loose-change bank, a talent show. What an outpouring of love and concern!

Every day is an opportunity to love "the least of these," wherever they may be.

Lord, bless the least of these and those who respond to their needs. Amen.

OCTOBER 27 KEEP A GOOD NAME

A good name is more desirable than great riches; to be esteemed is better than silver or gold. *(Proverbs 22:1 NIV)*

Shakespeare wrote, "What's in a name?"

Our name reflects who we are. Our reputation is in our name. Our name is associated with what we say and do.

Take the name "Judas." There were several men in the Bible named Judas. The apostle Thaddeus was also known as Judas. Likewise, Jesus' half-brother was named Judas (Matthew 13:55; Mark 6:3), but some scholars say that biblical translators changed the name to Jude (Jude 1) when the name was disgraced by Judas Iscariot, who betrayed Jesus (Matthew 26:49).

It may take many years to build our character and good reputation. But it takes only a moment of indiscretion or a poor choice to destroy our good name.

As grandmothers, we can teach our grandchildren the importance of making and keeping a good name. We should warn them about the company they keep. We can tell them how the language they use defines them. To keep a good name, our grandchildren can ask, "WWJD?" (What would Jesus do?).

Lord, help our grandchildren to follow a path that will keep their good name. Amen.

OCTOBER 28   HOLD YOUR TONGUE

The tongue also is a fire, a world of evil.... It corrupts the whole person.   *(James 3:6 NIV)*

James wrote a treatise on the tongue. He gave examples of how small things control large things—a bit in the mouth of a horse makes it obey, and a rudder steers a ship. Then he characterized the tongue as "a small part of the body...[that] makes great boasts" (3:5 NIV), "a fire, a world of evil" (3:6 NIV), and "a restless evil, full of deadly poison" (3:8 NIV).

We used to say, "Sticks and stones will break my bones, but words will never hurt me." This is not true. Words, unwisely used, can set fires of anger, doubt, jealousy, and hate. We can ruin our reputation with a few ill-chosen words. Once a word is spoken and heard, it cannot be retrieved.

James acknowledged that we use our tongues to praise God in one breath and spread evil or hurt someone in the next breath. What hypocrisy! "How can both blessing and cursing come from the same mouth?" he asked.

Not only must we "watch our mouth," but we also must teach our grandchildren that controlling their tongues is a sign of a disciplined life.

Lord, help me to guard my mouth so that I will be an example to my grandchildren. Amen.

OCTOBER 29   LIVE TO PLEASE GOD

God... [called] us... to live a holy life. (1 Thessalonians 4:7 NIV)

In 1 Thessalonians 4, Paul gave us guidelines for pleasing God. We must control our bodies in ways that are "holy and honorable" (v. 4 NIV). We must not mistreat our brother (or sister) or take advantage of him (or her). And we must love one another. Throughout the Scriptures, we are given ways to please God:

"Do the will of God." (Romans 2:7a TLB)
"Live peaceful and quiet lives in all godliness and holiness." (1 Timothy 2:2 NIV)
"Obey his commands." (1 John 3:22 NIV)
"Offer your bodies as living sacrifices." (Romans 12:1 NIV)
"Without faith it is impossible to please God." (Hebrews 11:6 NIV)
"The prayer of the upright pleases [God]." (Proverbs 15:8 NIV)

Ways of pleasing God are not intended only for us adults; they also apply to children. A few are even directed specifically to them, such as Colossians 3:20: "Children, obey your parents in everything, for this pleases the Lord" (NIV).

Not only must we live to please God, but we also must teach our grandchildren how to do the same.

Thank you, Lord, for teaching me what pleases you. Amen.

OCTOBER 30   TRUST THAT THE LORD WILL PROVIDE

God . . . richly provides us with everything. (1 Timothy 6:17 NIV)

When I was a child, I heard my mother say, "The Lord will provide," and "I'm gonna trust in the Lord." I didn't know what she meant then, but I experienced the truth of her words as I matured in the faith.

On two separate occasions, my granddaughter and I witnessed God's provision for his creation. One beautiful autumn day we were returning home from shopping when, suddenly, the sky became dark. We realized that the darkness came from hundreds of chirping birds praising God as they flew south for the winter. It was a thrilling sight.

Another day, we saw a flock of geese flying in a "V" formation. When we returned home, I did some research and discovered that this is God's plan for efficiency. As each goose flaps its wings, an "uplift" is created for the birds that follow. By flying in a "V" formation, the whole flock adds 71 percent greater flying range than if each bird flew alone.

Just as God provides for the safety and security of his feathered creatures, so also he provides for us. If only we would trust him!

Lord, help me to teach my grandchildren how to trust in you for everything. Amen.

OCTOBER 31   GROW AS JESUS GREW

Jesus grew in wisdom and stature, and in favor with God and men.   (Luke 2:52 NIV)

One of our most important tasks as grandmothers is to help our grandchildren become like Jesus so that they will have a personal relationship with God. Just as they will behave differently in each level of their physical and mental development, so it is with their spiritual development. God's ultimate goal is to make them—and us—like Jesus.

We have considered some of the ways that we can help our

grandchildren grow as Jesus grew. Jesus grew mentally, physically, spiritually, and socially. To help our grandchildren grow mentally, we can teach them about God in his Word and in his world. To help them grow physically, we can help them understand that they are "fearfully and wonderfully made" (Psalm 139:14 KJV). To help them grow spiritually, we can model prayer and encourage them to have their own quiet time with God. To help them grow socially, we can teach them the Golden Rule (Matthew 7:12).

Becoming Christlike is a progressive experience that we *can* help our grandchildren achieve!

Dear Lord, guide me as I teach my grandchildren how to grow as Jesus grew. Amen.

November

Messages of Hope

SYLVIA M. CORBIN BERRY

NOVEMBER 1   THE SHEPHERD AND THE LAMB

The LORD is my shepherd; I have everything I need. He lets me rest in fields of green grass and leads me to quiet pools of fresh water. He gives me new strength. He guides me in the right paths, as he has promised.   **(Psalm 23:1-3 GNT)**

I recall a picture from my childhood of the Lord carrying a lamb in his arms, protecting it from harm. He was walking across a green pasture, taking the lamb back to the flock.

We grandmothers are like the lamb, for we, too, need the Lord's guidance. The Lord promises that he will give us everything we need. When we are tired or discouraged, he will give us rest in fields of green grass. We can rest, without fear of harm or danger, by trusting in him. Then the Lord takes us to the quiet pools of fresh water to renew our strength and hope.

We grandmothers are also like the shepherd. We care for and protect our grandchildren; and when we see them straying on the wrong path, we must gently nudge them in the right direction.

This month I will bring messages of hope—hope that comes through love, peace, courage, and strength. We will recall the many times the Lord has guided us and given us strength, remembering that we continually need renewed strength. And we will explore the many ways that we, in turn, can guide and strengthen our grandchildren.

Lord, thank you for meeting our needs. Give us the strength and wisdom to guide our grandchildren on the right paths. Amen.

NOVEMBER 2   TREASURES OF LOVE

And to all these qualities add love, which binds all things together in perfect unity.   *(Colossians 3:14 GNT)*

The fall of the year is one of the most beautiful seasons. Vibrant colors cover the earth with a radiance and glow that is warming to the heart. As evening approaches, the night air becomes cool and we look forward to a cup of hot tea or a warm, cozy blanket.

The love of God is all around us as he kisses our faces with the cool breeze, soothes our souls through the windows of our eyes, and embraces our hearts with love. The sights and smells of the fall are treasures of love from God. Families also come together to share treasures from God. Tonight, I will teach my granddaughter how to make sugar cookies. We will share the treasures of love by spending time together. As we mix the ingredients of the sugar cookies, I will tell her the most important ingredient is love.

Heavenly Father, bless us with the treasures of love so we may come together in unity. Amen.

NOVEMBER 3   YOU CAN REST

There were so many people coming and going that Jesus and his disciples didn't even have time to eat. So he said to them, "Let us go off by ourselves to some place where we will be alone and you can rest a while."   *(Mark 6:31 GNT)*

Jesus demonstrates how much he loves us through many unselfish acts of kindness. He also reminds us to take time for ourselves. We grandmothers have so many new responsibilities; some of us are raising our grandchildren as well as caring for our elderly parents. We do not possess the same strength and energy we had when we raised our children. Yet, from deep within we are able to be a strong center of support.

When I go shopping or take time out for me, I sometimes feel so guilty. It is difficult to go into the store to shop without buying clothes for the grandkids. When our grandchildren call, we grandmothers are ready to drop everything and tend to their every need. One of our prayers is to see our grandchildren grow up. So, we must take care of ourselves, physically and spiritually. Let us start today by taking time out for ourselves. After all, we want to be there to watch our grandchildren grow up!

Sometimes we feel a little tired and grow weak. Lord, give us the strength to be the best that we can be. Let us know when it is time to get some rest. Amen.

NOVEMBER 4   GOD LOVES VARIETY

Then God commanded, "Let the water be filled with many kinds of living beings, and let the air be filled with birds."
(Genesis 1:20 GNT)

I have six grandchildren with individual personalities. The beauty of creation is that God created each one of us to be different. It is obvious that God loves variety.

I enjoy the beauty of creation through each of the seasons. My grandchildren are like the seasons. Jasmine is like the spring because she smiles like a buttercup. Braxton is like the winter; he is cautious and stands back. Thomas III and Tyler are like the summer, full of fun with vivid imaginations. Ethan and Christian are like the fall because they are just learning to walk.

To enjoy life is to be a part of life. Look inside yourself and see the variety God has placed in you. Look at your grandchildren and marvel at how God put a little bit of different family members in each grandchild. We are all such beautiful creatures formed and designed by God to add variety to life.

When you are feeling a little down because of changes, remember that change is variety, and variety is life.

We are exceedingly happy; we are blessed to witness God's love for variety through our grandchildren. Thank you, Lord. Amen.

NOVEMBER 5   SHARING GOD'S GIFTS

"All I have is yours, and all you have is mine."
                              (John 17:10a GNT)

I cannot imagine a more perfect expression of love and sharing. Jesus is saying he is giving us all of him; in return, all that we have belongs to him.

It is a wonderful feeling to share and to teach others how to share. As grandmothers, we need to demonstrate sharing and teach our grandchildren to share, as well. Because they are so innocent and caring, children often *want* to share when they see someone in need.

Jesus teaches not only that we are to give of ourselves but also that those we give to should be willing to give of themselves. Remind your grandchildren of all the wonderful things you do together, and then ask them to share with you. Depending on the age of a grandchild, he or she might read you a story, cook a meal for you, or take you for a drive.

The strongest illustration of sharing is Jesus dying on the cross so that we might be saved. Today let us tell one another the words that Jesus told his disciples: "All I have is yours."

Father, prepare us to teach our grandchildren to share, and to give back to those who share with them. Amen.

NOVEMBER 6   FOREVER GOD'S WORD

"All human beings are like grass, and all their glory is like wild flowers. The grass withers, and the flowers fall, but the word of the Lord remains forever." **(1 Peter 1:24-25a GNT)**

Do you hear the quietness in the air? The leaves are falling from the trees without making a sound. The grass is drying up, and everything that once seemed alive appears to be decaying. When we look around, there is a lot taking place quietly. Everything is changing in a quiet, natural way.

Our grandchildren are growing up right before our eyes. If we go several weeks without seeing them, there is a noticeable change.

There is comfort in knowing that the Word of God remains forever. We can give our grandchildren something that will last forever, something they can pass to their children, as well: God's Word. I gave my first grandchild a Bible. In it there is a word for every occasion and an answer for every question.

We will not always be a physical part of our grandchildren's lives, but through God's Word, we will always be a spiritual part of their lives. There is no better way to teach our grandchildren about the goodness of the Lord than through God's Word.

Father, we are going through many changes. Thank you for allowing us to give our grandchildren your Word, which never changes. Amen.

NOVEMBER 7   COMFORT IN HIS LOVE

Your life in Christ makes you strong, and his love comforts you.
(Philippians 2:1 GNT)

When life is painful, we sometimes want to hold back the tears because we want to appear strong for our loved ones. But it is OK to cry and ask for comfort. When my grandchildren fall and hurt themselves, I immediately want to help them. Christ feels the same way about us. He feels our pain and suffering and wants to comfort us.

I tell my grandson that it is OK to cry. Sometimes boys are told not to cry because it is a sign of weakness. Actually, to cry is a sign of strength. Through our tears we are acknowledging that we need Christ. Through our tears, we reach out to the Lord for comfort and love. Through our tears we release tension, frustration, and stress.

Go ahead and let tears fall from your eyes when struggles seem to get you down. Likewise, go ahead and let tears fall because you have so much to be thankful for! Thank the Lord for allowing you to see your grandchildren cry and to smile when they are comforted.

With joy in our heart, we thank you, Lord, for allowing us to share tears and joy with our grandchildren. Amen.

NOVEMBER 8   FROM THE VALLEY TO THE MOUNTAINTOPS

He rules over the whole earth,
 from the deepest caves to the highest hills.
He rules over the sea, which he made;
 the land also, which he himself formed. (Psalm 95:4-5 GNT)

From the depths of the sea to the height of the highest mountain, God is there.

A trip to the mountains with the grandchildren proved to be a lesson in experiencing the omnipresence of God. We decided to go on a picnic to catch the last warm days of the season. There were a number of scenic views on the long drive to the top. The splendor of watching the mountains touch the sky was breathtaking. (It is there that I feel closest to God; the mountains are so majestic and remind me of God's majesty.) We finally reached a peak of over three thousand feet and found a picnic table where we could eat our lunch. The grandchildren were having the time of their lives as they ran through the piles of leaves.

I watched them enjoy every aspect of what God has given us. As we walked to the scenic spot and looked down, one of them asked, "Are we in the sky?" I told them we were very close to God. I explained that God is all the way from the valley to the mountaintops—and beyond.

Indeed, God is everywhere!

Thank you, Lord, for being with us wherever we go. Amen.

NOVEMBER 9   THE LIGHT OF THE WORLD

"I am the light of the world," he said. "Whoever follows me will have the light of life and will never walk in darkness."
 (John 8:12 GNT)

The lighthouse shines a beacon of light for ships that sail at night. The light is a guide that leads seamen to safety. I can only imagine how happy they must feel if they are lost and have been tossed and turned on the dark sea, and then suddenly a light appears out of nowhere; they know there is hope. When I am going through some dark moments, I focus on the light of Jesus. When I focus on him, I realize I am not alone.

My grandchildren do not like sleeping in the dark. They are afraid of what they cannot see. I tell them that Jesus looks after them always—even when it is dark. Jesus is the light of the world—like the light shining from the lighthouse. I place a special night-light for them, and also leave a light on in the bathroom. This makes them feel a little more secure. I reflect on how the light of the Lord makes me feel secure as well. I know that there is never darkness because of his light.

Bless our grandchildren, keep them safe from harm, and let your light continue to light their way. Amen.

NOVEMBER 10   THE HARVEST IS GOOD

"As long as the world exists, there will be a time for planting and a time for harvest. There will always be cold and heat, summer and winter, day and night."   **(Genesis 8:22 GNT)**

I remember working in the garden, planting and picking vegetables with my brother and sisters. We would have the prettiest garden around. My mother was so proud of all we produced and thankful for the blessings God gave us. We had a bountiful harvest in the fall that would see us through the winter.

Explaining the harvest to my grandchildren is challenging. They kind of understand how hard we worked in the garden. However, to tell them about canning food is an entirely different story. It is difficult for them to understand putting food in a jar and referring to it as canning. They understand the concept of gathering and coming together to share in the harvest. Thanksgiving is coming soon, so there is some anticipation of the big feast. I have a large picture of them with a beautiful harvest background, in which they all have big smiles and are seated by the produce of a harvest. The large orange pumpkins and cornstalks give the picture a real farm look. However, when I look at my grandchildren, I see the harvest of our family tree.

Lord, we are thankful that you have blessed our family with a good harvest. Amen.

NOVEMBER 11   REJOICE

Let all who worship him rejoice!   **(1 Chronicles 16:10 GNT)**

Nature rejoices in praises to the Lord every day. We see it when rain and snow fall from the sky. The sun rejoices every time it rises and sets with magnificent beauty. The trees rejoice, bowing down to the Lord gracefully. I love praising the Lord through worship, and I rejoice at the gifts of life through my grandchildren.

At a sleepover, the grandchildren carried their sleeping bags to my recreation room and made beds across the floor. If I hadn't known better, I would have thought there were more than four children in the room. When they are in the house, there is always laughter and joy. What a wonderful sound and an extraordinary way to lift up the Lord. My grandchildren were taught at an early age by their parents to pray. Although they are never ready to go to sleep, I ask them to turn in and say their prayers. Their little voices sound in unison as they pray to the Lord. My husband and I rejoice at the sounds of their thanks and requests to watch over them and their family.

Heavenly Father, we rejoice at the great gifts you have given our family through our grandchildren. Amen.

NOVEMBER 12   BEARERS OF GOOD FRUIT

"I am the real vine, and my Father is the gardener. He breaks off every branch in me that does not bear fruit, and he prunes

every branch that does bear fruit, so that it will be clean and bear more fruit."   *(John 15:1-2 GNT)*

Our heavenly Father takes good care of his garden by breaking off branches that do not bear fruit. When we ask him to, he carefully removes those things that destroy us. I can visualize the image of Christians being connected to the vine, which is the Holy Spirit. We must stay connected to the Holy Spirit to be productive Christians who bring disciples to Christ.

I love fresh peaches straight off of the tree. They are so juicy and sweet and actually tantalize the taste buds. If a branch on the tree dies, the fruit dies as well. We are the tree, and the heavenly Father is the gardener. It is important that we be bearers of good fruit.

Our grandchildren are good examples of the fruit we bear. They are extensions of us, just as we are an extension of the Father. We must teach them to be connected to God to bear good fruit. Share some sweet fruit with your grandchildren today.

Father, you have given us grandchildren who are examples of good fruit. Thank you. Amen.

NOVEMBER 13   A MEAL WITH THE MULTITUDE

Then he took the seven loaves and the fish, gave thanks to God, broke them, and gave them to the disciples; and the disciples gave them to the people.   *(Matthew 15:36 GNT)*

Through Christ all things are possible. He fed four thousand people with only seven loaves of bread and a few small fish.

Now that the weather has changed, it us not unusual for my daughter-in-law to call, saying they are coming by after they finish shopping. On one occasion, I thought this was a good time to cook spaghetti. A meal that will feed my multitude is spaghetti, garlic bread, and tossed salad. When the grandchildren, my children, and husband were ready to eat, there was enough for everyone. We even topped it off with apple pie and ice cream.

The disciples gave thanks and broke the bread. I always ask my grandchildren to bless the food. As they give thanks for the food they are about to eat, I give thanks for my family coming together to break bread like the multitude.

Take time and share a meal with your family or another family. God supplies our needs every day; we should see to the needs of others as well.

Lord, it is a blessing to share a meal with our multitude. Thank you for blessing us in such a special way. Amen.

NOVEMBER 14   COURAGE IN GOD'S PRESENCE

We have courage in God's presence.   ***(1 John 3:21 GNT)***

It is raining so hard today, as though the bottom has fallen from the sky. The raindrops are forming little pools of water in the yard. A little brown rabbit is scurrying across the back yard, trying to seek shelter from the rain. I remember when the rabbit was very small and my grandchildren laughed as the little bunnies ran quickly to find cover with their mother. Now the little rabbit has grown up, and he knows that he must seek shelter without his mother guiding him. It took courage for him to dash out on his own, not knowing if there is any danger close by.

Even the smallest animals belong to God and have courage that is inborn. They realize that there is a presence much greater than them, just as we recognize the presence of God in everything we see. His presence is all around us, and that presence gives us courage to face whatever obstacles come our way.

As grandmothers, we can enjoy watching our grandchildren gain courage each day.

Father, grant our grandchildren courage, and keep them forever in your presence. Amen.

NOVEMBER 15   SELF-CONTROLLED AND ALERT

You must be self-controlled and alert, to be able to pray.
       (1 Peter 4:7 GNT)

My grandson wants to take his bath, watch TV, eat a snack, and say his bedtime prayer at the same time. I explain the importance of giving God that personal one-on-one time. When we finally get through the bath and everything else, it is time for him to settle down for bed. Self-control is so important, and teaching this at a young age is the building block of a solid foundation.

It is important to teach little ones that there is a time for everything, and the time we give God is so important. I explain to him how God keeps us and watches over us while we are asleep. Therefore, we must take special time to pray and ask for his protection through the night. My grandson wants God to wait until he finishes his day. I am teaching him that the day belongs to God, as does the night. We must give him all of our attention, and the only way to do that is to put everything aside and take time out for God.

Lord, show us ways to teach our grandchildren to have self-control, to be alert, and to pray from the heart. Amen.

NOVEMBER 16   A MESSAGE OF PEACE

Christ's message in all its richness must live in your hearts.
(Colossians 3:16 GNT)

Have you noticed that when you travel from one state to another there are all types of billboards or signs to get our attention? There are messages about vacations, cheap tickets, shopping centers, restaurants, and so forth. When I travel with my grandchildren, we look for signs as a game to see who will find the next sign first. The next part of the game is to read the sign and try to figure out the message.

Just picture a large billboard with the message of peace from Christ. The billboard would have a message of peace that calls us together in one body. It would be strategically placed to cause a positive impact in the lives of others.

Living together in peace means more than just living. As we and countless others would read the message over and over, it would be planted in our hearts. And as that happened, we would become the billboard of peace.

Look at your grandchildren as a message of peace.

Lord, let our lives be examples of a message of peace for our grandchildren to emulate. Amen.

NOVEMBER 17   PEACE IN THE WATER

A stream flowed in Eden and watered the garden; beyond Eden it divided into four rivers.   *(Genesis 2:10 GNT)*

Watching the waves of the ocean is so peaceful and relaxing. The water comes up on the beach and washes all the prints away. All of a sudden there is a smooth, clean surface—a fresh, new beginning.

Life is like the waves: You never know when they are going to come up over you and almost sweep you away. The waves also remind me of how quickly troubles in our lives come and go.

When we pray, there is a connection to God that flows like a stream within us. We are being nourished like the stream flowing into the Garden of Eden. We continue the flow as we communicate with our grandchildren the wonders of God.

This summer we took four of our grandchildren to the beach. They were so amazed at the size of the ocean, and so inquisitive about the source of the water. "Where did all of that water come from?" they asked. As they watched the waves peacefully come and go, washing away their footprints, they realized the greatness of God.

Thank you for the opportunity to show our grandchildren the source of the stream that is great in you. Amen.

NOVEMBER 18   NEVER GIVE UP

They were hungry and thirsty and had given up all hope. Then in their trouble they called to the LORD, and he saved them from their distress.   *(Psalm 107:5-6 GNT)*

Never give up hope, no matter how desolate the situation may appear. Often there will be times in our lives when it seems there is no hope. Trouble pops up out of nowhere and causes so much pain and distress. When we concentrate on the trouble, it becomes a part of our lives. Concentrating on the problem is like giving life to it.

When we are hungry, we eat; and when we are thirsty, we drink. When we are in trouble and feel hopeless, we must pray.

There have been times in my life when I felt like giving up. As I look back on my life, I remember there was hope in every situation. The Lord brought me through each one, and he will bring my grandchildren through, as well.

My seven-year-old granddaughter is the first to tell you that the Lord will see you through. She has heard her mother tell her about the power of prayer. When she told me how the Lord had answered all of her prayers, I thanked God for being a witness to such a wonderful blessing.

We should pray with our grandchildren and let them know that through God, the impossible becomes possible.

Thank you for allowing us to see and hear our grandchildren pray and speak of never giving up. Amen.

NOVEMBER 19   HIS WORD

"My word is like the snow and the rain that come down from the sky to water the earth. They make the crops grow and provide seed for planting and food to eat." **(Isaiah 55:10 GNT)**

All across the fields are large bales of hay, which are remains of the summer's successful crops. I see the blackbirds landing in the fields to collect pieces of grain. They are gathering in large numbers as though bad weather is approaching. The blackbirds have a beautiful contrast against the golden fields. Suddenly, the wind blows the leaves across the road. Some of the trees have a few dangling leaves left that seem to move back and forth but never blow completely off. In a few months, the rain will turn to beautiful flakes of snow and decorate the fields like a warm blanket.

Can you imagine looking up into the sky and seeing God's Word coming down from the sky? We can run in the fields like the birds and catch his Word as it falls from the sky.

Take time to enjoy the crisp air and the beautiful fall days with your grandchildren. As you walk and play outdoors together, tell them to look up as God's Word comes down around you.

Oh, what a beautiful day to let the Word of God cover our grandchildren and us. Amen.

NOVEMBER 20   CHILDREN AND TRADITIONS

But Jesus called the children to him and said, "Let the children come to me and do not stop them, because the Kingdom of God belongs to such as these."   *(Luke 18:16 GNT)*

The holiday season is quickly approaching. I can feel it in the air and see it everywhere I go. This time of year is so special and makes me feel so warm inside, thinking about the family and the fun we will have this Thanksgiving. My mother is coming to dinner, and she will be the guest of honor with all her great-grandchildren present.

We are keeping and starting new traditions with each generation. My mom has the best recipes for candied yams and home-made pound cake. She makes the cake from real butter and fresh farm eggs. I can smell the food cooking and see the men watching the football game. What a wonderful time of the year to be in the presence of the Lord with all of the children around.

The Lord reminded the disciples of how special children are by calling the children to him. Teach your grandchildren the traditions that were taught to you. Remember it is a blessing to have children around you.

Father, keep us mindful of all of the wonderful blessings we have in our grandchildren. Amen.

NOVEMBER 21   WORDS TO GROW BY

Be alert, stand firm in the faith, be brave, be strong. Do all your
work in love.   *(1 Corinthians 16:13-14 GNT)*

Listening to the news can be very discouraging. There are so
many terrible things happening around us. Sometimes I think it
would be better not to know. Realistically, however, we must be
aware of what is going on so we can be alert and able to help others. We cannot shut our eyes and ears to trouble. We must pray for
our communities and the world.

When children learn of the tragedies around them, they become
very concerned and sometimes afraid. As grandmothers, we must
teach our grandchildren to be alert always; to be aware of their
surroundings. We also must teach them to stand firm in their
faith, which will help them in life.

My grandchildren are aware of the dangers in the world, but
they are comforted and assured because we look out for them and
pray for them every day. As God watches over us and protects us,
he does so in love. We can give our grandchildren the words to
grow by as God has given them to us.

Lord, thank you for all you have done in our lives and the lives
of our grandchildren. We're grateful that our faith keeps us
strong. Amen.

NOVEMBER 22   MANNA FROM HEAVEN

It was as delicate as frost.   *(Exodus 16:14b GNT)*

Early in the morning I start cleaning upstairs and work my way
downstairs. As I look out the window, I stand in awe at the frost
that lightly kisses the grass. It looks like fine, woven linen. In the
Scriptures, the manna from heaven is described as delicate frost.
When the Israelites saw the covering on the grass, they stood in
awe. God had blessed them with plenty to eat.

There will be plenty of food on the table in a number of house-
holds on Thanksgiving Day. Many people will take this time to

share with others. Wouldn't it be nice if we shared with others less fortunate all the time? God has blessed us with manna from heaven, yet some of us keep it to ourselves.

Our heavenly Father has taught us to show love for one another. No matter the age of our grandchildren, it is never too late to teach them to appreciate and to share what God has done for them.

Today is a good day to tell our grandchildren about the manna from heaven—either in person or by phone.

Heavenly Father, thank you for the gift of frost that reminds us of your provision. Amen.

NOVEMBER 23   THE DEEPNESS OF YOUR THOUGHTS

A person's thoughts are like water in a deep well, but someone with insight can draw them out. **(Proverbs 20:5 GNT)**

When my mother was in the hospital, I tried to maintain a positive attitude even though I was worried. This was the first time I had seen her so ill, and I was afraid that I would lose her.

One day the great-grandchildren came in with laughter and energy. They climbed up on her bed and asked all kinds of questions about her health. One, however, tried not to come too close. I asked him to come and give Grandma a big hug. He came over with a worried look in his eyes, so I asked him what he was thinking. He said he was afraid his great-grandmother would stay sick and never get out of the bed. I should have known that if I was afraid, he, too, must be afraid.

In situations of illness and trouble, it is best to ask our grandchildren how they are feeling or what they are thinking. Though they may be very young, their feelings and thoughts are as real and valid as our own.

Heavenly Father, give us the insight to know when to ask our grandchildren about their thoughts. Amen.

NOVEMBER 24   BOW DOWN AND WORSHIP

The heavenly powers bow down and worship you.
(Nehemiah 9:6d GNT)

When I was nine years old, I would preach to the trees, blades of grass, and birds. I would imagine that they were bowing down to the Word of the Lord. The majesty and greatness of the Lord is so awesome that even nature bows down.

My granddaughter wanted to fly a kite when she was about three years old. She could not understand why we needed a strong wind in order for the kite to fly. We ran back and forth, trying to get enough wind to lift it up so that it would fly. Our efforts seemed hopeless, when suddenly a little breeze came from nowhere and gently lifted the kite in the sky. The wind lifted the kite for about a minute, which was enough to make her smile. The kite bowed down and came gracefully back to the ground.

Small things in life, like a breeze, can mean so much and be so special to a little child. I like to think that an angel blew her breath and made the kite fly.

When we begin to forget how small things are important, remind us of the day the kite bowed down. Amen.

NOVEMBER 25   HAVE FAITH

To have faith is to be sure of the things we hope for, to be cer-
tain of the things we cannot see.   *(Hebrews 11:1 GNT)*

On my desk at work is a mustard seed with the scripture from Hebrews 11:1-2. This is one of the most powerful scriptures in the Bible. It is my faith that gets me through trying situations. When my father passed away, it was my faith that got me through that period in my life. Faith is attempting the impossible, knowing that it is possible because of our faith in God.

When my grandson was very young, he had several seizures after an illness. He was rushed to the emergency room. When my husband and I arrived, we were stunned to see him lying there so helpless. My daughter-in-law and son had a look of desperation. We prayed in the hallway with a stranger, and we prayed with my son and wife's pastor. My faith gave me the strength to get through and to know that, whatever the outcome, God was in control of the situation. I kept saying to myself, "Have faith; he's going to be all right." My grandson fully recovered, and everyone gave thanks.

A gift of wisdom for our grandchildren is the message to have faith.

We pray that the message of faith reaches the hearts of our grandchildren and stays planted there forever. Amen.

NOVEMBER 26   LOVE ONE ANOTHER

Dear friends, let us love one another, because love comes from God. Whoever loves is a child of God and knows God.
(1 John 4:7 GNT)

The telephone is ringing, and I know it is one of the grandchildren. When they call our house, they ask to speak to my husband or our teenage son.

I answer the telephone to hear the voice of my grandson, who ends every call with, "I love you." When the other grandchildren call, they end the call the same way. Our family members love one another and know that love comes from God.

We should always begin and end each day with love. Although the price of everything has soared, love doesn't cost a thing. God gets the glory when we love one another.

So, how can we bring love where there is hate? We can start each day with a prayer, asking God to somehow let those we meet feel the love we have inside. Our love comes from God, so we must share that love.

Sometimes I make my grandson a bowl of hot chicken noodle soup. He loves sipping one noodle at a time. Soup warms the body, and love warms the soul.

Father, use us as vessels to show others it is good to love one another. Amen.

NOVEMBER 27   TEACH THEM WHILE
                               THEY'RE YOUNG

Teach me, LORD, the meaning of your laws,
*   and I will obey them at all times.*
Explain your law to me, and I will obey it.
                               (Psalm 119:33-34 GNT)

My husband and I visited our grandchildren's church to worship with them. They were lively but attentive. The pastor smiled at them as they came up for altar call and gathered around his legs. When they returned to their seats, each one gave us a big smile. As the service continued, they tried to follow along by reading their Bibles. I noticed an excited look on their faces as the message was delivered. They told us they know the Lord watches over them. My grandson proudly confessed that he has asked the Lord to forgive him for talking too much at school and getting a time out.

After church, they came to our house for dinner and discussed the service. Each one had his or her own interpretation of the message. This was a valuable time to teach our grandchildren about God's Word as we listened to their comments.

When we teach our grandchildren the meaning of God's Word, it truly becomes planted in their hearts. They are eager to learn if we will take time to teach them.

Lord, thank you for opportunities to teach our grandchildren your Word. Amen.

NOVEMBER 28   TWO OR MORE

"For where two or three come together in my name, I am there
with them."   *(Matthew 18:20 GNT)*

Today is a celebration of life. My house is full of the sounds of laughter and squeals as four of my grandchildren come together for playtime. They are up and down the stairs from one room to another just having fun. I am going to make a lemon double-layer cake for a treat.

My two youngest grandsons decide to jump up and down by the oven, shouting, "The cake sure smells good!" They quickly run outside for more fun and adventure. When I open the oven door, the cake is as flat as a pancake. I decide to frost it anyway.

The grandchildren finally come inside for some cake and talk on the speakerphone to their great-grandmother. My mother asks if we are having a party. I say, "No, whenever there are two or more, there is always a celebration."

The Lord is always present when we are together. You can have a celebration of life by joining together in everyday fun. Bake a cake or paint a smiley face and tell your grandchildren you love them today.

Lord, we pray for everlasting communion between our grandchildren and us. Amen.

NOVEMBER 29   PHYSICAL STRENGTH

I prayed, "But now, God, make me strong!"
(Nehemiah 6:9b GNT)

Exercising is good for our health and physical endurance. I have decided to watch what I eat and to exercise. At first it was an uphill battle. However, I know that God wants us to be strong, and I want to stay strong and healthy for my grandchildren.

So, I rolled up my sleeves and headed for the recreation room. First, I warmed up and tried the exercise bike; later I almost crawled to the treadmill. I learned that I must build my physical endurance, so I began to use weights a little at a time.

My grandson came over one evening while I was on the bike and just stared at me. He asked if I was okay, and I told him to go away for a while. He decided to watch, and finally he ran downstairs to tell his grandfather that I was sick. At that moment, I realized how important it is to get in shape.

After a period of time, I started to see results! My goal is to stay healthy and strong to enjoy my family and grandchildren.

Father, we pray for health and strength so that we may enjoy our families and grandchildren. Amen.

NOVEMBER 30   IN THE RIGHT DIRECTION

Even storks know when it is time to return; doves, swallows,
and thrushes know when it is time to migrate.
                                        (Jeremiah 8:7a GNT)

The sky is full of blackbirds flying south for the winter. Suddenly
they descend upon my holly tree and start stripping the bright red
berries one by one. Some of the birds are landing in my yard and
on my deck. It appears that they are driven with the desire to
return to some far-off place.

Birds instinctively fly in the right direction to reach their des-
tiny. They generally migrate in order to survive. The survival
instinct is borne inside them at birth.

We humans were given a survival extinct; unfortunately, it often
leads us in the wrong direction! If we had a natural instinct to go
in the right direction to avoid trouble, we would have much fewer
heartaches and headaches.

My grandson has been talking at school when he should be listening to his teacher. He explains to me that sometimes his friends
ask him questions. He will have to learn which "direction" is the
right one to take. In the process, he will learn that when we take
the right direction, there are always rewards.

Father, give our grandchildren a sense of direction that will
keep them always headed in the right direction. Amen.

December

Evidences of God's Love

SYLVIA M. CORBIN BERRY

DECEMBER 1 THE BEST CHRISTMAS EVER

May the Lord lead you into a greater understanding of God's love. *(2 Thessalonians 3:5 GNT)*

When I think of understanding God's love, I think of all the things surrounding me. God shows his love for me in so many creative ways. In a few weeks, our families will celebrate the birth of Christ. What a wonderful time of year filled with evidences of God's love.

As I put away the fall decorations, my excitement grows for the Christmas season. I go to the boxes in the attic marked "holiday decorations." I am looking for the box that has decorations made by my three children when they were very little. The box is all the way in the back, and I have to reach to get it. Inside it are evidences of God's love—made by my children's hands and inspired by God. Oh, there are also decorations made by the grandchildren. This box is the most precious of my ornaments.

This is going to be the best Christmas ever. I say that every year because each year with my family is a gift of love from God. I am going to bring the box down now and wait for my husband to bring in the Christmas tree!

Heavenly Father, open my eyes to the evidences of your love all around me. Amen.

DECEMBER 2   DO NOT BE AFRAID

"Do not be afraid, little flock, for your Father is pleased to give you the Kingdom."   *(Luke 12:32 GNT)*

One of the most empowering evidences of God's love is his promise to give us the kingdom of heaven. We are often afraid of what life will bring—afraid to live for fear of dying.

Our Father refers to us as his little flock. He is so much bigger than us and anything we could possibly fear. He tells us not to be afraid but to step boldly into the blessings that are ours alone. Then what is there to fear?

My grandson Braxton is very cautious of what he does not know. Sometimes he appears to be afraid and very shy. Little children are afraid because of what they have seen or heard from adults. We can actually place our fears in them. When we do that, we prevent them from growing and experiencing all that God has planned for them.

As grandmothers, we must examine our words, hearts, and minds before we speak. The words we say to God's littlest of the flock may have an everlasting impact. We can teach them to trust God and not be afraid.

Lord, we hear your words that rebuke fear. Let your words empower our lives and the lives of our grandchildren. Amen.

DECEMBER 3   BEING HUMBLE

"Happy are those who are humble; they will receive what God has promised!"   *(Matthew 5:5 GNT)*

God wants us to be humble. If we are proud, we will not see God in what we receive but will be consumed by what we have, forgetting the loving One who so graciously gives. God has promised us a great reward if we are humble, and no material item can replace or measure up to what God has for us.

I picked up my grandson Tyler from day care, and he told me he had some good news and some bad news. I asked what the bad news was, and he said, "I got a time out today—and the good news is I got to get up." As I looked at him in the rearview mirror, I realized that, to him, getting out of time out was more important than any material thing he might have received.

God showed me how humble a four-year-old can be in comparison to an adult. He was punished, but he was allowed to start over. This is a gift that God gives us every day—a gift that should humble us.

Dear God, help us to remain humble. When we forget, may we remember the humble example of a child. Amen.

DECEMBER 4   CELEBRATE WITH JOY

They all decided to celebrate for another seven days. So they celebrated with joy.   **(2 Chronicles 30:23 GNT)**

A celebration that lasts for seven days is quite a worship service! When we look throughout the Bible, we see that the number "seven" is very significant. The Sabbath is on the seventh day, and there were seven years of plenty, to name just a few.

My granddaughter turned seven this year. She was so excited because turning seven is a big thing in a little girl's life. This means she will be in second grade and be allowed to make some new choices, such as how to wear her hair or what outfit to wear to school. We went shopping and purchased some cute items for a girl who is a princess. I'm sure she would love a seven-day celebration for her birthday, but we will celebrate for only one day.

As grandmothers, we can make every day of a grandchild's life a celebration. Go ahead and celebrate every day of the week, giving thanks that God has blessed you with grandchildren. God is worthy to be praised each and every day. There are so many more reasons to celebrate than to complain!

Lord, it is our pleasure to celebrate each day of the joy you give through grandchildren.

DECEMBER 5   PRAISE THE LORD

Praise the LORD, you heavenly beings; praise his glory and power.   *(Psalm 29:1 GNT)*

The sound of a children's choir singing praises has to be the closest thing to the sound of angels' voices. I remember the year my granddaughter Jasmine sang in the Christmas play at her day care. She asked her Grandfather and me to come. We had such a busy schedule, but we took the time to attend. What a delight as we were seated to see her standing on the third row, surrounded by twenty or more children. When the musician gave the queue, their little voices rose together in praises for the birth of Christ. I knew the Lord had to be pleased to hear such angelic voices coming from his littlest "angels."

We are often very busy, and sometimes it is difficult to attend all of our grandchildren's recitals or activities. However, we must take the time to show them that we support them and love them—even if we can attend only half of a function or if only one grandparent can attend. Through our love they will see God's love.

The smiles on our grandchildren's faces are priceless. Surely, their smiles are praising the Lord.

Father, thank you for the privilege of showing our love and support to our grandchildren. Amen.

DECEMBER 6   TRUE NAME

For this reason I fall on my knees before the Father, from whom every family in heaven and on earth receives its true name.
                                            (Ephesians 3:14-15 GNT)

We praise and honor God because he has blessed us with our true name. Everyone on earth and in heaven has an identity because of our Father. We are all family because Christ makes his home in our hearts.

My grandson Thomas Peyton Berry III (Trae) is named after my oldest son and my husband. When a family name is passed down, it carries with it history, love, memories, and the lineage of family. The scripture says that every family in heaven and earth receives its true name.

It is our responsibility to tell our grandchildren about the importance of their names. We must let them know that the names they were given were not chosen by chance. Their parents took time to select their names—perhaps even waiting until they were born to make their choice. My youngest grandson's name is Christian, and from the day he was born, I believe Christ had his hands on him—as he does all of us.

Tell your grandchildren a story about how they received their names. Complete the story with a prayer on your knees.

God, we are grateful for the gift of our true name. May the name of Christ be a home in the hearts of our grandchildren. Amen.

DECEMBER 7   WELCOME STRANGERS IN
                                                YOUR HOME

Remember to welcome strangers in your homes.
(Hebrews 13:2 GNT)

Who is a stranger? I believe a stranger is more than a person you do not know. A stranger is a person who does not know God. When we are one in Christ, we all have a connection. We are not strangers.

As Christians, we are called to bring others to Christ. We can welcome others because we are part of the family. When others confess their sin and accept Jesus as their savior, they are no longer strangers. They have become part of this wonderful family.

One of the greatest privileges we can have as grandparents is telling our grandchildren about Christ and welcoming them into Christ's family. Then, when the time comes for them to go into the world, we can be careful to tell them—as we told our own children—to take God with them wherever they go. If and when they come upon another child of God, they will be welcomed.

Lord, help our grandchildren and us to recognize those who are "strangers" so that we may tell them about you and welcome them into the family. Amen.

DECEMBER 8   A GIFT FROM GOD

*Who made you superior to others? Didn't God give you every-
thing you have? Well, then, how can you boast, as if what you
have were not a gift?*   *(1 Corinthians 4:7 GNT)*

We cannot count the many gifts our loving God has given us. Of
course, the most perfect gift God has given is his Son Jesus. Yet,
often we're too busy to take time to give thanks for all God's wonderful gifts.

So many people boast about how much they have, and others
complain because they think they need more. We can celebrate
every gift God has given us. All we need to do is take time to look
around. The Christmas decorations are beautiful; God has given
us the gift(s) to see, touch, or feel them.

As grandparents, we can teach our grandchildren about gifts
from God by encouraging them to write a letter to Jesus—or by
writing one on their behalf if they are too young—telling Jesus
"thank you" for all their gifts: laughter, a home, parents, vision,
and taste, just to name a few.

We should all begin to look at everything we have as a gift from
God. When we do that, we can earnestly celebrate our gifts from
God.

*Heavenly Father, help us to teach our grandchildren to be
thankful for all the gifts you have given them. Amen.*

DECEMBER 9   LIKE A LIGHT

"You are like light for the whole world."   *(Matthew 5:14 GNT)*

Jesus is the Light of the world, and his light radiates within us.
Even when there is darkness, the light of Jesus prevails throughout the world. And it can never go out.

As we celebrate this Christmas season, let us not forget to reflect
on the Light of the world. May we celebrate the birth of Christ
through prayer and praise and in all our holiday activities. Even as
we decorate, we are capturing the beauty of the Light for a season.

We always put clear lights on the tree in the dining room. When we turn off the ceiling lights, the reflections from the tree lights dance across the china cabinet to the chandelier. Although it is dark, the room is illumined with the twinkling lights.

We can be lights in our grandchildren's lives. We are able to provide light even in their darkest moments because we have the light of Jesus in us.

This year, let us decorate our Christmas trees with clear lights and remind our grandchildren of the Light of the world, our Savior. The lights may go out on the tree, but the light of the Lord lasts forever.

Dear God, we give you honor and praise for the light you give to light the world for our grandchildren. Amen.

DECEMBER 10   BLESSING OF RAIN

It is your father's God who helps you, The Almighty God who blesses you With blessings of rain from above.
(Genesis 49:25 GNT)

After such a dry and hot summer, rain is truly a blessing. Tonight they say the rain will turn to snow, which is early for this time of year. I can hardly wait because the grandchildren have already called to share their excitement about the prediction.

We are blessed with so many different kinds of gifts. Something as simple as the rain can be as valuable as precious jewels. God is continually looking after us and providing for us. We don't have to ask him; often the blessings just come.

If the rain turns to snow, my grandchildren will be outside building a snowman—and I will bring them a scarf. Isn't it wonderful how one blessing can give so much pleasure to so many!

Thank you, Lord, for the blessing of rain and for all your good gifts. Amen.

DECEMBER 11   FAITHFUL TO YOUR PROMISE

Faithful to your promise, you led the people you had rescued;
by your strength you guided them to your sacred land.
                                        (Exodus 15:13 GNT)

Oh, what jubilation the Israelites must have felt to be led into the
promised land! Finally, they were free to live and worship their
God. There must have been a sound of jubilation that could be
heard for hundreds of miles.

This story reminds us that God never lets us down. He is always
faithful. He will lead us and rescue us when we are in trouble. In
fact, we should feel jubilation right now because God is leading
us!

Our grandchildren listen to every word we say—and believe it.
They have faith in us and look up to us to lead and rescue them
when they are in trouble. To them, the things we say are like the
promises of God. They often believe that we can do anything, and
that we are always right.

So, we must never make a promise we cannot keep. It is better
to say "I will try" than to say "I will" and later let them down. We
can tell them God is faithful to all his promises, but we will do the
best we can for them.

Dear Lord, we want to be careful to tell our grandchildren that
we are only human but that you are divine and will be faithful
to your promises. Amen.

DECEMBER 12   THE HEART: A TREASURE OF
                                              GOOD THINGS

"A good person brings good out of the treasure of good things
in his heart."   *(Luke 6:45 GNT)*

The heart contains a "treasure of good things" more valuable
than all the gold in the world, because this treasure comes straight
from God. The "good thing" of a smile can mend a broken heart.
The "good thing" of saying thank you each time you receive some-

thing can change another's coldness to warmth. The "good thing" of consideration or concern can lift one who is down. A person brings good out of the treasure of his or her heart each and every time he or she elevates someone else.

Grandchildren have a special way of bringing good out of the treasure of good things in their hearts. When they say thank you, we feel good inside. When they ask if they can help us with a chore or activity, we feel good inside. When they look at us with love in their eyes and tell us from the bottom of their hearts that they love us, we feel good inside.

Grandchildren have the biggest hearts and are always ready to bring us good things. We, in return, can give them good things by giving them a card with a personal expression of how good they make us feel. Our grandchildren constantly show us the good inside of them. Let us always show them the good things in our hearts.

Father, you have given our grandchildren a treasure of good things in their hearts. Today, we thank you from the bottom of our hearts. Amen.

DECEMBER 13   A BLADE OF GRASS

"What did you expect to see? A blade of grass bending in the wind?"   **(Luke 7:24 GNT)**

There is always one piece of grass that survives even the harshest weather. No matter how much frost, snow, or ice, the blade of green grass stands out. Perhaps this piece of grass was just too stubborn to turn brown and wither away.

This little blade of grass represents how a Christian withstands the tests of life. Although there may be confusion or chaos everywhere, we can stand tall like the little blade of grass because God is our strength. Just as the grass bends when the wind blows and then stands back up, determined to persevere, God gives us the ability to persevere through even the most difficult trials.

Our grandchildren, too, are like a blade of grass bending in the wind. When they are little, they show us determination by learning to tie their shoes and make it to the bathroom on time. When they're older, they show perseverance when they keep on trying until they master a particular skill. They are like the blade of grass that bends in the wind: When they are down, they quickly get back up.

May we continue to encourage our little blades of grass.

Lord, give our grandchildren the strength they need to continue to be blades of grass that bend in the wind. Amen.

DECEMBER 14   THE BEAUTIFUL TREE

How beautiful the tree was—So tall, with such long branches. Its roots reached down to the deep-flowing streams.
(Ezekiel 31:7 GNT)

The scripture compares a country with a cedar tree. We can almost see the beauty of this tree.

The tree is not just tall, it is "so tall." The roots are not just long, but they are long enough to reach "deep-flowing streams."

How many lives have we touched through our "branches"? The branches are our family tree. When we look back, we can see that the streams from our past run like rivers through our family.

Our grandchildren are receiving nourishment from the roots of the family tree. How beautiful is the family tree! Each branch has its own family, and each family has its own roots.

This month we can draw upon the beauty of the Christmas tree to tell our children how it resembles the family tree. We trim the tree with the past and the present. The strands of lights that run through the tree resemble the streams. At the bottom of the tree is the source of nourishment—the water that keeps the roots alive.

This Christmas, tell your grandchildren about their roots and how they connect to the deep-flowing streams of the family tree.

Father, we thank you for the beauty of the family tree. Amen.

DECEMBER 15   CLAP YOUR HANDS

Clap your hands, you rivers; you hills, sing together with joy before the LORD, because he comes to rule the earth.
(Psalm 98:8-9a GNT)

When the water of the river rages and the rocks fall from the mountains, it is all praise. We can imagine the high waters rising up and suddenly clapping against the rocks in a sound that is glorious. Then, as the rocks tumble down the mountainside and land on the hills below, the sound rings out like a xylophone. The tune is joy to our ears. All the earth is praising the Lord.

The musical instruments of the marching band fascinate my grandson. He asks my son about the instruments he plays and says he wants to play in the high school band. Of course, he is only four and has to wait quite a while! However, just as the earth has found a way to praise the Lord, so also my grandson has found a way to praise the Lord by creating his own symphony sound. The clap of his hands and the hum of his lips are all praises.

This holiday season, let us encourage our grandchildren to clap their hands with joy before the Lord!

Lord, it is our prayer to hear the same music that children hear when they clap their hands with joy before you. Amen.

DECEMBER 16   WRITE ALL OF THIS

"Tell us, now, how did you come to write all this?"
(Jeremiah 36:17)

I love to tell stories and to write them down. Keeping a journal of my ministry has also been meaningful. When we write, we share our deepest emotions and our love.

The Holy Bible contains written accounts from at least forty different authors. The words are inspiring and life changing. We are so thankful that someone took the time to write them down. We would have missed so many blessings if it were not for the written Scriptures.

Today's scripture verse reveals that Jeremiah wrote it all down. Likewise, Moses also kept a journal. We, too, can give a priceless gift of our love in written form to pass down for generations to come.

Buy a journal and write down all of your special moments with your grandchildren. Then, go back and read the stories in your journal occasionally. You will find the words rich and full of blessings. The words also are life changing and can be passed down to your grandchildren—a gift they can keep always. One day they will share it with their own grandchildren.

Go ahead and write it all down, beginning today!

Dear Father, help us to begin the discipline of writing down our moments with our grandchildren, because they will last a lifetime. Thank you. Amen.

DECEMBER 17   AN ANGEL

"Then why do I see four men walking around in the fire?" he asked. "They are not tied up, and they show no sign of being hurt—and the fourth one looks like an angel."
(Daniel 3:25 GNT)

I love to collect angels. They are in my family room, living room, and dining room. Angels are God's messengers. The Bible provides many instances of angels coming with a message. One of the most powerful and life-changing messages is found in the gospel of Luke: the proclamation of Jesus' birth.

Another scripture describes an angel in a fiery furnace (see Daniel 3). This is a reminder that the Lord is always present in times of intensity. There is nothing more intense than a blazing fire. We all have experienced how life sometimes comes at us with such a bold intensity that it engulfs us. Yet the Lord shields us from the pressure, and we get through.

We can share the story of Daniel and his three friends with our grandchildren, who are going to face some very intense moments in their lives—some as intense as a fiery furnace. We also can share our own life-changing experiences and tell them how the Lord always has been and always will be with us.

In this season of angels and shepherds and a baby in a manger, we celebrate that God is always with us. The one who went through the fire with Daniel and his friends—and who goes through the fire with us—looks like an angel. We know it's the Lord.

Lord, thank you for being with us through the intensity of life. Amen.

DECEMBER 18   NEVER LET THEM GET AWAY

My child, pay attention to what I say. Listen to my words. Never let them get away from you. Remember them and keep them in your heart. **(Proverbs 4:20-21 GNT)**

These are incredible words of wisdom to live by. We must pay attention to God's words and never let them get away. God gives us the gift of wisdom through his words.

God wants us to listen to his words and keep them in our hearts. The heart is so important because this is where we "hear" God; God speaks to our hearts. The heart also is the place where we store all eternal gifts from God.

We must never let God's words get away. Nor should we let our grandchildren "get away" without God's words. We teach our grandchildren to memorize nursery rhymes. Why not teach them to memorize the Scriptures? Even older children and teens will be blessed by hiding God's words in their hearts.

One day our grandchildren will remember the Scriptures we have taught them because they will keep them in their hearts. And if they have scripture in their hearts, they will never let God's words go!

Our Father, help us to teach our grandchildren to keep your words in their hearts. Amen.

DECEMBER 19   OFFERING GIFTS

"For the others offered their gifts from what they had to spare of their riches; but she, poor as she is, gave all she had to live on."   *(Luke 21:4 GNT)*

Some people brag about the gifts they give to others. Others try to make our gifts or offerings seem insignificant compared to theirs. Still others give and turn around and tell others what they gave and to whom. Jesus reminds us that when we give all that we have from our hearts and out of sincerity, this is the largest of all gifts or offerings. This is the gift that Jesus sees.

Our grandchildren are quick to give us their love. Especially when they are little, they sincerely want to give us everything they have. When they have a cookie, they bring it to us to take a bite. When they have a toy, they ask if we want to play. Even as they get older, they give us their love by calling us on the phone and asking how we are. My mother is eighty-one years old, and when my grandchildren see her, they run to her and ask if she needs any help.

Our grandchildren are examples of the woman in the scripture. They give from the heart all that they possess. Jesus loves the offering of their gifts.

Father, when we select gifts or choose to give, may we remember the woman who gave all she had. Amen.

DECEMBER 20   BLOW TRUMPETS

Sing praises to the Lord! Play music on the harps! Blow trumpets and horns, and shout for joy to the Lord, our king.
(Psalm 98:5-6 GNT)

Praising God through musical instruments is a beautiful tribute to God's holiness. My husband and I love to hear our son, Philip, play Christmas carols on the trumpet. The sounds of the trumpet are regal and majestic. We can imagine Christ walking our way in all his glory as we listen to the melodious sound. Musical notes from the trumpet set the tempo for praise.

All of my grandchildren love musical instruments. Perhaps it is because their parents and grandfather play musical instruments. Each one has been given some type of instrument—from drums and keyboards to little horns—to play. When the grandchildren come together in concert, the sounds are very interesting. Although we cannot tell the tune sometimes, God recognizes the praise because all music is made in heaven.

This year we will give the youngest two grandchildren toy trumpets to blow in an announcement of the birth of Christ. How sweet it is to blow trumpets and horns in praise to the Lord with our grandchildren.

God, thank you for the gift of music. May we celebrate and praise you through musical instruments with our grandchildren this Christmas season. Amen.

DECEMBER 21   MAY THE LORD BLESS YOU

May the LORD bless you and take care of you;
May the LORD be kind and gracious to you;
May the LORD look on you with favor and give you peace.
                                   (Numbers 6:24-26 GNT)

This prayer of blessing, peace, and favor is one of the most beautiful and generous prayer requests in the Bible. Moses and Aaron did as God commanded and prayed this prayer of blessing over the people of Israel. Even though it contains only a few words, it has so much meaning and power. The message of the prayer is not only life changing, it is empowering.

I believe one of the ways the Lord shows his favor is by blessing us with grandchildren. We can be like Moses and Aaron and constantly pray this prayer over our grandchildren. We can ask the Lord to bless them each day and to give them peace and favor. When they go to school, we can ask the Lord to go with them and bless their every step. When they are upset or disturbed, we can pray for peace so that they may be in harmony with the Lord. And when they grow up and go out into the world, we can pray for favor so that life will be kind and gracious to them.

Heavenly Father, we are praying for blessing, favor, and peace for our grandchildren. Hear our prayer, O Lord. Amen.

DECEMBER 22   THE LORD IS ALL-POWERFUL

I know, LORD, that you are all-powerful;
that you can do everything you want.   *(Job 42:2 GNT)*

Is it really nearing the end of the year? It seems that the older I get, the quicker time passes! I'm also realizing how precious time is for all of us. Every moment we have with our loved ones is truly precious. We should take every opportunity to show our love because we can never go back and do something differently. The Lord has given us the gift of family for a season, a time. Especially this time of year, we come together to celebrate family and friends.

We know the Lord is all-powerful and that he can do everything—if it is his will. So we pray that we are there to see our grandchildren grow up, graduate from college, and get married. It is as if we are praying the same prayers for them that we prayed for our own children. Grandchildren, after all, are an extension of our children and ourselves. In a way, we are starting all over.

So, we should thank the Lord for every day he gives us with our grandchildren. It is as though we are doubly blessed. Yes, the Lord is all-powerful!

Lord, we thank you for the double blessing of our children and our grandchildren. We praise your holy name. Amen.

DECEMBER 23   OPEN YOUR HOMES

Open your homes to each other without complaining.
       (1 Peter 4:9 GNT)

Nothing compares to the warmth and coziness of home during the winter months. The fragrance of pine and the smell of cinnamon are everywhere. On the beds are large, warm comforters. The candles have a soft light that gently scents the house. Even the bathrooms have a warm, inviting atmosphere. The delicious smells of the best cookies and cakes made for family and friends fill the kitchen.

The family is excited because there are shorter days and longer nights to sit by the fireplace and tell stories. The grandchildren hope every day for enough snow to keep them home from school for the rest of the winter. Chicken noodle soup warms us when we come inside from the cold, brisk air.

We readily open up our homes to friends and family this time of year without complaining, yet often we forget to open up our hearts to those in need throughout the year. We are eager to help the needy during certain times of the year. However, there is a real need for help each day of the year.

We can teach our grandchildren to be mindful of the needs of others. We can help them to understand that giving should take place all year long.

Father, help us to open up our homes and hearts year round. Remind us to be cheerful givers. Amen.

DECEMBER 24   A CHILD OF GOD

Whoever believes that Jesus is the Messiah is a child of God.
(1 John 5:1a GNT)

My grandchildren believe that Jesus is the Messiah. They celebrate his birthday with a birthday cake every Christmas. Each of them gathers around the table as we light the candles on a special cake for Jesus. They blow out the candles and sing "Happy Birthday." They created the tradition themselves as they thought about how they celebrate their own birthdays. They wanted to make sure there was a cake for baby Jesus, too.

We have taught them that Jesus is the Messiah, that he came to save the world, and that we must praise him with all of our hearts. A birthday party helps to teach them about Jesus in a meaningful way that they can understand—and that will have an everlasting impression on them.

All of us are children of God because we believe in Jesus.

Teaching our grandchildren that all of us have Jesus in common is teaching them about equality and self-esteem. A lesson that changes their lives forever is a lesson about Jesus.

We're never too young or too old for this lesson. So this Christmas, find an age-appropriate way to teach your grandchildren about Jesus.

Father, we are thankful that you call all of us who believe in Jesus your children. Amen.

DECEMBER 25   GLORY TO GOD

"Glory to God in the highest heaven, and peace on earth to those with whom he is pleased!"
(Luke 2:14 GNT)

Today our voices ring out as we thank God for the birth of our Savior! On that glorious day long ago, an army of angels appeared, suddenly singing praises and shouting "Glory to God!" And each day thereafter, the heavens and earth have given praises to God's name. On Christmas Day, the happiness and joy we feel is overwhelming.

The happiness and joy I felt as I watched my grandchildren come into the world was glorious. When I saw the first sight of their heads, my heart skipped a beat and I jumped for joy. Nothing compares to witnessing the birth of a child. We can see why the angels shouted, because the birth of Jesus was no ordinary birth. His birth changed the world forever; and his life, death, and resurrection have had a profound impact on every living creature.

Today, our grandchildren will open and enjoy their gifts. Whether we are with them in person or by phone, let us take time to tell them of the birth of Jesus. If we were blessed to see their births, we can tell them of that glorious day, as well. Together let us shout, "Glory to God!"

God in the highest heaven, we give thanks on this special day for every gift you have given us, especially the gift of Jesus. Amen.

DECEMBER 26   AN EXPRESSION OF JOY

All this was an expression of the joy that was felt throughout the whole country.   *(1 Chronicles 12:40c GNT)*

Real expressions of joy come from within. When children feel joy, they do not hide it. Their joy bubbles up and spills out! Their joy is also contagious. When we see them smiling, we cannot help smiling. And suddenly our problems just melt away.

One expression of joy was the excitement both of my grandchildren showed when I visited their school. It was "Eat lunch with your grandchildren day." When I went to my grandson's class and looked in, he could not contain himself. Likewise, my granddaughter stood up and giggled when she saw me. Both of them were so happy to introduce me to their teachers and friends. The lunch was a real treat for all of us. They gleamed as they ate and looked at me with pride. This was truly an expression of joy.

If possible, take time to eat lunch with your grandchildren one day soon. Whatever their ages, they are sure to make you feel loved. An expression of everlasting joy is the face of a happy grandchild.

Dear Lord, a happy smile from our grandchildren is such an expression of joy. Thank you for the joy! Amen.

DECEMBER 27   THE LEFTOVERS

When they were all full, he said to his disciples, "Gather the pieces left over; let us not waste a bit."   *(John 6:12 GNT)*

We learn from this story that even the leftovers can be used. Often in life, certain people are chosen over others, and those who remain are considered the "leftovers." We think of leftovers as something we do not need or something that can be stored away and later thrown away.

There are two lessons we can teach our grandchildren. First, they shouldn't be concerned about being a "leftover." During selection for games, children often choose their friends or those who are considered "cool" first. When this happens, other children are left standing around, feeling inferior. We should be the first ones to tell our grandchildren that God has use for everyone. Being a "leftover" is not bad. We can remind them that in the story of the feeding of the multitude, the leftovers were gathered for future use by Jesus and the disciples. Likewise, God has a special plan and purpose for each of them.

Second, we should teach our grandchildren not to worry about whether they are chosen by others. Jesus made the most important choice when he chose them for his kingdom.

Now, we have given our grandchildren more reasons to celebrate this season!

Heavenly Father, we thank you for wanting to use all of us, regardless of who we are. Amen.

DECEMBER 28   FINISHED

When the repairs were finished, the remaining gold and silver was given to the king and Jehoiada, who used it to have bowls and other utensils made for the Temple.
(2 Chronicles 24:14 GNT)

A half-built home that was left to rot and decay is a discouraging scene. Even more discouraging are people who want to give God half their time and, in return, want all of God's time. We must be willing to give God our all. One important way to do this is to finish the assignments we are given—especially when they come directly from God. We cannot serve God completely when we do a job halfway.

Children get bored quickly and are ready to go to the next adventure before the last one is finished. We must teach and encourage our grandchildren early in life to finish their assignments so that they won't become adults who do things halfway. When they have the kind of healthy pride that makes them want to do their best and be their best, it is pleasing to God.

Our grandchildren are watching us with very curious eyes and are emulating us, as well. One day we will celebrate that they finish what they start because we taught them early.

Lord, we want to finish what we start and to teach our grand-children to do the same. Amen.

DECEMBER 29   I LONG FOR YOU

As a deer longs for a stream of cool water, so I long for you, O God.   *(Psalm 42:1)*

A common sight in the country is deer. When they scurry across the field, they do so with graceful elegance. Watching a deer run across an open green field is a beautiful sight.

When we were children, we would watch the deer from a hilltop in the forest. The lush, green leaves would hide us from their view. When the winter came and the trees had lost their leaves, we would have to stoop down low or cover ourselves to catch a glimpse of God's beautiful creatures.

During hunting season, deer run for safety and then are thirsty for a cool drink. As soon as it is safe, they bow their heads, looking around carefully as they drink from the cool, running streams.

Our need for God is as intense as the panting deer's need for a cool drink of water. In fact, we need God even more. When we receive God, it is like satisfying an overwhelming desire to quench our "thirst."

We can help our grandchildren to understand how much we need God by comparing the thirst of a deer with our need for God. To long for God is to always be humble and grateful, like a gentle deer.

God, we long for you every day. Help our grandchildren to feel the same need so that you may become their very lives. Amen.

DECEMBER 30   ADD GOODNESS

For this very reason do your best to add goodness to your faith; to your goodness add knowledge.   *(2 Peter 1:5 GNT)*

When we add goodness, faith, and knowledge, we have an almost perfect recipe for love. And when we add love to these other wonderful qualities, we are sure to see the face of Jesus.

Our two youngest grandchildren, Christian and Ethan, walk with a wobble and always have a big smile. When I look at them, I see the qualities of goodness. These two little guys do everything to please everyone. They are too young to know that there is any evil in the world. They both live in a world that, to them, is perfect; they show it on their happy faces.

We grandparents want our grandchildren to live in a safe world filled with goodness. The day inevitably comes, however, when our little ones learn there is evil in this world. When that day comes, we can add goodness, faith, and knowledge of the Lord Jesus Christ, who never leaves or forsakes us.

Heavenly Father, we thank you for all of the gifts in this recipe of love. Amen.

DECEMBER 31   NAMING THE ANIMALS

So the man named all the birds and all the animals.
(Genesis 2:20a GNT)

By now, everyone is beginning to get bored with their toys and bored with movies, so we decide that a trip to the zoo would be a fun excursion. As we pull into the parking lot, the grandchildren have all decided which animals they want to see first. Of course, the monkeys and elephants are a must-see. As we begin our tour, the children are reminded of the creation story from Genesis. They discuss how Noah got all of those animals in the boat. One says, "It must have been a big, big boat, all right." When we see the giraffes and elephants, the kids are so excited. We finally reach the monkeys and watch them swing and jump. The children love them because the monkeys are very active.

Our trip to the zoo with our grandchildren makes us feel young again. We laugh and run with them—especially when they start naming the animals. They read the little signs to the best of their ability, renaming some of the exotic animals. Antelope become deer and the baboon becomes a gorilla.

As the year comes to an end and the winter months set in, let us treat ourselves to being young again by doing something fun with our grandchildren—perhaps even a winter's day trip to the zoo!

Heavenly Father, thank you for fun times with our grandchildren and for sharing together the beauty and wonder of all your creation. Amen.

Breinigsville, PA USA
08 March 2011
257160BV00003B/25/P